THE DEVELOPING CHILD

Bringing together and illuminating the remarkable recent research on development from infancy to adolescence, for students of development psychology, policy makers, parents, and all others concerned with the future of the next generation.

Series Editors

Jerome Bruner
New York University

Joseph Campos
University of California, Berkeley

Michael Cole
University of California, San Diego

Annette Karmiloff-Smith
Neurocognitive Development Unit,
Institute of Child Health, London

WHAT WE KNOW
ABOUT CHILDCARE

Alison Clarke-Stewart
Virginia D. Allhusen

HARVARD UNIVERSITY PRESS
Cambridge, Massachusetts, and London, England / 2005

Library of Congress Cataloging-in-Publication Data

Clarke-Stewart, Alison, 1943–
    What we know about childcare / Alison Clarke-Stewart, Virginia D. Allhusen.
        p.   cm.—(The developing child)
    Includes bibliographical references and index.
    ISBN 0-674-01749-8 (alk. paper)
    1. Child care—United States.   2. Child care services—United States.
3. Child development—United States.   I. Allhusen, Virginia D.   II. Title.
    III. Series.

    HQ778.63.C583 2005
    362.71'2'0973—dc22   2004060668

CONTENTS

Preface		*vii*
Acknowledgments		*ix*
Abbreviations		*xi*
Introduction		1
Part One: A Nation Transformed		5
1	Making the Best of Difficult Choices	9
2	The Evolution of Childcare in the United States	27
3	Childcare in the United States Today	43
Part Two: A Quarter Century of Research		63
4	Studying Childcare	69
5	Effects of Care	83
6	Variations in Care	105
7	The Caregiver's Role	127
8	The Family's Place	150
Part Three: Looking to the Future		165
9	Making Better Childcare Choices	169
10	Planning Better Childcare Research	191
11	Implementing Better Childcare Solutions	206
Notes		*219*
Index		*291*

This book represents a brand-new version of a book that first appeared in 1982. It updates, expands, and deepens discussion of the issues set out in that book and reflects our current state—and lack—of knowledge about childcare. Two decades ago, when the first edition of *Daycare* was published, it seemed unlikely (to the authors, at least) that we would still be discussing issues of childcare twenty years later.[1] In 1982, "daycare" was a concern for both parents and psychologists, but solutions seemed just around the corner. Parents and psychologists wanted to know whether a young child should be put in care, and, if so, at what age and in what kind of care. They wanted to know what research says about the effects of care and what policies would improve its quality. They were concerned about the lack of high-quality care available and thinking about ways to remedy the situation. Today, childcare is as much a concern as it was twenty years ago. In fact, the situation may be worse. There is more care available, and more parents are using it, but the quality of care is not uniformly higher, and parents still have trouble finding and recognizing good care. More studies have been completed and more articles written, but for any questions about childcare that have been answered, other questions have arisen, and psychologists still debate whether care has positive or negative effects on children's well-being. It seems unlikely that childcare will cease to be a concern anytime soon. It is because of this continuing concern that we have written this book. The earlier editions were directed exclusively toward parents and attempted to answer relatively simple questions. This book includes discussions of interest to students and researchers as well as parents and addresses more complex issues and questions. It illustrates how difficult it is for researchers to study childcare and how difficult it is for parents to weigh the evidence from different studies as they choose a childcare arrangement—or decide to stay home. Because the study of childcare is important and the use of childcare has real consequences for real children, we have tried in this book to provide useful information for all readers who are concerned about the future of the nation's children and their own. For better or worse, childcare is here to stay; therefore, as a society, we should make it the best that we can. When parents decide that they should both work in full-time jobs, they should make the best childcare arrangement possible for their children. We hope that this book will help promote success for parents and society as a whole.

ACKNOWLEDGMENTS

We extend our sincere thanks to the National Institute of Child Health and Human Development and in particular to its able leader, Dr. Duane Alexander, for their years of support for the NICHD Study of Early Child Care and Youth Development. Dr. Alexander believed in this study from its earliest days and long after others tired of it—and in so doing he made a great gift to childcare research and policy. We are also grateful to our colleagues on the study, alongside whom our ideas about childcare and maternal employment have evolved over the past decade.

We appreciate the many hours of clerical and research assistance from our staff: Wayne Roemhild, Erin Gordon, Nathalie Carrick, Sarah Roper-Coleman, Josie Aye, and Rachel Smallman.

Last but not least, we thank our loving and supportive families, who patiently waited for this book to be completed. They say that behind evey successful man is a woman; but as we found in writing this book, behind some successful women there are indispensably helpful men and maybe also a few darling children.

CCDBG	Child Care and Development Block Grant
CCDF	Child Care and Development Fund
CDA	Child Development Associate
CQO	Cost, Quality and Child Outcomes Study
ECERS	Early Childhood Environment Rating Scale
FDCRS	Family Day Care Rating Scale
FIDCR	Federal Interagency Day Care Requirements
FMLA	Family and Medical Leave Act of 1993
HOME	Home Observation for Measurement of the Environment
ITERS	Infant/Toddler Environment Rating Scale
NAEYC	National Association for the Education of Young Children
NICHD	National Institute of Child Health and Human Development
NLSY	National Longitudinal Study of Youth
ORCE	Observational Record of the Caregiving Environment
PPVT	Peabody Picture Vocabulary Test
PRWORA	Personal Responsibility and Work Opportunity Reconciliation Act
TANF	Temporary Assistance for Needy Families
TEACH	Teachers of Excellence for All Children

WHAT WE KNOW ABOUT CHILDCARE

Industrialist Henry Kaiser has opened a series of manufacturing facilities around the Pacific Northwest. His product is in
high demand, so he keeps the plants running twenty-four hours a day
and mobilizes his workforce to deliver units as quickly as possible.
Realizing that nearly a third of his employees are women and that
those who are mothers have been missing more hours of work than
their childless counterparts, primarily because of childcare problems, Kaiser decides to arrange for on-site childcare for children ages
eighteen months to six years at two of his manufacturing sites. He
hires an architectural firm to design state-of-the-art, child-centered
facilities. When the project is complete, they are the world's largest
childcare centers, truly innovative models of child-centered construction. Fifteen playrooms surround a cheerful courtyard. Windows in the playrooms are kept low to the ground and feature views
of the manufacturing sites so that the children can watch their parents at work. Everything from the furniture to the bathroom fixtures
is designed from a child's point of view.

Naturally, the childcare program itself is every bit as top-notch as
the physical space it occupies. Sparing no expense, Kaiser consults
with Lois Stoltz, a Stanford professor of early childhood education,
to oversee the development of the curriculum. Teachers have degrees
in child development and at least three years' teaching experience.
Recognizing the importance of this work, Kaiser rejects the prevail-
ing low preschool-teacher wages and instead pays his teachers professional wages comparable to those he pays his skilled factory laborers.

The care and education these children receive is therefore first-rate, and many of them show enormous cognitive gains during the time they are enrolled at the center.

The family benefits of this innovative program are endless. The centers are open twenty-four hours a day, seven days a week to accommodate the shift work of the plant employees. In addition to the highly trained teachers, the staff includes nurses who provide sick care and well-child care (giving immunizations and checkups), nutritionists who oversee meal planning, and family consultants who provide various types of family support. Families can drop off their laundry, get a tear in their child's pants mended, and even have their child's ever-growing feet fitted for new shoes. Workers on traditional shifts are greeted at pick-up time with a hot dinner to take home to the family.

Is this a model childcare program of the new millennium, developed at long last in response to the stresses and strains facing working mothers? Is it a figment of the imagination of childcare advocates? It may come as a surprise to learn that, in fact, this visionary program was developed well over a half century ago, in the early 1940s, in response to the war effort.[1] Henry Kaiser was in the business of building the ships that the military desperately needed after the United States entered World War II in 1941. Kaiser managed to speed production to a record-breaking seventy-two hours for completion of a ship, but this pace required round-the-clock work and the absolute minimum of absenteeism among his workers. He therefore built these model childcare centers at his shipyards, charging his workers a mere seventy cents per day (an equivalent of about $7.00 in 2005 dollars) for childcare and passing off the rest of the cost to the federal government by adding it to the price of his ships. During their short tenure, the Kaiser Shipyard childcare centers served nearly four thousand children. Yet despite the program's success, the end of the war also meant the end of the centers; with wartime needs no longer pressing, women were expected to return to their homes, dust off their aprons, and get back to their "natural" duties as providers of a warm and welcoming hearth and home.

And so it has gone in the United States over the past half century, with women slowly and steadily fighting their way into the workforce but facing childcare challenges and cultural resistance at every step of the way. This book discusses the issues women have faced in that battle, describes the state of childcare past and present, reviews the massive body of research that has sprung up around this controversial topic over the last quarter century, and provides suggestions for future directions for childcare practice, policy, and research.

The narratives that punctuate the three parts of this book were solicited from friends to reflect some of the diversity involved in childcare decision making. They illustrate how different women have dealt with childcare issues, depending on their individual circumstances.

In Part I of this book we present the history of childcare as a social phenomenon in this country from the 1800s through present day. In the first chapter, "Making the Best of Difficult Choices," we discuss the often thorny decisions today's parents face regarding work and family: whether to work at all, what to do about childcare if they are to work, and how to balance work and family obligations. In the next chapter we review the history of American childcare from its earliest roots as a service for the working poor and a form of enrichment for the more entitled, and we discuss the evolution of childcare financing and regulation. In the third chapter we turn out attention to the state of affairs of childcare in the United States today: the different circumstances that have given rise to the tremendous need for childcare, and the features of the childcare parents choose.

In Part II of the book we distill the results of three decades of research on childcare. In the first chapter, we describe the research methods that have been used to study childcare effects, and highlight three excellent, contemporary studies. The next chapter explores a central question: Are children better or worse off—intellectually, socially, and emotionally—when they are in childcare rather than exclusively at home with their parents? The chapter "Variations in Care" follows up this discussion with an analysis of the effects of being in different *kinds* of care. For example, does it matter if childcare involves many other children, has a structured curriculum, or takes place in a well-appointed facility? The next chapter, "The Caregiver's

Role," focuses on the key component of childcare: the adult care-provider. Here we ask how caregivers' backgrounds are related to the quality of their caregiving; for example, do caregivers with more experience provide better care? In "The Family's Place," we deepen the discussion by showing how childcare has different consequences for children from different families.

In Part III we look into the future in three different ways. In "Making Better Childcare Choices," we offer a set of guidelines for parents on how to make better childcare choices in the future—how to choose the right kind of care for the individual child and family and how to identify a good childcare setting and continually monitor its quality. In "Planning Better Child Care Research" we discuss the kinds of research that are still needed if we are to find out all about childcare. We have made great strides since the topic first came to researchers' attention in the late 1960s. Many dollars and hours have been spent probing deeper and deeper into issues of childcare. We have come up with answers, albeit provisional ones, to many of the questions that interest parents, psychologists, and policy makers. But although substantial progress has been made, there is still a need for new and better studies. In this chapter, we suggest the direction that these studies should take. Last, in "Implementing Better Childcare Solutions" we glimpse into the future of childcare itself. We have discussed many of the difficulties faced by working parents and the problems inherent in the current childcare situation in the United States. In this final chapter we consider ways of solving the childcare problem by making parents' lives easier and childcare better in the coming years.

PART ONE

A NATION TRANSFORMED

Back in the 1950s and 60s when I was raising a family, there was never a question of how I would do it. It was a matter of course that I would meet the man of my dreams, get married, settle down, and start a family; my future would almost certainly contain all of those elements, and unquestionably in that order and no other. My vocation from the start was to make a safe and comfortable home for my husband and, eventually, our three girls. It was what my mother had done, and her mother before that, and it was what I knew how to do. Working in a job outside the home was no more my lot than taking out the trash or mowing the lawn. You know, young people today see June Cleaver on the television and they get a good laugh out of how simple she is, and how downtrodden. But that was the black-and-white reality that we grew up in, and we were happy.

So I stayed home with the girls, and I expect somewhere in the back of my mind I thought some day they would grow up and have a life similar to mine, only maybe with a little more money. I taught them all the things they needed to know: how to sew, how to bake a prize-winning apple pie, how to keep the family peace. And I will tell you one thing: raising children is no walk in the park as the young people would say today. I may not have had a traditional "job," but I sure did have my hands full between taking care of them and keeping our home in order. That's the one thing I wish some of these mothers of today would understand.

In retrospect I guess I could have gone out into the world of work once the girls were in school full time, but by then what was I going to do? I had no training, no experience, no education by today's standards. I can hardly imagine what I could have been good at. So I kept my job as a homemaker. But by then change was in the wind. Women's roles were changing in ways I had never dreamed of. Now mind you, I did not agree with some of those outspoken women pressing for all that change; if you ask me, they seemed a little bitter and maybe more than a little unhappy with their own lives. But slowly and surely the ideas they were spouting took hold in one small way or another, and we started to redefine our dreams for our own children's future. Now all of a sudden it seemed very important for them to have a good college education, not just to have a chance to meet the men of their dreams, but to start a career. So we saved what we could to help them pay for college. I remember my husband telling them that if they had their own good professions, they could still be happily married, but they would never have to feel like they were dependent on someone else. Not bad for a couple of old timers like us.

And sure enough, today I am proud to say that my girls are all accomplished young women and mothers of the new century. They have each forged their own path, making their own unique set of circumstances work for them. Two of them work full time; one stays home with her little boy. I have to admit I worry about the working moms, and about my grandbabies. But they certainly do seem happy, and I give my girls a lot of credit for what they have accomplished, both professionally and personally in their home lives. The children are bright, polite, happy. They love their babysitter, but they know who their mommy is and they are always glad to see her at the end of the day. It's the twenty-first-century family in living color, and they're just as happy.

—Sarah, age 70

I didn't have a choice—never mind Dr. Laura. Well, Dr. Laura wouldn't have approved of me anyway, because I was a single mother. I definitely needed to work and I definitely needed childcare. After the baby was born, I had a month to relax and recover from my episiotomy. I didn't even sit at my desk the entire month (because of the baby, not the episiotomy). But then I had to get some childcare help. I had to get back to work. I had a career; I had responsibilities. One time, the baby's father looked after him while I ran to the office. But when I got home, I discovered that he was holding a business meeting instead of the baby. Clearly this was not a solution to my need for childcare!

Maybe there are more choices now, but I was on the leading edge of the childcare and maternal employment wave, and the pickin's were pretty slim. My first "childcare" was a young student who came to my house several hours a week. Usually I ended up sending her to run errands for me, because the baby was always asleep when she arrived. It was helpful to have a personal shopper, but it wasn't childcare. I started interviewing nannies—quite a few nannies. I finally found one that I liked. She had a young child herself and she seemed kind and knowledgeable. She sure seemed to know more about babies than I did. But when I called to offer her the job, I discovered that the rate that I thought was for the month was for the week! That woke me up in a hurry. I wasn't going to be able to afford an in-home caregiver. I looked in the paper for women who watched children in their homes. There weren't very many in the neighborhood, and being in the neighborhood was important to me. Eventually, I found a woman who stayed home because she had a toddler herself, and she wanted to care for one more child to make a little extra money. It sounded promising; it was affordable and there was only one other child, so I was sure that my son would get plenty of attention. Within a month, though, this woman had taken in another child, and soon she said she was looking for another one. That wasn't the direction I wanted to go, so I got on the childcare carousel again. I found another home with a woman who was staying home with her own toddler. This worked well . . . until she got pregnant and decided she wouldn't do childcare anymore. I was back to the now all-too-familiar task of interviewing care providers. My first choice—a wonderful woman with a background as a nursery school teacher—had changed her mind by the time I called to hire her. She was going to do something entirely different. I don't remember what it was now—maybe making jewelry. So I went to my second choice—a young woman who had just graduated from college with a degree in animal science. I was her second choice too. She hadn't been able to land a job at the zoo, so she thought that taking care of babies would be the next best thing. She wasn't ideal, but I needed someone right away, and she worked out okay, I guess. She was shy and quiet, and she didn't talk to the baby as much as I would have liked. But she was careful and caring. She took my son to the park; she played with him in the yard. He was safe and seemed content.

At the end of the year, though, my job required me to move across the country. So back on the childcare carousel I went, before my son had even had his second birthday. This time, I went to the university and checked with a childcare expert. She recommended the childcare home where her son had gone. We tried it. It was clean and there were lots of toys. The care providers were very professional. But before the end of the year, I decided to look into nursery schools. My son was almost three, and I thought he would benefit from a more educational program. I was lucky to find the wonderful Buttons 'n' Bows program and talk the director into accepting my son even though he wasn't toilet trained. "Never mind," she said, "he soon will be." She was wrong about that (every day I picked up a little wet baggie when I picked up my son), but she was right to take him. He enjoyed it and thrived. But six months later, it was time to move again, and the childcare search recommenced. I looked for Montessori schools, because that's what Buttons 'n' Bows was, and that narrowed the search to a single program in the town where we lived. I liked it. The director was intelligent; the teachers were fabulous—full of ideas and energy. Unfortunately, my son did not share my opinion. Every morning it was a struggle to leave him inside the gate in tears. (Buttons 'n' Bows had let me come in and settle him with a friend and an activity; the new school didn't.) So once again, we moved to a new center. It was also a Montessori program, and although it was a longer drive, I had met the owner and liked her. She helped my son get integrated into the new class and watched out for him there. He was never really happy about going, but he tolerated it, and we stayed there until he started elementary school. At long last, after a dizzying five-year, eight-childcare-arrangements ride on the childcare carousel, I was able to jump off and move on.

—Kathleen, age 60

1

MAKING THE BEST
OF DIFFICULT CHOICES

The issue of nonparental childcare is a complex and controversial one for parents, researchers, and policy makers alike. No topic lights up a cocktail party conversation or a call-in radio program's switchboard like the question of whether a mother should stay at home with her baby or return to the workforce. A young parent or parent-to-be, upon facing this question for the first time, is greeted with endless advice from well-intentioned friends and family members regarding the best course of action—advice most typically guided by these other people's personal experiences, successes, and struggles with their own children. Turning to the childcare "experts" for a more objective perspective, the conflicted and confused parent finds, to a large extent, more of the same—no shortage of opinions, no shortage of convictions, but no apparent consensus either. Why has the topic of childcare continued to be such an emotional one for parents? Why has the United States been so seemingly reluctant to address childcare needs at a national level? And why have the "answers" regarding the effects of childcare proven to be so elusive? These are the central issues fueling the continuing concern about childcare.

To Use or Not to Use

Perhaps the first question a parent asks herself is whether to use non-maternal childcare at all. At the root of this never-ending national debate in the United States are the different beliefs we hold about the role of parents, and especially of the mother, in a young child's life. Ask ten adults on the street for their opinions on the latest world political crisis, and at least a few of them will have no opinion at all. It would be far more difficult, however, to find one adult who does not have a strongly held belief about childcare and maternal employment that he or she will gladly share, perhaps even trying to convert the pollster to the "right" camp if necessary. The parent facing decisions about childcare carries a heavy load of worry, doubt, and uncertainty. What makes the issue of childcare so impossible to sort out? The answers lie within our own personal, deep-rooted feelings about the care of young children, as well as the beliefs that are imparted to us by our friends and neighbors, family and colleagues, advisors and experts, and, indeed, society as a whole.

BIOLOGICAL TIES

To a large extent, decisions about leaving one's child in the care of another are weighted heavily with the mother's primal connection to her child. In all but a small number of cases, the mother is crowned the first and most important person in the child's life by virtue of biology. She begins her relationship with her child in private, from the earliest days of pregnancy, as she carries around her constant companion. As the weeks and months go by, she becomes increasingly aware of the child within her as a unique little person—first with the sight (via sonogram) of a small, beating heart no larger than a grain of rice, which brings home the reality that a new human being has begun to form inside her; later with the gurgling, whooshing sounds of a heartbeat transmitted via Doppler; then with the first flutters of movement from within her growing belly; and still later with the sight of a perfectly formed baby in shadowy form on the ultrasound screen. By the time her precious bundle is delivered into the outside world to meet the rest of his admirers, the mother has already established a relationship with her baby. Over the course of nine months she feels she has already learned something of the little one's personality—smart, feisty, quiet, caring—and may even think she recognized Uncle Henry's powerful soccer legs in the nighttime pummeling from within as her baby kicked and squirmed about. By the time the physical bond between mother and child is cut, their emotional one is well in place, aided perhaps by a healthy dose of maternal hormones. The new mother typically keeps her child near, hovering and protecting, ready to jump at the slightest indication that her baby needs her.

The baby, too, has spent nine months getting to know his mother, listening intently to her ever-present (if muffled) voice.[1] Infants show an almost immediate preference for their own mothers; even as newborns they can discriminate their mother's voice and scent from those of another woman.[2] They will turn their heads preferentially to her sound or smell, and in research studies newborns have even been shown to "work" (by sucking on a special pacifier) to hear her voice. They also seem to be able to recognize and prefer their own mother's face, even after limited exposure to it.[3]

To be sure, the lucky child has others who love him and who have been eagerly awaiting his arrival. Fathers too have a chance to get to know their little ones before birth, strategically placing a hand on the mother's belly to experience a swift fetal kick, talking to their partner's ever-growing midriff to make sure that the baby within recognizes his voice too—but these encounters are mere interludes in the twenty-four-hour intimacy experienced by mother and child. The depth of the father's bond with his child will continue to grow to profound levels over the course of the child's early years of life, but the mother has a jump start on all of this. Indeed, the idea that the mother by biological destiny must take center stage in the child's life has roots in sociobiological theory, that is, the theory that adults are more likely to care for and protect those who will carry their genes into the next generation.[4] In support of this idea, researchers have found that adults express stronger feelings of kinship to biological relatives than to nonbiological relatives, that most prospective parents see adoption as a "second-best" last resort when natural conception fails, and that children are more likely to be abused by stepparents than by natural parents.[5]

The intense bond between a mother and her baby is perhaps the central factor that makes the issue of childcare such an agonizing one for the new mother. She feels fiercely protective of her child, views the baby as vulnerable and delicate, and demands only the best for him or her. In the context of those feelings it is easy to see why the question of "to work or not to work" outside of the home is an immensely difficult one for a mother who has a choice. If the child is to be entrusted to another's care, either by choice or by necessity, the mother worries endlessly about finding the right person to care for her child and provide the loving, doting attention she wishes for him or her.

THE MOTHER-CHILD RELATIONSHIP

Beyond the central anxiety about being able to trust another person to care for her baby, the other primary concern fueling a mother's anxiety about childcare is the threat that the mother-child attachment relationship may be compromised, either because the child spends too *little* time with the mother or because he or she spends too *much* time with the nonmaternal caregiver, developing an even stronger bond with this "other woman." Indeed, since the earliest days in the United States, when mothers first began their mass exodus out of the home and into the workplace, this question has been the single greatest source of concern and scientific investigation. Attachment theory has therefore been considered by many experts to be central to the issue of childcare and its potential effect on children's well-being.

In his theory of attachment, John Bowlby emphasizes the centrality of the infant's relationship with a primary caregiver to the child's subsequent psychological development.[6] Based on the quality of the interactions between caregiver and child during the earliest years of the child's life, Bowlby suggests, the infant constructs an "internal working model" of the attachment figure—that is, a set of expectations concerning that person's availability and a complementary view of the self as strong or weak, worthy or unworthy of love and affection, capable or incapable of confidently venturing out into the world to explore and learn.

Although he recognized that the child can form attachments with multiple adults, Bowlby's focus was almost exclusively on the mother as the *primary* attachment figure, mainly because at the time he was developing his theory (in the mid-1960s), in cultures throughout the world it was the mother who served as the infant's primary caregiver.

A large body of empirical work, inspired by Bowlby's theory, thus focused upon the mother as the primary attachment figure and examined the relation between the quality of that relationship and the infant's subsequent psychological development.[7] Attachment theorists developed their models of the centrality of the mother-infant relationship within the social and cultural context of the traditional maternal role: the mother at home rearing children.

As more mothers of very young children began to participate in the workforce, increasing attention was given to the fact that young children can and do form attachments to several people, including fathers and other caregivers.[8] However, the mother-infant relationship was still assumed to be at the core of the child's attachment "hierarchy," with other important people playing more distant roles; it was this primary relationship that was thought to retain the greatest impact on children's subsequent social-emotional development and to influence the quality of the child's relationships with others.

The idea that the mother holds a special place in her child's emotional life over and above all other attachment figures, and the associated question of whether extensive daily separations from the mother place the child at risk for later emotional maladjustment, have been at the heart of the empirical controversy regarding the effects of childcare on young children. Certainly it is one of the primary issues that haunts parents and gives detractors of childcare a loud voice.[9]

CULTURAL BELIEFS, SOCIAL PRESSURES

But worries about the parent-child relationship are not the only sources of conflict for the parent facing decisions about childcare. The notion of childcare goes against traditional views of family and child rearing that American society has espoused for generations—family-oriented views that dominated the upbringing of most of today's young mothers themselves. Under this view, the day-to-day rearing of children has been considered the primary responsibility of the mother, with father as breadwinner and mother as homemaker and child rearer. Over the past quarter of a century, however, major shifts have taken place in the social landscape of the United States. It has become increasingly difficult to hold onto that utopian view of the two-parent nuclear family living in the suburbs with Father working nine to five while Mother bakes cookies and children play happily in a neatly manicured yard. Today, the cookies are baked at midnight or bought at the grocery store (also, perhaps, at midnight); there may or may not be a father living at home; and the majority of mothers have found paid employment outside the home.

Despite these changes, the working mother feels pressure from society to stay home and see to her primary responsibility, the care and nurturing of her young children. She meets with the disapproval not only of many of her elders, who hold on more firmly to traditional views about mothers' roles, but also of her contemporaries who have made choices (and perhaps economic or career sacrifices) to stay home with their own children. If the perception from outsiders is that there is financial flexibility to make a choice to work or stay home, the mother who "chooses" to work may face criticism from others, who may wonder why she had a baby in the first place if it was not her intention to stay at home to raise it. Working to achieve "mere" personal fulfillment, much less to be able to afford a larger house or nicer car, is viewed as selfish and myopic. Nor can the mother fall back on her own childhood experiences regarding maternal work and childcare for guidance, as life was different for women in the days when she herself was a young child.

Friends, co-workers, family members, and acquaintances are not the only source of disapproval confronting the working mother. Journalists and reporters are quick to report every childcare horror story—the childcare facility located in the public building that was the target of a terrorist attack, the nanny caught on video slapping the face of an infant who did not want to eat, the childcare provider accused of sexually abusing children while in care, the child who wandered off and drowned in a fountain located on the grounds of the childcare home—the list can unfortunately go on and on. Stories such as these, unrepresentative as they may be of the daily experiences of millions of children in the United States, are terrifying enough to make the color drain from anyone's face. But to the parent whose child is in someone else's care as the story breaks, the anxiety can be overwhelming. The not-so-implicit message for those looking for reasons to disapprove of childcare is that children are safest when they are under their own mothers' watchful eyes.[10]

Yet another source of concern for mothers deciding whether to use childcare is the history of childcare provision and use in the United States as a service for the poor or incapable. The earliest childcare facilities in the United States—overcrowded and custodial—sprang up in the nineteenth century primarily as a service for low-income women forced to enter the workforce by industrialization and urbanization.[11] Thus the concept of group care may be tinged in the minds of some parents by images of children in large institutions and fears that such "maternal deprivation" would cause the same negative kinds of child outcomes that had been reported for children reared in orphanages.[12] These fears create a difficult climate for parents' decisions about childcare use.

Women who work outside the home are not alone in feeling cultural pressures regarding work and childcare, however. Today's mothers are caught in a crosscurrent of slowly changing values, needs, and beliefs. The stay-at-home mother may be just as likely to experience real or perceived disapproval from others regarding her choice to stay at home with her children. Is she being lazy "just" to stay at home instead of toiling at a paid job? How can she sacrifice a career into which she has already invested so much? How hard could it possibly be to take care of a child or two? Isn't she worried that her brain will turn to Jell-O if she trades in her *New York Times* for *Goodnight Moon?* Society seldom recognizes the investment of stay-at-home mothers into the country's "human capital," that is, the nurturing of young people to grow to be skilled, productive, enterprising contributors to society.[13] It seems, then, that regardless of what choice she has made, the young mother today is likely to encounter both those who support her decisions and those who do not.

INCONSISTENT EXPERT OPINIONS

The educated mother, in search of the "truth" about childcare, might reasonably turn to the "experts" for answers to her dilemmas. And indeed, she will find no shortage of such advice, from chapters of baby-care books to parenting magazine articles to entire volumes dedicated to the topic.[14] But, unfortunately, these experts do not themselves agree. Some believe that long hours away from the mother in the earliest years pose an unacceptable risk to children's healthy development.[15] Others point to the potential benefits of high-quality childcare and maternal employment not only for children but for mothers and families as well.[16] Because of this lack of consensus, expert opinions, published in books and magazines and expressed on radio and television shows, only add to parents' confusion and anxiety. What gives rise to these different opinions about the effects of childcare? The answer lies in part in the complexities of studying the effects of childcare on children's development and in part in the difficulties in understanding the "real-world" significance of statistically significant results.[17] Adding to the complication is the unavoidable tendency of experts, like anyone else, to interpret seemingly objective data in line with their own personal values, beliefs, and experiences, as the values of society at large continue to change. There is no single answer emanating from the scientific psychiatric or psychological community—leaving parents even more at the mercy of their own personal feelings and their own personal advisors as they sort out decisions about childcare.

When There Is No Choice

Although certainly there are parents who have the flexibility to choose whether to work outside the home or to stay home with baby, to work many hours or few, in millions of American homes the economic reality leaves no choice—some mothers simply must work to sustain the family. In one large-scale study of childcare in the United States, the vast majority of working mothers of infants and toddlers (80–85 percent) said that they worked because they needed the income to support their families.[18] So mothers may find themselves in one of several situations where they feel they have no choice but to use childcare: they are single parents; they need to supplement their husband's income to make ends meet; they have limited leave time; or they are reluctant to exit the workforce for fear that it will be impossible to get back in. Of course, some of these pressures are more internal than absolute; there's a difference between doing one's best for the child, as opposed to making sure the child has food to eat and shoes for her feet. But the net effect is the same: childcare is a complex issue that keeps most mothers always wondering if they are doing the right thing. Indeed, it may be the case that women who consider themselves to have no choice but to work are in the majority among employed mothers. A handful of recent local and national polls, conducted by organizations such as Public Agenda (a national polling agency), the *Los Angeles Times, Parents Magazine,* and the I Am Your Child Foundation, all suggest that about two-thirds of mothers, if given a magical choice, would prefer to stay at home with their children rather than to work outside the home and place their children in childcare of any type.[19]

Having It All

Today's American workforce thus includes some mothers who are there by choice and others who are there by necessity. But regardless of the reasons for using childcare, the common outcome for all working mothers is that they are stretched to their limits as they try to balance work and family life.

COMPETING DEMANDS

Perhaps the greatest challenge facing today's working mother is finding the time in a mere twenty-four hours to take care of all the responsibilities that pile up around her each and every day. Working mothers must schedule their activities rigidly. They may do less housework than they would if they were not working, or complete their chores in less time, or sleep fewer hours, or buy frozen prepared meals, or hire someone else to help with at least some of the domestic tasks. Indeed, studies have shown that working mothers have adjusted their responsibilities by using a variety of time-saving alternatives for household tasks and by taking on less housework than in previous generations, from a high of about twenty-seven hours per week in 1965 to about fifteen hours per week in 1995.[20] But many tasks are unassignable, either because it is not possible for someone else to do them or because the mother prefers to do them herself.

Chief among the tasks in this category are those relating to the children; working mothers spend almost as much time taking care of and interacting with their children as they would if they were not employed. Indeed, although partners (when available) do take up some of the slack, childcare and the household remain primarily the working mother's responsibilities, in effect creating a second full-time job for her.[21] Adding to the stress is that—unlike traditional men's household roles like repairs and home maintenance tasks, many of which can be completed at the husband's convenience—most traditional women's roles (like making dinner) are nonnegotiable and must be done at specific times.[22]

Another complication for the working mother's schedule is that even when she is at work, she cannot put her home responsibilities on hold until she gets home. In particular, even when she is at work, the mother is still usually the one "in charge" of the kids: she must arrange for and continually monitor the quality of the childcare, and she worries about it while she is at work—and that's on a good day. On a bad day a childcare crisis erupts just when she has a big deadline at work: the baby is sick, the nanny quits, the childcare home is flooded, or the center is closed for a holiday that the working mother's employer does not observe. And in most families, the responsibility for piecing together an alternate strategy or simply staying home from work falls squarely on the mother's already overloaded shoulders.[23]

QUALITY TIME

Yet the working mother does her best to keep all these balls in the air. And chief among her priorities is making sure her relationship with her child is not lost in the shuffle. As maternal employment became the norm in the United States, a new catchphrase entered the everyday vernacular, namely, "quality time." Working moms may spend fewer hours with their children, so the argument goes, but the time they do spend is quality time. They are not cooking dinner (Pizza Hut takes care of that), paying bills (this can be done after the kids are tucked in bed at night), or watching an aerobics video (this can be done before the kids get up in the morning). Instead, they get down on the floor, play dominoes, color a birthday card for Grandma, help with homework: in short, they compress a day's worth of interaction into the few hours between the five o'clock whistle and the eight o'clock lights out. Working mothers work hard to make time for their children; in fact, in one recent study, even though mothers reported spending more time on the job than they did twenty-five years ago, they also spent more time with their children than they did twenty-five years ago.[24] But others argue that the concept of quality time is nothing more than an invention meant to assuage the guilt of working mothers and allow them to go right on neglecting their children. From this perspective, quality time cannot be scheduled to happen in the way a business meeting can be scheduled; rather, one has to be available in the child's presence around the clock so that when the opportunity presents itself, the parent is standing by ready to seize the moment. Research has yet to be done to actually confirm this hypothesis, but that fact does little to dissuade those who espouse it.

Of course, if a mother is at home all day with her child, she obviously spends more time with the child than if she were away at work all day. And indeed, to quantify this difference, in one recent study working mothers were found to spend about a third less time with their infants than their nonworking counterparts spend. But this differential had no apparent effects on the quality of observed interaction between mother and child or on the quality of their attachment relationship.[25] In another study, the children of working mothers actually reported that they received *greater* amounts of verbal and physical affection from their mothers than did the children of stay-at-home mothers.[26] A study in Germany suggests the same: The mothers of toddlers who were enrolled in full-time childcare had more social interactions with them during nonworking hours than did the stay-at-home mothers with their toddlers.[27]

But not all studies show this difference.[28] We don't know how common these special times are or how often working mothers' interactions have this stimulating quality. When researchers have asked mothers to come to a room at a university and play with their children, dress them, and read to them, or when they have asked mothers questions about their behavior with their children at home, they have found no differences between working and nonworking mothers; the quality of mothers' interactions with their children was the same.[29] However, these researchers have also found that working mothers are less positive and sensitive when they play with their children in front of the researchers' video camera if their children spend more hours apart from them in childcare.[30]

What seems likely is that the end of the day is an especially social time for working mothers and their children and not for mothers who are at home all day, but that at other times (e.g., weekends) the quality of mother-child interactions are similar. However, if the child is in care for many hours each week, the mother may be less skilled at reading the child's signals.

HELPING HANDS

With working mothers apparently stretched to their limits in balancing work and family, one might reasonably ask how fathers fit into this insane equation. Despite the fact that mothers by and large retain their responsibilities as primary organizers of childcare and household-related tasks, fathers have increasingly taken on at least a small share of the burden. In 1965, fathers spent on average just five hours per week on childcare and household tasks, compared to mothers' twenty-seven hours per week. By 1995, not only had men increased their participation in household tasks (albeit slightly), but they were doing proportionately more of the total housework, taking on eight hours per week as compared to their wives' fifteen hours.[31] Fathers in dual-earner families are more likely to participate in childcare than are fathers with stay-at-home wives, and, to the extent that they do, couples report greater marital satisfaction.[32]

But fathers, like mothers, face pressures to give their undivided attention to their paid employment, certainly at least during the hours of the traditional workday. In fact, they might face even greater difficulties than their wives in balancing the work-family tension.[33] Working fathers, like working mothers, have limited time available for childcare and household tasks. Early in the social revolution that saw mothers entering the workforce in increasing numbers, it was perhaps to be expected that change would not occur overnight and that working mothers of that transitional generation would be saddled with the overwhelming task of taking on the whole new world of work while also retaining responsibility for hearth and home, and this was indeed the case.[34] But even after thirty years of a strong maternal presence in the workforce, traditional roles dictated by our culture would still have us believe that the care of children and maintenance of the household are the wife's primary responsibility, and providing for the family financially is the husband's primary responsibility: Thus, employers are far less accommodating to a man's request to take time off to deal with family issues, and male employees are less comfortable even making such a request.[35] Fathers, too, having been socialized to view themselves as the primary breadwinners of their families, are victims of the pressures of a fickle economy and of our increasingly high expectations about acceptable standards of living.

Even as conflicting traditional husband-wife roles are blurring, men retain a tendency to define their success in terms of how well they provide for their family financially.[36] In a literal sense, then, they feel they cannot afford to help out with childcare matters on the home front. In fact, in one study, fathers who reported greater personal responsibility for childcare tasks had lower earnings than those who did not.[37] In another study, only those who had advanced in their careers enough to be able to relax a little were able to devote more time and attention to family matters.[38]

Of course, as little childcare help as married working mothers might get from their husbands, at least it is still something. But in a disturbingly large number of American households today, there is no husband present to help out. Ideally, fathers would be bound to their children regardless of whether they are married or living in the household. But in reality, out of sight is apparently out of mind for many out-of-home fathers. In one recent study, over a quarter of nonresident fathers had had no contact at all with their child in the last year.[39] Even when the father lived in the home, those who were

not married to the mother were shown in one study to be less positively involved in their children's lives than married fathers were.[40]

ROLE SATISFACTION

To a large extent, it appears as though a woman's success in the quest
for "having it all" depends in large measure on her ability to be able
to choose whether she wants to stay home with her children or work
for pay outside the home. Indeed, research has shown that it is not so
much whether a woman is a working mom or a stay-at-home mom
that predicts whether she will be happy, but whether she is satisfied
in her role, whatever it may be.[41] Of course, this observation is not
rocket science; it hardly seems like something that needs to be demonstrated empirically. But in the context of a society with a long, valued tradition of mother at home, this logic is often lost in the heat
of arguing for passionately held positions on what the mother's role
should be.

If a woman is not satisfied with her role, it is reflected not only in
her own well-being but in her behavior with her child. Women who
are not happy have been found to be less involved, affectionate, playful, and effective with their children, and their children in turn have
been shown to have more behavior problems and lower cognitive
ability.[42] In one Canadian study, Margaret McKim and her colleagues
found that employed mothers who preferred to stay home were more
depressed and that their children were more likely to experience un-
stable care than mothers who were working and wanted to work.[43] In
a study by Ellen Hock, if a mother who was not working thought it
was better to be working, or if a working mother thought she should
be the baby's exclusive caregiver, the child's relations with mother
were disturbed.[44] The children of these dissatisfied and conflicted
mothers were likely to respond to the mother's approaches with
avoidance or crying. Another study also found that infants of mothers who were homemakers and preferred it that way were more sociable than those of discontented homemakers who wished they were
working.[45]

In a much larger study of more than one thousand families in the
United States, likewise, when mothers of children in full-time care

believed that maternal employment was beneficial for children's development, children did better on cognitive tests; when mothers of children who were not in care held the same opinion, however, children did more poorly.[46] Poorer social outcomes (less-secure attachment, poorer social skills, more behavior problems) were also reported in a study of children in 120 childcare centers, when parents reported more work-family interference (e.g., "when I get home, I am too tired to do very much with my children").[47] With school-age children, too, it has been found that children's self-esteem and adjustment are better when the mother is satisfied with her role as worker or housewife.[48] These findings suggest that when maternal attitudes toward care coincide with mothers' actual employment status, children benefit, whereas when attitudes and employment are at odds, children suffer.

In one careful study on this subject, researcher Anita Farel interviewed 212 mothers of kindergarten children from eight schools, half of them working mothers and half nonworking. She also tested their children's persistence, creativity, curiosity, intelligence, consideration, and sociability. As expected, mothers who were not working but who thought it would be better if they were had children who did more poorly on almost all of these tests. Surprisingly, though, children whose mothers were working but who thought they should not be working (another dissatisfied group) did not do more poorly on the tests.[49]

Why did these children not show the expected problems? Perhaps the reason was that these children were not exposed to as much of their mother's dissatisfaction, since she was away from them more, at work. Perhaps it was because these children had special times with their mothers that compensated for her dissatisfaction. Perhaps it was because they were in childcare arrangements that provided the stimulation and care the mother could not. Perhaps it was because the message conveyed by unhappy working mothers was basically accepting of the child—these mothers wanted to be with their children more—whereas the message of discontented full-time mothers was more rejecting—by working, they would have had more time away from the child. Or perhaps mothers wanted to spend less time with children who were not developing as well. Whatever the reason, it is clear that the mothers' work status alone did not determine the children's development. How the mother felt about her roles as worker or mother, not simply the fact that she worked, predicted children's development and well-being.

These studies all suggest that maternal employment status per se is not the driving factor in a woman's satisfaction with life, but rather the woman's perceived level of support and stress. We all know women who feel suffocated at home, maybe scream a little too much at their kids, and long for a little adult contact during the day. Likewise, we also know women who cry into their coffee at their desk, toiling at a job they do not enjoy, worrying about their kids, and wishing they could just go home and be the one to change the diapers and see the proud smiles of achievement when her child figures out which shape block fits into which hole. It seems, then, that it is not so much a question of all mothers belonging at home or all mothers being just fine at work but rather finding the harmonious fit that works for the individual woman and her family.

THE RESULT: STRESS AND STRAIN

Working mothers typically have so many balls in the air at one time that they inevitably feel a high degree of stress trying to balance all their responsibilities. The stress level is especially acute for mothers with limited financial or emotional resources. Mothers with financial pressures must deal with the stresses of inadequate living conditions and concerns about how they will survive, in addition to the stresses of combining work and parenthood. Without a partner to share the load, single mothers must cope with the dual demands of work and parenting, enduring the physical strains of doing everything by themselves; the psychological strains of isolation, loneliness, and bitterness; and the economic strains of reduced family income.

But even with adequate resources and a partner's help, working mothers experience stress as they cope with physical fatigue, with conflict between their work and their husband's, and with the challenge of balancing their maternal, spousal, and employee roles. Three-quarters of mothers who are employed in full-time jobs claim they don't have enough time to do everything. They often cope with the situation by giving up time for themselves; they have no free time at all. In fact, in one recent study working mothers reported having less than an hour a day for themselves, only about half of what they said they had twenty-five years earlier.[50]

This "overbooking" almost inevitably results in physical and psychological stress.[51] As a result of their constant efforts to juggle the demands of family and job, most mothers holding full-time jobs feel overtired, overworked, and harried. There are benefits to employment, of course. Most working mothers feel good about getting out into the world, having new experiences, and enjoying the successes of their careers. They feel more independent and in control of their own lives. For example, in one study of working-class families, employment was found to buffer against maternal depression, presumably because the associated financial security gave women a sense of empowerment to control their own destinies.[52] But benefits aside, working mothers also feel rushed and pressured, especially when they are first adjusting to their dual roles.

Employed mothers might also feel that they are not doing anything well, because of their inability to devote 100 percent of their effort to any one "occupation"—as a worker, a mother, a wife. On the work front, they may feel constrained by their effort to protect their family time and keep work from encroaching on those precious moments. In one recent survey, 16 percent of working mothers reported having turned down a promotion at work, and nearly a third said they cut back on their work investment or refused to work overtime.[53] Some mothers, in an effort to strike a balance, choose part-time employment. But this "solution" creates new difficulties of its own: part-time jobs in traditionally female occupations are typically lower paid and lower status. Thus, a woman in such a position is not likely to have the flexibility to set or change her work hours to accommodate ever-changing family needs or to deal with the inevitable sick child or school holiday. She is therefore faced with the no-win choice of finding last-minute childcare or calling in sick, either of which results in added stress for the mother and a sense of being pulled in too many different directions. Whether she forges on in full-time employment or elects part-time work, these decisions are not without consequences: compared with men or even working women who do not have children, working mothers are levied a "mommy tax" in the form of lower salaries and fewer opportunities for advancement.[54]

And on the home front things are just as stressful. Although reporting lower levels of emotional investment in their maternal role than nonworking mothers, working mothers worry more about the time they spend with their children and feel guilty about leaving them to go to work. These mothers feel deprived of their children's company. They feel confused and worry about the harm they might be doing their children.[55] Near the start of the precipitous rise in maternal employment, in the late 1970s a national panel of experts concluded that parents felt "the sense of having no guidelines or supports for raising children, . . . of not being in control as parents, and . . . personal guilt for what seems to be going awry."[56] A quarter of a century later, a new generation of mothers experience all the same stress, guilt, doubt, and confusion. All these kinds of stress—fatigue, frustration, worry, guilt, uncertainty—take a physical and emotional toll on working mothers, leaving some to question whether it is worth the strain. Yet despite all the hardship, somehow working mothers do seem to manage it all. In one recent survey, for example, men and women were about equally likely to report feeling successful in the work-family balancing act, with 85 percent reporting that they felt at least somewhat successful in managing both.[57] Tired but triumphant, working mothers are indeed finding a way to balance their dual roles.

2

THE EVOLUTION OF CHILDCARE
IN THE UNITED STATES

Beginning in the 1970s and continuing slowly but surely through the 1980s and 1990s, a social revolution of sorts unfolded in the United States. Mothers of young children began to enter the work force in droves, and more and more children found themselves in the care of someone other than their mothers at younger and younger ages and for longer periods of time per week. Yet despite these somewhat dramatic shifts in childcare usage patterns over a relatively short period of time, the institution of childcare in this country is not new. Indeed, the history of childcare in the United States goes back well into the 1800s, even though the popularity of nonparental childcare has waxed and waned over the years, as sociocultural, economic, and political circumstances have changed.

From its earliest days, "childcare" has taken two basic forms in the United States: as a place for the basic care and nurturing of the young child, most often to allow the mother to work outside the home; and as a means for intellectual and social enrichment. As we shall see, in the earliest days of childcare in the United States these two goals were for the most part independent, with any given childcare facility focusing on one type of service or the other. In more recent times, however, these functions have merged so that many of today's childcare facilities strive to satisfy both kinds of goals.[1]

Childcare as a Service for Working-Class Parents

Throughout the first half of the nineteenth century, the United States experienced a flood of immigration that brought more than 5 million newcomers to the United States in search of more favorable economic, social, and political conditions. During that same period, industrialization and urbanization created a working class that took women out of their homes and into factories. Young children were left to fend for themselves—locked up at home, allowed to roam the streets, or put under the casual supervision of a neighbor or relative. The situation was ripe for philanthropic intervention, and wealthy women and well-meaning service organizations, appalled by the neglect and squalor, organized "day nurseries" to provide care for these children. The first American day nursery was opened in Boston in 1838, followed by a trickle of additional day nurseries in cities such as New York, Detroit, and Cincinnati over the next several years. The post–Civil War era brought a new and even larger wave of immigration by Europeans (over 10 million strong), and with it came an increase in the number of day nurseries in cities such as Philadelphia and Chicago. By 1898, about 175 day nurseries were operating in various parts of the country, enough to warrant the creation of the National Federation of Day Nurseries.

Day nurseries were considered a last resort for children who couldn't be cared for at home, in an effort to at least keep working class families intact. As such, most day nurseries did not enjoy broad ideological support and certainly lacked the financial backing necessary to develop high-quality programs. Instead, most day nurseries were simply custodial in nature, with the primary goals of keeping children safe and meeting their basic physical needs. Day nurseries were most often set up in converted homes and were open six days a week, twelve hours per day. They were operated primarily by untrained women with one or two assistants, whose daily responsibilities included not just the care of the children but also such household tasks as laundry, cooking, and cleaning.

A few day nurseries with more energetic directors offered not only clean, safe places to keep children but something of interest to occupy their time. Since the clientele were largely immigrants, these centers taught children manners and hygiene in the American tradition. Children were trained to use a napkin, to eat in silence, and to march in line. They were given tickets that they could exchange for

articles of clothing if they exhibited the American virtues of punctu-
ality, obedience, industry, cleanliness, and good behavior. Beginning
in the 1890s, some of the better day nurseries also began to offer a
modest educational program, by hiring kindergarten teachers to
teach the children for several hours a day. The curriculum was extended in these exceptional day nurseries to include weaving, sewing,
reading, spelling, and paper folding.

These early day nurseries were founded on the notion that these
working-class mothers needed help, and clients were selected on that
basis. Consequently, in the better day nurseries, working mothers
were also offered services beyond a place to leave their children. They
were offered classes in sewing, cooking, English, and childcare; access
to job training and opportunities; and help with practical as well as
psychological family problems.

The Great Depression of the 1930s created a renewed interest in
group childcare, not necessarily because the service was in greater demand, but rather because it was identified as a way of creating jobs
for unemployed teachers, nurses, cooks, and janitors. In 1933, President Franklin Roosevelt initiated an economic recovery act and the
Work Projects Administration, and federal funds for childcare became available for the first time. By 1937 over nineteen hundred day
nurseries were in operation (a tenfold increase over the number operating at the turn of the century), caring for forty thousand children
of working families. These nurseries were most commonly located in
schools and followed school hours; there was increased participation
by teachers and an increased emphasis on the older, more educable
preschool child.

This temporary expansion of childcare services was short-lived,
however. With the demise of the WPA in 1938, the number of day
nurseries declined again until World War II. Then, with the massive
mobilization of women into war-related industries and renewed financial support provided by the Lanham Act of 1942, day nurseries
flourished once more. By 1945, more than 1.5 million children were in
childcare. However, this childcare boom, too, ended as precipitously
as it had begun, with the end of the war, the withdrawal of Lanham
funds in 1946, and the expectation that mothers would leave the work

force and go back home. Nearly three thousand centers closed, and by 1950 only eighteen thousand children were in childcare centers, or about 1 percent of the enrollment figures just five years earlier.

From 1950 to 1965, childcare again became a marginal service for the poor with an emphasis on social work and problem families. Un-expectedly, however, although the centers had closed, many women continued to work, and those who were not poor enough to qualify for publicly supported childcare used the few available private child-care centers or made other arrangements with relatives, neighbors, or housekeepers. Only in the mid-1960s did attitudes toward childcare begin to become more positive, as it was recognized that mothers were already working and that provision of childcare would appar-ently allow more women to get off the welfare rolls.

Convergence and Expansion of Day Nurseries and Nursery Schools

At about the same time as the use of day nurseries expanded among working-class families, a parallel movement began to take hold among more affluent families. Nursery schools first began to pop up all across the United States in 1915, in cities small and large—Pasa-dena, Detroit, Chicago, New York, and Cambridge, Massachusetts, to name just a few—primarily as a means of providing cognitive and social enrichment for young children and social contact and child development education for their mothers. The idea quickly gained popularity, and many more schools were created over the fol-lowing two decades. Most of these early nursery schools were private programs for children as young as eighteen months. They were most often located in converted residences and supported by parent fees and participation similar to the modern-day parent co-op. Parent education was often part of the program, but nursery schools were above all for children. With blocks, sand, clay, and paints, the schools offered a rich physical environment, where children could play under the kindly guidance of a teacher whose purpose was to help the chil-dren develop impulse control, verbal skills, and knowledge about the world.

By the late 1960s day nurseries and nursery schools were starting to look more and more alike. Day nurseries (later called "childcare centers" or "daycare centers") were generally still full-day programs with the primary purpose of allowing parents to work; nursery schools (later called "preschools") were generally part-day programs with the primary goal of intellectual and social enrichment. Despite these differences, they began to resemble each other from the standpoint of the daily curriculum offerings. In the case of childcare centers, the curriculum shifted away from basic care and unstructured play toward a more formal, academic orientation for at least a part of the day. This change came about primarily as an outgrowth of renewed national interest in early childhood as a critical period for stimulating intellectual development; group childcare settings were seen as the perfect forum for offering such enrichment. Parents ate it up. In one short decade, from 1965 to 1975, enrollment in licensed childcare centers doubled, and enrollment in nursery schools and voluntary kindergartens increased (from just over one-quarter to nearly one-half of all three- to five-year-olds).[2] Through the 1970s childcare began to enjoy a more favorable reputation as a potential source of enrichment for children's development.[3]

In arguably one of the most significant shifts of the twentieth-century American social landscape, the period from the 1970s through the end of the century saw enormous growth in mothers' participation in the labor force and children's attendant participation in childcare. In 1977, approximately 4.3 million American children under age six were cared for by someone other than their mothers for a significant portion of each week. Less than ten years later, that figure had more than doubled to 8.8 million. And although the increase was not quite as steep, the upward trend continued through the next decade, with 12.4 million young children (63 percent of the nation's youngsters) enrolled in regular child care of some type in 1997.[4] By the close of the century, childcare participation had extended to fully two-thirds of the population, with 68 percent of children under the age of six in some form of regular childcare.[5] Interestingly, this figure aligned exactly with the end-of-the-century projections that had been made as early as the mid-1980s.[6] The groundwork was laid for childcare to become one of the more pressing social issues of the 1990s and beyond.

Government Involvement in Childcare: 1960s to 2000

Unfortunately, this unprecedented growth in childcare consumption took place for the most part in the absence of any type of comprehensive national system for increasing the availability of childcare, providing financial assistance to families or facilities, or monitoring childcare quality. Despite nearly forty years of urgings and efforts on the part of child development and early childhood education experts, family-centered politicians, and policy makers to develop a childcare system in the United States, "childcare" continues to be a veritable hodgepodge, varying in form and quality from state to state and family to family. Woven throughout the patchwork quilt of programs and services are the long-held cultural beliefs that the family is sacred, that the rearing of children is the sole responsibility of the family, and that the long arm of the government has no place in this inner sanctum. And while we're at it, some would add, do mothers really belong in the work force at all? Why do we even need public childcare for our youngest citizens? Taken together, the result of these attitudes has been that federal, state, and local governments have sidestepped responsibility in the matter of childcare, and families have been left to work out their childcare needs mostly on their own.

This is not to say, however, that the government has done nothing at all. From the time women first started to flood the workforce, the federal government has been involved to varying degrees in financial support and quality regulation of childcare. This involvement has been slow and reluctant, however, with pieces of legislation being added here and there in the absence of any kind of unified approach. The result was that by the early 1990s, more than ninety different federal childcare and early childhood education programs were in operation, managed by eleven different federal agencies and twenty different offices.[7] And despite the plethora of small Band-Aids being given to the childcare problem, gaping wounds still exist, both in financial support and quality regulation.

FINANCING CHILDCARE

A variety of childcare programs were first funded in the 1960s; over the next thirty years, support for these and later programs ebbed and flowed. Major trends include a notable decline in funding during the mid-1980s and a warmer climate of generosity beginning in the mid-1990s. Federal financial support for childcare has taken three basic forms: direct provision of childcare for low-income families (most prominently in the form of the Head Start program), subsidies to help lower-income families pay for childcare, and tax benefits for middle- and higher-income families. According to the U.S. government's own General Accounting Office, the total federal spending on childcare was more than $16 billion in the year 2000.[8]

Head Start

The flagship of federal childcare programs is Head Start. Created in 1965, Head Start is a comprehensive support program for low-income families that includes education, health, nutrition, and mental health services for children and their families. Originally designed as an eight-week, part-time experimental program to promote the intellectual growth of children from low-income families, Head Start was the first ongoing, nonemergency government program that focused on supporting early childhood development. Because of its ambitious scope and prominence, Head Start alerted the public to the importance of early childhood education for all young children, not just those in affluent families.

Head Start has widely been hailed as a critical success in the power of the federal government to make a difference in young children's lives. Studies on the long-term impact of Head Start and similar early childhood programs have shown that children who participate in such programs are less likely to be held back in school or to be placed in special education classes; they are also more likely to perform well on tests of cognitive development, more likely to succeed in school, and more likely to be rated as socially competent.[9]

These successes notwithstanding, others have pointed to the limitations of Head Start—its relative lack of focus on academic preparedness for children; its lack of sustained, long-term positive effects; and its only modest demonstrated gains. Perhaps the most significant limitation of Head Start, however, has been that it has been limited in its reach. Even though it has served over 20 million children since 1965, because of funding constraints not all eligible children can actually participate. Beginning in the mid-1990s, however, Head Start funding was markedly increased, reaching an annual budget of $6.7 billion in 2003. Head Start services now reach about 60 percent of eligible children.[10] In addition, an Early Head Start component was added in 1994 to serve infants and toddlers, and this component has thus far met with success in giving children cognitive advantages and helping parents learn more productive parenting techniques.[11]

Nevertheless, Head Start was never intended to be a source of childcare that allowed mothers to work outside the home. On the contrary, one of the founding principles of Head Start was that parents (usually mothers) would be intimately involved in the program, with the hope that such involvement would give them additional parenting skills and a sense of empowerment. To this end, few Head Start programs offer full-day care, which working mothers usually require. Thus, although it remains a watershed in the long struggle to get the government involved in early childhood, in reality Head Start is more about providing optimal enrichment opportunities for at-risk youngsters than about helping working parents meet their childcare needs.

Subsidies

A second means through which the federal government has provided childcare assistance to lower-income families is through a variety of government subsidy programs. The earliest of these was Title XX (now known as the Social Services Block Grant), begun in 1974. This program provides states with monies for a variety of human services. Many states use some of these funds (approximately 13 percent) to subsidize childcare, although this practice is becoming less common as demand for other social services grows and separate pools of funds specifically for childcare become available.

As an outgrowth of the heated debate throughout the 1980s regarding the needs of families for childcare assistance and the proper role of the federal government in assisting those families, a slew of reforms and initiatives swept through Congress in the late 1980s and through the 1990s.[12] The Family Support Act of 1988 was a major welfare reform initiative that included expanded childcare assistance for welfare families and those leaving the welfare rolls. In 1990 two new state childcare grant programs were enacted: the Child Care and Development Block Grant (CCDBG) and the At-Risk Child Care Program. The CCDBG was established to help families that earn less than 75 percent of their state's median income pay for childcare. In addition, this block grant allows for a small portion of the funds to be set aside for childcare quality improvements, including increased capacity and availability.

In 1996, as part of the Personal Responsibility and Work Opportunity Reconciliation Act (PRWORA), these programs were consolidated into an expanded Child Care and Development Block Grant (which later became the Child Care and Development Fund, or CCDF). The PRWORA brought together several different funding sources, including those previously offered for welfare recipients in job training programs (JOBS Child Care Program), families who left public assistance for paid employment within the past year (Transitional Child Care Program), and families at risk of returning to public assistance (At-Risk Child Care Program). The CCDF is currently the primary federal program for subsidizing childcare. With funding of $4.6 billion in 2001, it supports childcare services for nearly 2 million children a year, enabling low-income parents and those receiving Temporary Assistance for Needy Families (TANF) to work or to participate in career-related educational programs.

The Child Care and Development Fund allows parents a great deal of flexibility in choosing their childcare arrangements. Except those who are providing care for a related child, such as a grandmother caring for her own grandchildren, childcare providers must meet all licensing or regulatory requirements applicable under state or local law to receive federal assistance. However, parents can enroll their child with a provider who has a grant or contract with the state to provide such services, or they can elect to receive a voucher that can be used to purchase childcare from an eligible provider of their own choosing. In 1998 vouchers were overwhelmingly the form of payment most used, serving over 83 percent of CCDF children nationally.

Not only has the CCDF provided subsidies and vouchers that enable families to select suitable childcare, it also has provided funding for quality-enhancement efforts, including supporting services for parents, quality care initiatives, provider development, childcare referral services, and childcare research.[13] Although a certain percentage of these special childcare funds is spent on increasing access to and capacity for childcare, the Administration for Children and Families has estimated that only 15 percent of eligible children actually attend childcare that has been subsidized by the CCDF.

A major effect of these government programs has been an increase in childcare usage, particularly of centers and licensed childcare homes. Easy access to subsidized or free childcare combined with a legal requirement for more parents to work outside the home has resulted in a greater demand for formal childcare arrangements. This pattern was clearly documented by a study in which mothers were randomly assigned to either a welfare-to-work program or a control group. Childcare enrollment in the welfare-to-work program rose from 46 percent to 78 percent in just two months, compared with an increase from 43 to 49 percent in the control group.[14]

Tax Benefits

Lower-income families are not the only ones to receive federal assistance to pay for childcare. Middle- and upper-income families benefit from two tax credit programs offered by the federal government: the Child and Dependent Care Tax Credit and the Dependent Care Assistance Plan. In fact, these two programs combined represent one of the federal government's most generous direct investments in childcare per se, at approximately $3.5 billion annually.[15]

Under the Child and Dependent Care Tax Credit, working parents may claim a tax credit of up to $2,400 for one child or $4,800 for two or more children to offset their childcare expenses. In 1997 an estimated 6.1 million families claimed this tax credit on their income tax returns.[16] The Dependent Care Assistance Plan allows working parents to deduct up to $5,000 from their gross annual income, thereby reducing their tax burden. Both of these programs are immensely popular with middle- and upper-income working parents, as the plans allow a great deal of flexibility in choosing childcare; the child-care provider or facility need not be licensed or registered to qualify under either plan.

The commitment of large amounts of federal monies to Head Start, CCDF, welfare-to-work programs, and tax subsidies has shaped a social landscape that depends upon formal institutions of nonpar-ental childcare. Social momentum is heading toward creating more capacity and relying more heavily upon childcare so that parents are free to return to the workforce. This tremendous demand is not without its darker side; in the study of childcare usage for welfare-to-work participants, half of the children were in settings that did not meet minimum federal guidelines for quality.[17] Clearly, if the government is going to encourage the use of formal childcare facilities, it must also show concern for the evaluation and regulation of those facilities.

REGULATING CHILDCARE

Government involvement in childcare has included quality regulation as well as financing. In fact, the first childcare licensing laws were on the books, at least at the state level, as early as 1885. And indeed, the first federal foray into childcare funding, in the 1960s, included provisions for ensuring that programs that received federal funds met at least the minimal state standards for health and safety. Because of the requirement that childcare programs have a state license to receive federal funds, states began to develop their own licensing standards. But by the late 1960s it was obvious that there were substantial differences among the states in the standards they were developing. Thus, in 1968 the Federal Interagency Day Care Requirements (FIDCR) were published, establishing requirements for childcare centers as well as licensed childcare homes. These new government standards were developed by the U.S. Office of Child Development, headed by Edward Zigler, a well-respected expert in the field of child development. The original version of the FIDCR was general and nonspecific, leaving too much room for interpretation and making regulation of federally sponsored childcare facilities difficult if not impossible. A revision of the FIDCR in 1971 specified levels of staff training, safety, health, nutrition, educational and social services, parent involvement, adult-child ratios, and group sizes. These revised standards would have been part of the Comprehensive Child Development Act passed by Congress in 1971, but the act was vetoed by President Richard Nixon. The FIDCR continued to limp along quietly; while compliance with FIDCR was never mandated, noncompliance was grounds, at least in principle, for a childcare facility's suspension or for termination of federal funding. In practice, however, such action was never taken. Facilities receiving federal dollars were supposed to be evaluated periodically, but no agent for evaluation was ever specified. Each federal agency that administered a childcare program was given responsibility for enforcing the FIDCR. But most agencies did not strictly enforce them because compliance was financially impossible for many programs and because enforcement would have meant a loss of federal funding, forcing programs to close. By 1980 the FIDCR standards were eliminated entirely. This decision was motivated in part by growing evidence that many of the requirements, particularly those having to do with childcare staffing, were simply too costly and, if enforced, would have resulted in as many as half of all existing federally funded programs being shut down. These closings would have created a childcare shortage of crisis proportions. Individual states thus inherited sole responsibility for regulating and monitoring childcare programs.

Overall, the results of the federal government's decentralization and deregulation were negative: discrepancies between states increased. In a handful of states, funding for childcare increased, but most states raised fees, cut back services, relaxed their quality standards, made the standards apply to fewer institutions (not to church-sponsored or part-time centers, for instance), and eased up on the enforcement of quality standards. These discrepancies led to an increase in the diversity of childcare options—a goal of a market economy held dear by most Americans—but it also led to a decline in the quality of care available.

Subsequent efforts of childcare researchers, providers, and policy makers formed the basis for a set of recommended standards sponsored by the National Association for the Education of Young Children (NAEYC) and widely endorsed by childcare advocates. These guidelines, established in 1985 and revised a number of times since, provided a means for individual childcare programs to voluntarily adopt recommended standards for high-quality care. Programs can seek NAEYC accreditation, a "gold star" rating that tells parents that the program is going above and beyond the mandated minimum in its quest for high quality.

The battle to adopt national standards for childcare was resurrected again in the late 1980s and early 1990s, when a coalition of some eighty groups—including NAEYC, the American Psychological Association, the American Academy of Pediatrics, and the American Federation of Teachers—joined forces behind the able leadership of Marion Wright Edelman, head of the Children's Defense Fund, to lobby for more support and legislation for childcare. Their efforts to legislate federal standards for childcare were unsuccessful yet again, however. Efforts were limited in part by political and economic issues (for example, by a belief that individual states could better adjust standards to reflect regional needs, and by a concern that federal standards would make childcare prohibitively expensive for many families) and in part by the strongly held American cultural bias toward keeping childcare a "family" matter rather than a matter for the federal government. At present, then, childcare regulation in the United States continues to be a responsibility held by each individual state, and childcare quality therefore varies enormously across the country.

Researchers tend to think of childcare quality in two principal domains: *structural* features of childcare settings, that is, features such as staff-child ratios, caregiver training, and various aspects of the physical environment that can be regulated with relative ease; and *qualitative* features, such as the quality of interactions observed between adults and children in the setting or the appropriateness of the daily curriculum. No state has a system in place for extensively monitoring these qualitative features. Instead, states regulate childcare primarily by setting standards for structural features. However, there is no agreement on the level of regulation or the standards that are followed, and standards thus vary widely from state to state and across different types of childcare settings (childcare centers vs. childcare homes).

Regulation of Childcare Centers

All states and the District of Columbia regulate childcare centers to one degree or another. In states with the most stringent childcare center standards, specific educational and training requirements are in place for lead teachers and assistants; staff-child ratios are very small (e.g., one caregiver for every three or four infants and toddlers); and the total group size is restricted in an effort to maintain a calm, quiet environment. At the opposite extreme, in other states there are no educational requirements at all for center-based teachers, staff-child ratios allow for one adult to supervise as many as ten or twelve toddlers, and group sizes are unregulated.[18] Overall, state standards for childcare centers tend to be barely adequate or less than adequate in comparison with NAEYC recommendations. More than a third of states set staff-child ratios at levels below NAEYC standards, while well over half allow group sizes larger than those recommended by NAEYC or do not regulate group size at all. Also, nearly two-thirds do not set minimum training or educational requirements for center-based childcare providers.

Regulation of Childcare Homes

States are also responsible for regulating licensed childcare homes. Discrepancies across states in the levels of childcare home regulation are even greater than those for center regulation, in part because there is such wide variability in what is considered a "childcare home" and what kinds of arrangements should be subject to licensing.[19] Most states define a "family childcare home" as a setting in which a provider takes care of a threshold number of children, with various associated definitions and exemptions. (For example, how many of the children are the caregiver's own children? Is the caregiver related in a more distant way to any of the children? How many different families of children are cared for?) Presently, all but three states license family childcare homes, but nearly one-third of those states consider an arrangement as "licensable" (that is, subject to licensing) only if five or more children are cared for in the setting.[20]

Allowable caregiver-child ratios and total group size (which are often one and the same in childcare homes) are even more variable across states than they are for childcare centers. Unlike centers, where children are usually grouped using a relatively narrow age range, the group composition of family childcare homes typically includes a wide age range of children, from infants to school age. Most states therefore do not set one single maximum group size or ratio but rather link the maximum to the age composition of the group, with more children allowed if all children are older and fewer allowed if some are infants. On average, however, states allow anywhere from five to ten young children in a family childcare home in the care of a single adult caregiver.[21]

Similarly, there is a wide range of standards regarding caregivers' training and education. Only sixteen states require either preservice training or orientation for family childcare providers (only one state requires both). Thirty-five states require some ongoing annual training after a care provider is licensed, but again the amount of training required varies widely from state to state, from as little as four hours to as much as twenty hours annually.[22]

These figures underscore how childcare homes are not stringently regulated in the United States. It is likely that the range of quality found in these settings is enormous. To add to this worrisome picture, most home-based arrangements used by parents in the United States are small and informal; either these arrangements are considered exempt from their state's licensing requirements, or they operate "underground" without taking the necessary steps to become licensed. Because these kinds of informal arrangements are so widely used, estimates are that as much as 90 percent of family childcare used in the United States is unregulated.[23] Indeed, in the multisite National Institute of Child Health and Human Development (NICHD) Study of Early Child Care, even among childcare homes with paid care providers and with at least two children unrelated to the care provider, 82 percent were not licensed.[24] The fact that family childcare is the most common form of childcare used by families with employed mothers for their children under the age of six years makes it all the more troublesome that care in these settings is largely unregulated and of unknown quality.

In summary, the period from the 1960s through the end of the twentieth century was marked by rapid, widespread changes in maternal employment and nonmaternal childcare use. Within this relatively short span of time the United States was transformed from a country of babies riding in strollers pushed along by their stay-at-home mothers to a society of babies riding in wagons with a cartful of age-mates pulled along by an unrelated caregiver who makes sure diapers are changed by the clock. In the next chapter we discuss some of the changes that precipitated this social phenomenon, and we describe the types of care most commonly used in the United States today.

3

CHILDCARE IN THE
UNITED STATES TODAY

It is difficult to present a single figure estimating the number of children in nonmaternal care in the United States today; depending on the source and the means of slicing the pie, these figures vary from 60 to 80 percent of the nation's children under the age of five.[1] Part of the complication is the fact that a significant proportion of the childcare used by working parents in this country is informal and unregulated, and thus "invisible" to those trying to count childcare participation. What is certain, however, is that within the span of a generation childcare has become a mainstay of American childhood for a majority of families, with no apparent reversal of this trend evident on the horizon. In this chapter we discuss some of the factors that have created the pressing demand for childcare, and we consider the different types of childcare options available in the United States today.

Childcare Demand

A number of social changes over the last half century have affected the modern family and created a new need for childcare beyond what the family alone can provide. The supply of high-quality childcare services has not expanded fast enough to fill this pressing and ever-growing need. The major social change affecting the need for childcare, of course, has been the dramatic increase in the number of women who are employed in jobs outside the home. Some women today find themselves in the workforce because they simply need the income to support their families; others are there in part as a function of the changing roles and expectations for women brought about by the women's movement of the mid-to-late twentieth century and the associated increased educational attainment of women. Still other women have no choice but to work outside the home, because they are single parents.

SINGLE MOTHERS

The rate of single-parent families in the United States has risen dramatically over the last fifty years. Currently, nearly one-third of all U.S. households with children are one-parent households, compared with less than one-tenth in 1960.[2] These figures translate into roughly 20 million children under the age of eighteen living in one-parent households in the United States today.[3] Furthermore, extrapolation from recent demographic trends suggests that, over the period from 1995–2010, the number of single-parent households will show the largest increase of all household types in the United States, with an increase from 11.4 million single-mother households in 1995 to an estimated 14 million by 2010.[4] As the sole potential wage earners in their households, single mothers need to work to sustain their families, and in fact government initiatives of the 1990s introduced reforms to make sure that as many single mothers as possible were actively participating in the paid labor force.[5]

This staggering increase in single-parent families is attributable in large measure to the rising divorce rate in the United States.[6] In addition, we have seen accompanying shifts in social attitudes toward marriage and parenthood. For example, in 1962 one survey revealed that about half of the women polled believed parents should stay in a marriage "for the sake of the children," but by 1985 that number had dropped to less than one fifth.[7] In a similar survey conducted in 1994, only 15 percent of the respondents believed that parents with marital difficulties should stay together for their children's sake.[8] Indeed, the presence of children has lost its effect of helping to protect a marriage from dissolution; the number of children newly affected by divorce each year has doubled from about five hundred thousand children per year in 1960 to just over 1 million children each year today.[9]

Not only are more children finding themselves in one-parent homes as a result of divorce, but a growing number of children are being born into single-parent homes. In fact, the number of never-married mothers now exceeds the number of divorced mothers.[10] In 1960, only 5 percent of all births in the United States were to unmarried mothers. By 1990, that figure had skyrocketed to 28 percent.[11] By 2000, one out of every three children born in the United States was born to a single mother.[12] Indeed, throughout the last quarter of a century there appears to have been a shift in young people's beliefs about the necessity of marriage as a precursor to childbearing: in a survey of adolescents' attitudes toward marriage and family, over half (54 percent) of the teen girls surveyed in the period from 1996 to 2000 agreed that having a child outside of marriage was "experimenting with a worthwhile lifestyle" or "not affecting anyone else," compared with just 33 percent agreeing with such statements in the period from 1976 to 1980.[13] Similarly, in a recent national survey of young men and women in their twenties, only 44 percent of the respondents agreed that it is wrong to have a child outside of marriage, and 40 percent of the young women surveyed agreed that, though the situation may not be optimal, they would consider having a baby outside of marriage if they had not found a suitable spouse.[14]

Regardless of whether they have chosen to give birth outside of marriage or find themselves raising children alone as a consequence of a divorce, most single mothers must work to support themselves and their dependents. Seventy percent of single mothers of preschool children are in the labor force, compared with 53 percent of married mothers.[15]

MAKING ENDS MEET IN A FLAT ECONOMY

Maternal employment and nonmaternal childcare are a reality borne out of economic necessity not just for single mothers but also, in a growing number of households, for two-parent families as well. The median family income for married couples in which only the husband works was at about the same level in 2000 as it was thirty years earlier, when adjusted to constant dollars.[16] Median wages actually dropped through the early 1990s, and although they began to rise modestly through the end of the decade, by 1998 the median family income was still slightly lower than it had been in 1980. In many American homes, families responded to this stagnation in male wages (and the concurrent threat that theirs might be the first generation not to improve its standard of living over that of their parents) by maintaining two wage earners in the family.[17]

At the same time that male wages were flat, the cost of living continued to go up. Not surprisingly, the dual-income family became the standard rather than the exception. This new standard now sets prices, making it virtually impossible for a family today to live on just one income; in most families the dual income is needed, not to pay for a minivan, or a fancy vacation, but to meet rising housing and day-to-day living costs. In fact, data on family income show that wives' incomes substantially reduce the likelihood of a family's living in poverty.[18] Financial dependence on the wife's income to keep the family out of poverty pushes mothers not only into the workforce but into the workforce sooner, while their babies are still very young. In one study, it was found that families who placed their infants in child care at the earliest ages (by three months of age) were more likely to be highly dependent on the mother's income.[19] Further binding many women to their jobs is the somewhat precarious nature of the economy over the last several years; fear of the husband's job loss results in the wife working harder.[20]

But even when the husband in a two-parent family earns a living wage and has job security, a new phenomenon is unfolding that makes it increasingly difficult for women to say no to paid employment. Women earn much more than they used to; the gender gap in wages is closing, and there are more opportunities for women in higher-paying jobs than ever before. The result is that in dual-earner families, the wife makes a significant contribution to the household income. In fact, in the span of just twenty years, the percentage of women earning more than their partners rose from just 15 percent in 1981 to nearly 25 percent in 2001.[21] Overall, the mean ratio of women's earnings to their partners' is about 3:4 in dual-earner families, and 55 percent of working women supply half or more of their family's household income.[22] Indeed, the cost of a woman leaving the workforce to stay home with her child has recently been estimated to be over 1 million dollars in lifetime earnings.[23] Given that today's woman provides such a significant proportion of the total family income, it is all the more difficult to leave the workforce, since doing so would likely result in the need for the family to substantially reduce its standard of living. Making this choice all the more difficult, the decision comes precisely when families are incurring significantly greater living expenses—as a result of adding a new member to the family.

PERSONAL FULFILLMENT AND ATTACHMENT
TO THE LABOR FORCE

Although financial considerations are perhaps the primary reason most mothers find themselves in the workforce, employed mothers also work because they like their jobs; because they want to have careers; because they want to get out of the house and meet people, have new experiences, avoid boredom, loneliness, or frustration; and because the feminist movement both made it easier for them to work and created the expectation that they would. The women's movement contributed to the increase of working mothers by bringing pressure against job discrimination, by encouraging new employment and educational opportunities for women, and by making it fashionable for women to work. Feminism encouraged women to be meaningfully and gainfully employed and made many feel guilty if they "only" stayed at home doing housework and raising children.

If the feminist movement brought women into the workplace, personal investment keeps them there. Some women who had established careers prior to having children perceive the need to stay in the workforce following the birth of a child, to avoid being derailed from their career track. In 1960, only 19 percent of married mothers with young children were in the labor force. Since that time, however, a number of demographic changes have converged to dramatically increase that figure. Women's attendance in college has increased to the point of eliminating gender differences in college participation and graduation rates, and the number of women in professional occupations has risen dramatically over this same period. Women have also delayed marriage and childrearing in the interest of completing their education and establishing their careers. Taken together, these changes have left educated, professional women firmly entrenched in occupations for which they have spent years preparing and which they are therefore reluctant to give up, by the time their first child is born. In fact, research suggests that professional women run a risk of experiencing a career derailment by taking the leap into parenthood: although young childless women now earn about 90 percent of their male counterparts' salaries for comparable work, women with children earn only about 70 percent.[24] Thus, a mother's decision to stay home or to reduce her employment to part time while her children are young has financial ramifications not just in the short run, in terms of the income sacrificed while she is home, but also in the much-longer term, considering the negative impact on her lifetime earning potential once she returns to the workforce.[25]

LIMITED FAMILY LEAVE

Whether women work out of choice or economic necessity (or both), another significant factor contributing to the increased need for childcare in the United States, and especially for infant care, is the country's limited family leave policy. The United States and Australia stand alone as the only holdouts among industrialized nations in a worldwide move to provide paid leave to women (and often their partners) following the birth or adoption of a child. In contrast, in other countries around the world women are given generous maternity leaves of anywhere from two months to over a year, at or near full pay and with a guarantee of having their job preserved for them while they are away.[26] These kinds of policies are not limited to just large, wealthy nations. On the contrary, paid leave is an employee benefit offered in over 120 countries around the world.

In the United States, maternity leave policies have been slow to evolve in comparison with the explosive increase in the rate of maternal participation in the labor force. In the early 1960s, nearly two-thirds of women quit their jobs once they became pregnant; by the mid 1990s, only a quarter of women made such a decision.[27] Prior to 1993, maternity leave policies were set by individual states. Proposals for federal maternity leave in the United States were made as early as 1942, when the Women's Bureau of the Department of Labor suggested that employed women be given fourteen weeks of leave (in line with proposals being adopted in many other countries around the world), but no such federal action was taken. By the mid-1980s, despite the dramatic increase in women's labor force participation throughout the preceding two decades, fewer than half the states had adopted unpaid maternity leave policies. By the mid-1980s, it was evident that this standard was inadequate for the needs of women, and in 1985 a bill allowing for maternity leave policies closer in line to those of comparable countries of the world was first introduced into Congress. The bill went through several iterations of downsizing, all of which were designed to minimize the economic impact of maternity leaves on businesses, but it was still vetoed by President George H. W. Bush.

Interestingly, the issue of maternity leave was a big applause-grabber in the presidential race of 1992, and when President Bill Clinton took office in 1993, the Family and Medical Leave Act (FMLA) was the first bill he signed into law. While still lagging far behind the generous policies of other countries, the FMLA extended the allowable period of unpaid leave to twelve weeks for full-time workers in companies with fifty or more employees, with continued health benefits during the leave and a guarantee of job security. Nevertheless, with its many restrictions, it is estimated that FMLA leaves over half of the nation's private-sector workers uncovered.[28] A further limitation is that even for workers who are covered under FMLA, few can afford to take the full twelve weeks without pay. In fact, in one U.S. Department of Labor survey it was found that two-thirds of FMLA-eligible workers who needed but did not take a leave indicated that they did not do so because they simply could not afford to go without a paycheck.[29] Thus, even though FMLA is clearly a step in the right direction, it falls short of providing the coverage that working mothers need and that their counterparts in countries around the world already enjoy.

LACK OF EXTENDED FAMILY

Yet another social change that has increased the need for childcare is the scarcity of extended-family members to provide childcare. In the late 1800s, nearly half of all mothers with young children had a mother, mother-in-law, or older daughter around to help out with childcare. By the end of the twentieth century, that figure had shrunk to one fifth.[30] Today's families are often geographically isolated from extended-family members; thus, few families have the luxury of having an aunt or grandmother nearby to pitch in with childcare assistance. Similarly, unlike previous generations very few American families today have older relatives living in the same household; the vast majority of American children live in a home with just one or two adults (their parents). But even when grandmothers or aunts live nearby or in the same home, they increasingly have lives and jobs of their own and are less likely to be available for childcare as a result of these other commitments. Last, families of previous generations were much larger, and the ages of their children were spread out; thus, older siblings were often available to care for younger family members. Today, by contrast, most families consist of just two children, close together in age, making sibling care another luxury of the past.

INCREASED FOCUS ON EARLY EDUCATION AND SCHOOL READINESS

Another cultural shift that has led to an increased demand for childcare has been an emphasis on the importance of the earliest years of childhood as a crucial period for brain development. An exciting new line of research in the mid-to-late 1990s grabbed the headlines and led parents to believe that they had better provide a cognitively stimulating, enriching environment for their children literally from the womb and certainly in those critical first five years of life.[31] Televised public service announcements now promote enrolling children in preschool if parents hope to have these children graduate from high school. An entire cottage industry has sprouted up around these findings: fetuses are now read and sung to; new mothers in some states leave the hospital with a free classical music CD to play for their newborns; the pastel bunnies and duckies that once dangled merrily from crib mobiles have been replaced by ostensibly more stimulating red, black, and white checkerboard patterns; and a video series entitled *Baby Einstein* is all the rage in children's home video sales. Riding the wave of this new hysteria have been the fields of childcare and early childhood education; even those children whose mothers are not employed outside the home now find themselves spending at least a year in preschool prior to entering the formal educational system. In 1965, for example, just 5 percent of three-year-olds and 16 percent of four-year-olds had some kind of preschool experience; by 1999 those figures had risen to 40 percent and 70 percent, respectively.[32]

Childcare Supply

All of these changes have converged over the last thirty-five years to create an ever-growing need for childcare. The childcare supply in this country, however, has grown in a haphazard manner. In this section we discuss the steps parents usually take in selecting care, and we present the most common types of care used by parents today, the availability and accessibility of care, the cost of care, and the quality of the care that is available.

HOW PARENTS CHOOSE CHILDCARE

Parents decide on a childcare arrangement by balancing three things: cost, convenience, and quality of care. Of these, not surprisingly, most parents report that high quality is the most important to them.[33] What parents care most about is their child's experience in the care arrangement—the warmth of the caregiver, the variety of daily activities, and opportunities for learning. Parents also value high quality in the facility (space, safety, security), staff stability (low teacher-turnover), and high quality in their own interactions with the teachers. Parents care for these qualitative factors more than they care about structural features of the program—such as group size, child-adult ratios, and provider training—and more than they care about cost and convenience.[34] Mothers in high-income families and those who work fewer hours are particularly likely to select a childcare arrangement based on quality rather than on practical concerns such as cost and convenience;[35] they are the parents most likely to find high-quality care and to be satisfied with it.

Yet despite this emphasis on high quality, most parents' childcare search in fact tends to be limited, informal, and unlikely to involve systematic data-gathering and assessment of pertinent information.[36] After parents decide what kind of childcare they want, they usually look only for settings of that type. They start by asking neighbors, friends, and relatives with children. Once an available childcare setting has been located, parents usually stop searching. Most do not comparison shop or evaluate an exhaustive list of childcare options; they are just glad to have found a place or person to provide care for their child. Children are usually enrolled in centers or childcare homes without extensive screening on the part of the parent; a brief visit or phone call is all the checking up parents often do. As a result, they are buying a "pig in a poke."

The friends who have recommended the caregiver or center have not usually known more than a few caregivers or visited more than one center. A "professional" (doctor or professor) who might have made a recommendation has not usually visited any centers. Telephone directories do not screen listed childcare facilities for high quality, and newspaper ads are clearly biased. The fact that a center or a home is licensed indicates only that it meets certain minimal physical standards, not that it offers high-quality care. Community agencies or referral services are not allowed to give parents recommendations or evaluations about childcare providers, even if evaluations are available. A phone call to the childcare center or babysitter is not very informative about quality unless the caller asks very astute questions and gets very accurate answers. Finally, even if parents visit the childcare facility, they often do not know what to look for. Suggestions given in women's magazines about how to identify a center that provides good care are usually vague, untested, and hard to interpret and observe (how can parents know what "optimal amounts of touching, holding, smiling, and looking" are or what "balances interaction with leaving infant alone" means?). For all these reasons most parents choose a particular childcare setting for the child on the basis of its physical conditions (whether it looks clean and smells good) and their rapport with the childcare director or provider.[37]

TYPES OF CARE MOST COMMONLY USED BY AMERICAN PARENTS

Three primary types of childcare are used by working parents in the United States: care in the child's own home, care in a family childcare home, and center care. In this section we describe these kinds of settings.

Care in the Child's Home

Care in the child's own home while mother works is most commonly provided by the father or another adult relative, such as a grandmother, or far less commonly by an unrelated adult, such as a babysitter, nanny, or au pair. The caregiver is usually untrained and is not subject to state licensing requirements. Except when the caregiver is the father, in-home caregivers tend to be older women (over forty). If the in-home caregiver is related to the child, this is the most economical and stable of all childcare arrangements; if the in-home caregiver is not a relative, this form of care is the least stable. If the caregiver is trained in child development—a professional nanny—in-home care is the most expensive kind of care. Educational or group activities with peers are uncommon in in-home care.

Despite these drawbacks, most parents, given a choice, prefer childcare in their own home, by a nonrelative adult babysitter.[38] Not only is this arrangement most convenient, but with an in-home care provider parents expect that they will have more control over the child's experiences and that the caregiver will be more respectful of parents' views and give the child the kind of discipline parents agree with.[39] In-home care with an unrelated adult, however, is usually the most costly kind of care. For that reason it is a relatively uncommon form of care in the United States. Relatives, on the other hand, usually do not charge anything for the care of the child. In addition, parents usually feel they can trust a relative more than a nonrelative to keep their children safe and well cared for. For these reasons, care by a relative is a popular type of care used in the United States, especially for infants and toddlers.

Family Childcare Home

A family childcare home is a care arrangement in which an adult (almost always a woman) cares for a small group of mixed-age children in her own home. Parents typically choose childcare homes located in their own neighborhoods. Therefore, this form of childcare is convenient, and it is also flexible, familiar, and comfortable. Parents can still exert some control over their child's experiences, and childcare homes are the least expensive of all types of care. In 2003 there were just over three hundred thousand licensed family childcare homes operating in the United States.[40] Childcare homes often operate informally; either they are not subject to licensing by their state's guidelines, or they choose to operate "under the radar," without going through the formal steps to become licensed. Thus, the actual number of family childcare homes operating in the United States is unknown but has been estimated to be as much as 80–90 percent higher than the number of licensed childcare homes.[41] In fact, in a study of family childcare conducted in the mid-1990s, 81 percent of the participating unregulated childcare homes were operating illegally.[42]

A number of research studies give us a picture of life in a "typical" childcare home.[43] Most childcare homes have no more than three or four children (aged eighteen months to thirty-six months) and one care provider present at one time, although most state licensing standards allow for six or more children in a family childcare home. (Of the three hundred thousand licensed homes reported in the 2003 survey, 15 percent were "group" childcare homes in which two or more caregivers provided care to a larger group of children.) The typical family childcare provider is a young married woman with young children of her own. She is a high-school graduate with six years of childcare experience, but she is likely to be untrained. She provides childcare because she is fond of children and because she wants to provide playmates for her own child while supplementing the family income. The childcare home is usually a single-family house with a designated indoor play area for the children, a sleeping area where portable cribs might be set up, and an outdoor play area. Childcare-home providers are unlikely to offer organized educational games or structured activities; rather, children in childcare homes spend most of their day in free play. The providers rarely follow a "curriculum" per se, although they might follow a rough schedule of activities. The typical day is relatively unstructured and may include free play, outside time, lunch and snacks, and nap time. Most home-care providers see their role as caring for children's physical needs and being "like a mother" to the children. They spend about half of their time interacting with the children and the rest of the time doing housework or personal activities. The main goal of most family childcare providers is to provide a warm "home-like" atmosphere for the children. In short, life in a childcare home is more like life at home than life at school, but unfortunately it offers children less interaction with an adult than they would probably have with their mother at home.[44]

Childcare Center

A childcare center is the most visible and easily identified childcare arrangement, and in recent years it has become virtually interchangeable with the term "childcare." A center may provide care for fewer than fifteen children or more than three hundred; on the average there are about sixty children in a center. Currently in the United States there are about 116,000 licensed childcare centers.[45] Unlike childcare homes, childcare centers are run under all kinds of different auspices, from for-profit conglomerates such as KinderCare Learning Centers, with a franchise in every neighborhood; to smaller, individually owned and operated for-profit centers; to corporate or government sponsored non-profit centers; to church-run or university-affiliated centers.

Parents whose goals for the child are supervision, stimulating play, and school preparation are most likely to choose a childcare center or preschool. They give up some convenience to achieve these goals—especially if the preschool is open only half days—but since costs run from relatively inexpensive to relatively costly, parents can often find a center program to fit their budget, especially if they are willing to be put on a waiting list until space is available.

About one-third of children in centers attend full time (at least thirty-five hours per week). They are usually divided into classes or groups according to their age. The average group size is seven infants, or ten toddlers, or fourteen preschoolers, but these sizes can vary enormously. Most children in childcare centers are three or four years old, although center care for infants and toddlers has steadily risen in popularity over the last thirty years. Teachers in the centers tend to be women (97 percent) under forty years of age. Most have attended college and have received training in child development.[46] They are likely to offer children educational opportunities and the chance to play with their peers in a child-oriented, safe environment that is rich in materials and equipment. The physical setting of a childcare center might be a converted space, or it might be a structure built specifically for use as a childcare facility, with such child-friendly features as low windows and high electrical outlets. There is usually a large, fenced outdoor play area offering play structures mounted over shock-absorbing surfaces; a covered area for shade; a sand pile; and plenty of outdoor toys and vehicles. Older children might have an outdoor play area separate from one for younger children, or different age groups might take turns using a common outdoor space.

In summary, there is a wide range of childcare used in the United States today, both in terms of the structural and qualitative features of the settings and the quality of care provided in those settings. It is a complicated task for parents to identify, choose, and monitor the quality of these different choices. As we discuss later in this chapter, unlike the building parents might work in or the restaurant they might lunch at, all these childcare settings have no government or private entity to make sure they are safe, good places for children to be.

CHILD AND FAMILY FACTORS IN CHILDCARE CHOICES
Two recent national surveys of parents' childcare use give us an idea of the types of care most often selected by working parents for their children today.[47] Infants and toddlers are usually cared for by their

own parents working opposite shifts (26 percent), by a grandparent or another adult relative (32 percent), or by an unrelated adult in the child's or caregiver's home (22 percent). Only 17 percent of this age group are cared for in centers. In contrast, older preschoolers (three- and four-year-olds) are more likely to be cared for in more formal or institutional types of child care (centers, preschools, or nursery schools), with about 34 percent of these children enrolled in this type of care. Indeed, in several studies of parents' childcare choices and preferences, it has been reported that parents are more likely to use home-based care settings for their younger children (up to two years of age) and centers for their three- and four-year-olds.[48] The inference has often been made from cross-sectional studies such as these that parents place their children in home-based settings in infancy and then "graduate" them into more formal preschool-type settings as they get older. However, in the prospective, longitudinal NICHD Study of Early Child Care, this pattern was not universally found to be the case; following the childcare history of individual children from birth through school age yielded no discernible pattern of care over the preschool years, and instead over four hundred different childcare paths were taken from birth through age five by the one thousand study participants.[49]

Differential patterns of childcare use are related not only to child age but also to such family characteristics as household composition and family income. For example, the more children in the family, the more likely it is that parents will use an informal home-care arrangement rather than more expensive center care.[50] Two-parent families and lower-income families tend to use center care less frequently than single-parent families or higher-income families. In fact, among low-income families, single-parent families are twice as likely to use center childcare as their two-parent counterparts (35 percent vs. 16 percent). In many studies, use of center care has been found to have a curvilinear relation to income, presumably because of the availability in many geographic locations of childcare subsidies or center-based early intervention programs for families in poverty; these programs and subsidies make centers accessible to low-income as well as high-income families.[51] Differential patterns of use are also found for relative care: two-parent families are less likely to use relative care (25 percent) than are single-parent families (33 percent).[52]

Of course, parental attitudes about child rearing and childcare also influence their childcare choices. Parents who value education highly and encourage literacy-related activities at home tend to use center childcare over home childcare.[53] Those who worry about negative effects of childcare on children's emotional development are more likely to use home care.[54] On the other hand, those who believe children benefit from childcare and who have positive views about combining work and family are more likely to use centers.[55] These differences in childcare use underscore the fact that childcare usage patterns are almost infinitely varied.

AVAILABILITY OF CARE

The number of licensed childcare spots for children has increased steadily in response to the growing number of mothers needing childcare for their children. For example, in the relatively short period of time from 1991 to 2003, the number of licensed childcare centers in the United States grew an astounding 35 percent, from 86,000 to 116,000. Similarly, the number of licensed childcare homes increased 32 percent, from 193,000 in 1988 to 254,000 in 2003.[56] Yet despite this surge in childcare supply, research suggests that gaps may still exist between childcare supply and demand, particularly for infant care and most acutely for the poor.[57] The problem, thus, is not that there is an overall shortage of childcare so much as that there are particular kinds of shortages—in the types of care individual parents want for their children, in affordable care, in high-quality care. For example, although there are a large number of centers in operation, many of them do not offer care for infants and toddlers, often because this type of care is the most expensive to provide. Only a minority of those parents who want center care can find openings for their children. At a highly regarded childcare center some mothers may wait in line through the night before registration day for the few childcare openings which are filled within hours. Other people put their names on a waiting list at a childcare center that takes infants the day they find out the mother is pregnant. Although that leaves nine months of lead time, the best centers commonly have more than a year-long waiting list. Many mothers thus end up having to find alternative care so that they can go back to work by the time their maternity leave is up; by the time the coveted spot opens up in the childcare center, the child has happily adjusted to a different childcare setting, and the mother is reluctant to pull her baby out of it.

Another problem parents face in trying to find childcare to meet their needs is that, as we have discussed, a lot of childcare is "invisible" to parents. That is, simply pulling open the local yellow pages will not give the parent an exhaustive list of available childcare options, although it will at least list the local childcare centers. Less formal types of childcare—which many parents prefer, especially for their younger children—are generally not readily accessible in any kind of directory, listing, or database. Many communities across the United States have in recent years put a lot of effort and funding into developing local resource and referral agencies. These agencies keep lists of licensed family childcare providers in the area, a veritable gold mine of information for the parent looking for family-based childcare. But going through the list by calling stranger after stranger, with an eye toward choosing the one whose home a mother might be willing to leave her little baby in all day every day, is a daunting task indeed. Perhaps for that reason many parents feel more comfortable choosing someone whom they have learned about through word of mouth; but the chance that the wonderful caregiver their neighbor used for her own small children is still in operation, lives nearby, and has an opening at the times the parent needs is usually very small.

COST OF CARE

One of the greatest childcare challenges facing young working parents is not just finding childcare that they like, that fits their needs, and that is reasonably convenient but being able to afford such care. Because it is a labor intensive service, childcare is expensive. The average cost of childcare for one child in 2003 was estimated at $4,000 to $6,000 per year, higher than the average cost of annual tuition at a public university in all but one state.[58] Care for infants can be even costlier. Trying to pay for childcare for one child, let alone two or more, therefore eats up a significant proportion of the working family's budget.[59] Childcare expenses take up 7 percent of the budget of a family above the poverty line and a staggering 20 percent of a poor family's income.[60] And though poor families would technically qualify for federal support to pay for care, only about 10–15 percent of eligible families actually receive such assistance.[61]

QUALITY OF CARE

In the richest country in the land and one with such careful regulations for the quality and safety of everything from carpet fibers to airline operations, it would be wonderful to think that it would be impossible to find poor quality in the childcare industry. Unfortunately, nothing could be further from reality. In 1991, the *Journal of Social Issues* identified childcare in the United States as "a national scandal" and "a most serious problem for children in our society."[62] Just how bad is the childcare that is available today? Of course, the quality of care found in childcare settings varies enormously; but a handful of studies conducted in childcare homes and centers paint a worrisome picture of the quality of care received by a majority of children in the United States every day. Furthermore, the situation appears to have grown worse, not better, in the same period of time that childcare use has increased exponentially, as Table 1 illustrates. For example, in one of the first studies of childcare quality, carried out in the early 1970s by the National Council of Jewish Women, 14 percent of the childcare homes included in that study were rated as poor, 48 percent as fair, 31 percent as good, and 7 percent as superior.[63] Twenty years later, another comprehensive study of quality in childcare homes found more dismal results: 13 percent of family childcare homes were rated as inadequate, 75 percent as minimal, and 12 percent as good.[64] As troubling as these findings are, there is cause for even greater concern: not only do a large number of American parents rely

Table 1 Childcare Quality Then and Now: Changes in Overall Quality from the 1970s to the 1990s

Quality	Childcare Homes		Centers	
	1970s	1990s	1970s	1990s
Poor	14%	13%	30%	12–21%
Fair/minimally adequate	48%	75%	43%	67–74%
Good or excellent	38%	12%	26%	12–14%

Sources: M. D. Keyserling, *Windows on Day Care: A Report on the Findings of Members of the National Council of Jewish Women on Day Care Needs and Services in their Communities,* report for the Educational Resource Information Center, 1972, ED 063 027; E. Galinsky et al., *The Study of Children in Family Childcare and Relative Care: Highlights of Findings* (New York: Families and Work Institute, 1994; Cost, Quality, and Child Outcomes Study Team, *Cost, Quality, and Child Outcomes in Child Care Centers,* 2nd. ed. (Denver: University of Colorado, 1995); Whitebook et al., *Who Cares? Child Care Teachers and the Quality of Care in America,* final report for the National Childcare Staffing Study (Oakland, Calif: 1990); J. M. Love, "Quality in Child Care Centers, *Early Childhood Research and Policy Briefs* 1 (1997).

on this type of care, but untold numbers of these family childcare arrangements today are unregulated and invisible to researchers and policy makers. They are therefore of unknown quality.

Like childcare homes, the quality of care observed in childcare centers has been found to range from poor to excellent. In the study by the National Council of Jewish Women, 30 percent of the centers visited were rated as poor, 43 percent as fair, 21 percent as good, and 5 percent as superior. Twenty years later, following a period in the United States when attendance in childcare centers had seen a sharp and steady rise, a handful of studies found that anywhere from 12 to 21 percent of observed childcare center classrooms offered care of inadequate quality (that is, care that was potentially unsafe or harmful to children's development), 67 to 74 percent offered minimally adequate care, and only 12 to 14 percent of observed centers offered care that was rated as good.[65] Researchers worry that experience in such kinds of care might have long-lasting negative consequences for children's development, and a great deal of effort has gone into studying this question in recent years, as we present in much greater detail in Part II of this book. But never mind the long-term effects: the reasonable parent might despair at having no other choice than to leave her child in a setting that simply does not seem like a nice place to spend the day, with caregivers who do not seem to care much.

National Reluctance, National Disgrace

Why is childcare in this country in such a sorry state? Why haven't government or private groups stepped in to support the improvement of childcare services? Why hasn't this been a higher priority in public policy? There are many reasons—reasons that involve economic interests, political agendas, and deep-seated social values and beliefs about parenting. Those opposed to federal involvement in or expansion of childcare point to the fact that significant increases have been made in the amount of childcare subsidies in the last ten years and that childcare subsidy programs for low-income families are seeing low rates of participation, suggesting that expansion is not needed. They worry that federal initiatives will unnecessarily limit states' flexibility to develop childcare programs to meet the unique needs of their populations. But others counter that while subsidies have indeed increased, so has demand and that supply has not kept apace. They argue that low subsidy participation rates are attributable not to a lack of need for childcare but a lack of availability of the specific kinds of care real families need: part-time care, care for infants or school-age children, care for sick or special-needs children, or simply care of reasonable quality in families' neighborhoods.

Childcare is not a simple issue. There is not even agreement among all American citizens that childcare *should be* expanded or improved. Childcare engenders controversies that go far beyond simply what is convenient or necessary for mothers and strike at the core of our social system and our personal ideologies. The sorry state of childcare reflects a national ambivalence about childcare. But despite this ambivalence, over the past thirty years, while childcare has been growing dramatically and growing out of control, researchers have been collecting data. They have been studying the effects of childcare on children's development and investigating just how much poor quality matters. This research is the topic we discuss in the next section.

PART TWO

A QUARTER CENTURY
OF RESEARCH

When my husband and I decided to try the adventure of becoming parents, I had years of long work hours behind me. I had finished school early by putting in many night, weekend, and early morning shifts, and I had advanced in my career by working fifty-five-plus hours a week on a regular basis. Therefore, working part time and staying home with a baby part time seemed at the time like an ideal change to me. My husband would have preferred for me to stay home full time with the baby, but he respected my wish to keep a foot on my career ladder. He agreed to care for our daughter Kaylee in the mornings when I went to work, and he truly enjoyed this one-on-one time with her. After a four-month maternity leave I was ready to go back to work part time. I felt like I had the best of both worlds; I could stay involved in my career and still have plenty of time to watch my daughter grow. I felt confident in my choice: all the research I was seeing on childcare in the local papers seemed to say that my baby would be just fine, that she would still love me, that I would feel more fulfilled, and what could be better? She was getting to stay home with daddy for some special bonding time anyway.

When Kaylee was nine months old, my husband's job situation changed, and he was no longer available to care for her while I was at work. We found a very sweet young woman with eighteen-month-old twins who watched Kaylee while we were both at work. Kaylee never cried when my husband dropped her off and was happy when I picked her up, and she was soon very attached to her daycare "family." But at about this time I started to feel less content about the situation. I felt I had too much on my plate, both at work and at home. My job responsibilities had been cut in half when I went down to part-time status, but trying to squeeze half of a fifty-five-plus hour workload into twenty hours was nearly impossible, and I wasn't motivated to work more than the twenty hours for which I was now paid. As a result, my work became stressful—I never had time to take a break or chat with co-workers, I constantly worked from one deadline to the next, and it never seemed like it was enough. Then I rushed to pick up our daughter from daycare. At home, I was now responsible for all household chores in addition to taking care of Kaylee. My husband's new job was financially rewarding but very demanding. He averaged a sixty-five-hour work week and worked many evenings and weekends. I felt lonely for the first time in my life. I thought about that research, and I knew this was not the life they were talking about that would be "just fine" for our family. I knew I had to make a change.

I finally talked to my husband about it, and we agreed to increase the daycare hours by adding two half-days. One afternoon a week my hubby and I would go on "dates," out for lunch, to the movies, etc. One other afternoon belonged to me. I was able to read a book, meet a girl-friend, or simply go to the grocery store without a toddler trying to climb out of the cart. This new arrangement gave me room to breathe and I loved my life again.

I would still have it this way if I hadn't been given another choice when Kaylee was two and a half years old: I was offered a promotion I couldn't resist. It was the career opportunity I had dreamed about for a long time. But it was a full-time position. To this day, three years after I accepted the position, I have not once regretted my decision. Sure, I had some compromises to make. When our son Brennan was born six months after I took the promotion, I felt I had to return to work after a short, two-month maternity leave because of the higher level work responsibilities. I have missed many moms' groups outings I would have loved to attend. I wasn't there for my daughter's preschool Christmas caroling or kindergarten Halloween party. My husband takes our son to his routine checkups, and the babysitter takes him to the park. I missed his proud smile when he went down the slide for the first time by himself.

But then again, I have gained much: I love my profession. I love going to work. I no longer stress out at work, because I have enough time to get all the work done and still take a few minutes to chat with co-workers and see to the little extras that make it a more pleasant place to be for everyone. I work from home two days a week, which saves me commuting time and gives me extra flexibility to do things like drive Kaylee and her neighbor friends to school and so return the favor to the neighbors who pick her up. We found a wonderful babysitter, and being able to trust her 100 percent is priceless in allowing me to feel so comfortable with my current situation. My employers, one of whom is a mother of young children herself, understand that a fifty-plus-hour work week is no longer an option for me. But years of experience have made me an expert in time management, and I use that skill to my advantage.

To be sure, life is very busy with two young children and a full-time job. I never take a break between 5:30 A.M. when I get up and 8 P.M. when the kids are in bed. But I feel happy and satisfied. I look forward to my time with the kids when I am away from them for a day. I am more patient, and I simply love being a mom. My husband and I have a date night once a week, and I no longer feel guilty hiring a babysitter for a couple of extra hours to run some errands by myself peacefully. The children are happy. We laugh and we dance together. Every single day.

—Andrea, age 35

I was in my second year of my graduate studies in psychology when I became pregnant with my first son, Nicholas. Ironically, I remember feeling nervous telling my professors, these experts in child development and family studies, that I would be interrupting my studies to have a baby. I was worried that they would think I wasn't committed to my graduate education, and I had some concerns of my own about how I would balance my baby with my grad school obligations.

I loved motherhood, but I felt some internal pressure to return to school when Nicholas was four months old. No one had told me it was time to go back, but my perception was that my professors would think it was time. I was pleasantly surprised when my advisor (a childless, middle-aged man who routinely worked well into the night) encouraged me to enjoy some more time at home with my baby and wait another quarter before coming back. I gladly took his advice and came back when Nicholas was eight months old. Fortunately, I was able to continue my studies on a part-time basis. It was comforting knowing that in my one-day-a-week absence Nicholas would be in the loving care of my husband, whose own work schedule is very flexible. I wasn't ready to turn my baby over to a "stranger," and we didn't have any grandparents or aunts or uncles living nearby. Paying for childcare would have proven difficult anyway, given our tight financial situation. When he was a little older, I started doing "babysitting exchanges" with the other moms from Nicholas's playgroup. Our playgroup felt like an extended family, and Nicholas spent many happy hours at his buddies' homes.

Despite some financial struggles and some late nights working after the baby was asleep, I felt happy at the way my life was organized. I was able to be with my baby most of the time, which was important to me. And I also squeezed in a moment or two to get my work done. The biggest work-family challenge for me was remembering when I was with him to truly be with him, to be in the moment—instead of stressing about when my next project was due.

When Nicholas was little, I read a book (OK—part of a book) called Sequencing *that described how mothers can think about their personal and professional life in terms of phases over a course of time. They can be professionals early on, take time out to be at home or work just part-time when their kids are young, and return to a fuller professional life as their children become older. The words really resonated with me. I was certainly on a career path, but I was not a high-level careerist who would lose out financially and professionally if I dropped out of the work world for a few years. I felt like I was making the right choices for me and my family to slow down on the career thing for a while.*

When I became pregnant with my second child, Jake, I decided to end my graduate program with a master's degree instead of finishing with the Ph.D. It was a tough decision. I felt good about stopping, but I wasn't really ready to leave it all behind. So I kept a foot in the water; I did a little writing, and I was able to collaborate with one of my old professors on some projects. Fortunately, she was a mother herself, and she totally respected and supported my decision to make my kids the primary focus of my life and fit in a little work on the side as icing on the cake, rather than the reverse.

When I think back on the different childcare and work choices I have made over the last five years, I guess it seems on the one hand hard but on the other hand oh so easy. I looked into my soul, and I knew what felt right for me and for our family. I was lucky that I was able to just go with those feelings. But it strikes me that it's not that way for everyone, and it's especially discouraging to see that so many people are so intolerant of other people's personal choices. I remember one morning reading in the newspaper about the new findings of some big, important national childcare study. The results were hard to understand. They seemed like a complicated web of various factors that were difficult to pick apart—and I was supposedly someone who was trained in psychological research! But everywhere I turned, journalists and moms were spinning the results this way and that to justify and validate their own beliefs and choices about childcare, or feeling guilty about the choices they had made. It was disheartening to see that working mothers and stay-at-home mothers felt pitted against each other. Childcare is such a deeply personal decision, with different scenarios working best for different families, and it seemed to me in the best of worlds that parents should be able to be supportive of each other's choices . . .

Nicholas is now five and a half years old and in kindergarten, and Jake is fifteen months. As I look back, I wouldn't have done it any other way. I love that I get to spend most of my time with them, and that I still manage to have some time each week to do my work from home, all without turning myself into a stress case or donning the proverbial "Supermom" cape. Recently, I decided to go back to grad school. Yet I can still be "helping mom" in Nicholas's class and take Jake to the zoo. I know that I am lucky to have the flexibility to do it all—it didn't come without tough choices and sacrifices, but I also recognize that they weren't exactly Sophie's Choice decisions, either. Nevertheless, I feel good about the se-

quencing, and I know I am doing the right thing for me and, above all, for them. One day I may be the famous psychologist that all the talk shows are clamoring for, but for now I am happy to be the one teaching a baseball unit to a bunch of grateful, adoring kindergarteners, with one especially proud, toothless little smile beaming up at me in the crowd.

—Annika, age 38

4

Social scientists have been studying the effects of childcare on children for three decades now. After thirty years of refinement, research approaches are more sophisticated, and statistical techniques are more sensitive and complex. Here, we describe the methodological progress researchers have made over the past quarter century and describe in some detail three special studies that represent the best of contemporary childcare research. The findings from these three studies are featured in the chapters that follow, and the studies themselves illustrate three different approaches to studying the complex issues of childcare.

Childcare Research the Old Way

For the first two decades of childcare research, in the 1970s and 1980s, the usual study of childcare involved locating two groups of children—those attending childcare and those at home with their mothers—and comparing how well they did on particular tests. If the average score for the group of children in childcare was higher than the average score for the other children, the researchers concluded that childcare had a positive effect on development; if it was lower, researchers concluded that childcare was damaging. This study design, however, turned out to be far too simple to do justice to the complex questions of childcare effects.

There were other limitations in this early research as well. For one thing, researchers were most likely to study university-based, well-funded, and well-run centers. These centers were convenient, open to research, and interesting because they reflected what experts believed was the best possible childcare, but they did not represent the kind of care most children were receiving. When researchers included in their studies childcare facilities from the community, they did not systematically observe and describe children's experiences in these facilities. Their research was mute about the nature and quality of care the children were receiving. However, one might assume that these facilities, too, would be of better-than-average quality, because care providers offering poor-quality care would be less likely to agree to participate in research. Thus, the results of early studies of childcare probably underrepresented low-quality childcare.

A third limitation of early research on childcare was that children in nonparental childcare differed from parental-care children in ways that the researchers did not or could not assess. Early researchers could not guarantee that the two groups of children were identical in every way except in the one variable being contrasted—attending childcare. Meeting this seemingly obvious requirement was a problem. For one thing, the researchers didn't investigate the childcare-like experiences of children who were not in the childcare group. Although these children were not enrolled in a formal childcare program at the time of the study, they may have had similar experiences in a playgroup or nursery school. In addition, although researchers could select for their two groups children who were of the same age, whose families had comparable incomes, and who lived in the same neighborhoods, it was not possible to rule out other differences between the two groups of families. These differences included such important factors as the mothers' work status and the parents' attitudes toward maternal employment.

Ideally, in a rigorous scientific study, researchers would randomly assign one group of children to go to childcare and another to stay at home. Although this design would completely eliminate any bias caused by preexisting differences between the two groups of families, it has seldom been used in studies of childcare.[1] It is not surprising that this design is rare—it is unlikely that most parents would be willing to have their work status or their child's care determined by the random roll of researchers' dice. Because families make their own choices about work and childcare and thus "self-select" themselves into childcare or home care conditions, it was not possible to say with certainty that the differences between groups of children observed in the early studies were caused by childcare. There may also have been differences in these children's experiences at home that made their test results different. This reality placed a further limitation on the findings from early studies.

A fourth limitation lay in the lack of precision in the instruments used for measuring children's development. Tools for assessing differences in children's development are often blunt. There is no exact yardstick for measuring children's social, emotional, and intellectual growth. We can make rough estimates, but they may miss subtle and important distinctions. One tool for getting such estimates is the standard intelligence test, which, in the preschool period, measures children's abilities to use and understand language (labeling objects, following instructions) and to manipulate and organize materials (putting pegs in holes, matching geometric figures, or copying complex designs with blocks). A child's score on such a test can then be compared to national norms for children of the same age. This measure tells us something important about how the child is progressing: in particular, by the time children are three or four years old, this test gives a reasonably good prediction of how well the child is likely to do in school. But it does not indicate anything about the development of social skills, emotions, creativity, or practical problem-solving competence. Measures of these qualities were less available, less reliable, and less frequently used in early studies of childcare.

In brief, then, early studies were limited by their simplistic and nonexperimental designs, their nonrepresentative samples, and their imprecise and narrow assessment procedures. These studies could not determine whether childcare caused differences in child outcomes, what outcomes were affected, and how childcare produced its effects.

Childcare Research Today

In the years since these early studies, researchers have become increasingly careful; their research designs have become correspondingly more complex. A major breakthrough was the recognition that what happens to children *during* childcare is perhaps more important than the mere fact that they are attending care. The *quality* of child-care became a research focus; researchers investigated how childcare of varying levels of quality affected children's development. Observers unobtrusively recorded children's experiences in their actual childcare environments as well as the characteristics of those environments. Measurements of quality became increasingly detailed and varied. They included structural aspects of quality, such as the number of children being cared for by a single caregiver, the caregiver's educational qualifications, and the safety and cleanliness of the physical setting—as well as interpersonal aspects of quality involving the nature of the caregiver's interactions with the children, the amount and type of stimulation he or she provided, and the emotional warmth and responsiveness of his or her behavior.

At the same time, researchers expanded their scope to include a wider range of community-based settings and extended their investigations to include different types of childcare, not just centers. They surveyed all the different types of care that parents use—nannies, sitters, neighbors, grandmothers—not just those caregivers who are most visible or accessible, such as teachers in centers. In this way, researchers could compare children's experiences in these different types of care and investigate whether apparent effects are caused by care per se or just by particular types of care.

Researchers also began to look at the child's history of care, not just at the kind of care the child was receiving at the time of the assessment. This approached allowed researchers to explore the significance of the amount and stability of childcare throughout the preschool period. They investigated childcare in the first year of life, which had been ignored in earlier studies because it was uncommon in the 1970s and 1980s for children to be in care at this age, and researchers also followed children who had been in care into the elementary school years to look for long-term consequences of care.

A wider array of measures to assess children's functioning found its way into researchers' hands. Researchers also began to rely on a wider set of evaluators—care providers, teachers, and parents—as well as testers and observers to assess children's abilities and behaviors. Childcare researchers were now going beyond the measures of intelligence that were used in earlier work; they also examined children's abilities to regulate their own emotions and behavior; to pay attention and sit still; and to share, take turns, and follow directions. They measured children's cognition with achievement and language instruments that are standardized and widely accepted. Also, researchers collected multiple measures for each child rather than settling for a single test.

Another important advance in childcare research followed from the realization that childcare effects are not independent of children's experiences at home. Family characteristics and parents' attitudes predict the age at which children enter care and the type and quality of care they are enrolled in. Parents *choose* care settings of better or worse quality. Researchers, therefore, began to assess family features, such as the parents' education and income, to investigate the effects of care in the context of these multiple, interacting factors. Childcare research was also advanced by the realization that childcare effects are influenced by the child's own characteristics, such as having an easy or difficult temperament. Researchers started to control family and child factors statistically in sophisticated analyses, which allowed them to investigate childcare associations above and beyond the influence of family and child characteristics.

Constructing models to study childcare effects in the context of family and child factors has raised childcare research to a new level. Now researchers ask questions about how family factors "mediate" childcare effects: that is, they ask whether observed differences in children's behavior are the result of different processes at home—for example, whether mothers using childcare pick up techniques of managing their children from the childcare staff and thus influence their children's behavior. They ask whether family factors "moderate" childcare effects: that is, they ask whether effects are different for different groups—for example, boys and girls, or children in high-income and low-income families. Researchers construct and test models of cumulative risk, asking, for example, whether low-quality care adds an additional risk for infants and toddlers who are already at risk because of biological vulnerabilities or family disadvantages, or whether high-quality childcare acts as a buffer to help young children overcome the negative aspects of being reared in a punitive or neglectful family.

Researchers also investigate what happens when children from stable families experience a "downgrade" from their well-functioning and stimulating home environments by attending mediocre childcare. Moreover, they ask whether children with difficult temperaments or physical handicaps, who may be more vulnerable to begin with, are more likely to suffer adverse effects from childcare. The layers of analysis in these models have increased exponentially since the early research using two-group comparisons. One relatively costly consequence of this increase is the need for larger samples than were common ten or twenty years ago. New studies are big and getting bigger.

Three Exemplary Studies

To illustrate the state of the art in childcare research, we have selected three projects to describe in detail. These three large-scale studies illustrate well the best in contemporary childcare research. Their findings are instructive, and we rely on them frequently in the chapters that follow.

COST, QUALITY, AND CHILD OUTCOMES STUDY

The first study we discuss here is the Cost, Quality, and Child Outcomes (CQO) Study.[2] This study, as its name suggests, was designed to examine relations among childcare costs, childcare quality, and outcomes for children in community childcare centers. The centers were selected randomly from four regions in California, Connecticut, Colorado, and North Carolina. These four regions varied widely in economic climate and the stringency of state regulations (for example, mandated staff-child ratios for four-year-olds varied from 1:10 in Connecticut to 1:20 in North Carolina). In each region, one hundred centers (fifty for-profit centers and fifty nonprofit centers) were recruited into the study. (It took a good deal of work to recruit these centers; refusal rates ranged from 32 percent in Colorado and Connecticut to 59 percent in North Carolina.) Two classrooms from each center were then observed. Whenever possible, these classrooms included a preschool class and an infant-toddler class. The final sample was made up of 224 infant-toddler classes and 509 preschool classrooms. Within the preschool classrooms, four children were tested.

Before data collection began, teams of data collectors from each state completed an intensive training session in Boulder, Colorado. The goal was to train all the observers to collect data consistently; it should not matter which observer was collecting data, because they would all respond in the same way. Such consistent observations are considered to be highly "reliable." To assess their reliability in the use of the observation instruments, site coordinators in each state went out on visits with their observers. When observers did not reach acceptable levels of agreement (approximately 80 percent agreement), they were given additional instruction. Then, to make sure that observations in different states were consistent, the four site coordinators traveled to the other states and tested the reliability of their observers. After all these reliability hurdles had been crossed, it was time to begin visiting centers for data collection.

At each center, a researcher interviewed the center director about the structural characteristics of the center. Then two observers visited the program to collect data on the quality of care in the selected classrooms. Observations usually started at about eight or nine o'clock in the morning and ended at two or three in the afternoon. The observers watched and calculated staff-child ratios and group sizes. They assessed the classroom environment using either the Infant/Toddler Environment Rating Scale (ITERS) or the Early Childhood Environment Rating Scale (ECERS).[3] They rated teachers' sensitivity with the Arnett Caregiver Interaction Scale, teachers' child-centeredness with the UCLA Early Childhood Observation Form, and teachers' responsiveness with Howes and Stewart's Adult Involvement Scale.[4]

The ECERS, which was developed to assess the quality of center care for children between two and five years of age, contains thirty-seven items in seven subscale areas: personal care routines such as diapering and toileting; classroom furnishings; opportunities for language development; activities to promote fine and gross motor development; creative activities such as art, music, and movement; opportunities for social development; and provision for adult needs. (The ITERS offers equivalent items for children aged two and younger.) The observer rates each item on a seven-point scale from inadequate (1) to excellent (7). In the Cost, Quality, and Outcomes study, researchers used a single average score from the ECERS to represent quality. This allowed them to determine whether the overall quality in the classroom was "poor" (scores from 1 to 2.9), "mediocre" (scores from 3 to 4.9), or "good" (scores from 5 to 7).

The Arnett Caregiver Interaction Scale consists of twenty-six items in four subscales: teacher sensitivity (e.g., speaking warmly to children); harshness (e.g., seeming critical of the children); detachment (e.g., not seeming interested in children's activities); and permissiveness (e.g., not reprimanding children when they misbehave). A single score from this instrument provided a reliable index of the teacher's positive behavior.

The UCLA Early Childhood Observation Form coded the child centeredness of the teacher's teaching style on the basis of five subscales: children initiate activities; the teacher's emphasis is academic; the teacher is a strong disciplinarian; there is performance pressure in the class; and the teacher gives negative evaluations. (The last four scales are reverse-coded to indicate the degree of child centeredness.)

Finally, the Adult Involvement Scale recorded the teacher's responsiveness to children on a single six-point scale ranging from the teacher ignores students to the teacher gives intense responses (positive physical interaction, conversation, play). Researchers used the percent of time that the teacher was at least minimally responsive as the measure of teacher responsiveness.

The researchers then found that scores from all four of these instruments were strongly intercorrelated, so they formed a single composite index of "quality of classroom practices," which they used in their statistical analyses.

Observers also distributed questionnaires to the teachers, asking them about their race, age, hours worked, wages, experience, education and training (see Figure 1); and researchers mailed the children's parents a survey about the family income, household composition, and parents' education.

Four months later, different researchers went back to the centers and tested the children. Two standardized instruments were used to evaluate children's language and math skills. The ability to understand language was measured with the Peabody Picture Vocabulary

Figure 1 **Childcare teacher education and training finding from the CQO study**

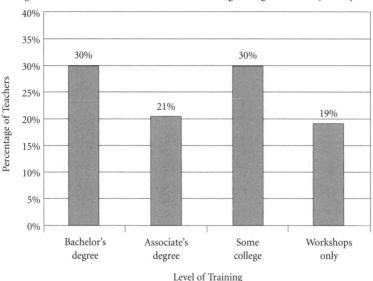

Test (PPVT), a test that involves having children point to a picture that matches the word spoken by the examiner.[5] Children's preacademic skills were measured using two subtests of the Woodcock Johnson Tests of Achievement: letter-word identification, which measures reading ability, and applied problems, which measures math skills.[6] Teachers were asked to rate the children using the Classroom Behavior Inventory.[7] This inventory tests three factors: cognitive ability, sociability, and problem behavior. Teachers also rated their own relationship with the child in terms of its closeness ("I share a warm, affectionate relationship with this child"), conflict ("This child easily becomes angry with me"), and overdependency ("This child reacts strongly to separation from me").[8] After the initial assessment for the Cost, Quality, and Child Outcomes study, follow-up information was gathered during the child's last two years in childcare (at ages four and five), in kindergarten, and in first and second grades.

This study is exemplary in a number of ways: it recruited a large sample of centers and children, included a wide range of different settings in four different states, used multiple instruments that are reliable and highly regarded, met a high standard for ensuring that the instruments were used appropriately, and followed the children over a period of years to look for later effects.

FLORIDA CHILD CARE QUALITY IMPROVEMENT STUDY

In the 1990s Florida provided a natural laboratory to study two important aspects of childcare: adult-child ratios and caregiver education.[9] In 1992, the state legislators in Florida mandated a change in teacher-child ratios from 1:6 to 1:4 for infants and from 1:8 to 1:6 for toddlers. In 1995, they imposed an additional requirement; for every twenty children in a childcare facility, there should be at least one staff person with a Child Development Associate (CDA) credential, or equivalent education or experience. Researchers seized the opportunity to conduct a study of these changes in childcare requirements, christening their efforts the Florida Child Care Quality Improvement Study. They randomly selected 150 licensed centers in four Florida counties, which were representative of childcare climates within the state. Within these centers, they focused on 450 classrooms and examined them before and after the legislation, in 1992, 1994, and 1996.

During the three years of data collection, researchers collected questionnaires, interviews, and observations. Center directors were asked about their perceptions of the effects of the mandated changes. Teachers were asked about their educational backgrounds. Observations in an infant class, a toddler class, and a preschool class in each center included adult-child ratios and group sizes, ECERS and ITERS assessments, and the Arnett Caregiver Interaction Scale.

Detailed assessments of two randomly chosen children in each class were made on an initial sample of nine hundred children. These assessments included the type of activities the child was engaged in—learning activities, creative activities, language arts lessons, gross motor activities, and playing with small objects—and the child's attachment to the teacher, assessed using the Q-set technique usually used for measuring attachment security with the mother.[10] Children's language proficiency was assessed with the Adaptive Language Scale, complexity of peer interaction with the Peer Play Scale, and complexity of cognitive play with the Object Play Scale.[11] Teachers also completed ratings of the child's behavior problems using the Preschool Behavior Questionnaire.[12] These child outcomes were measured in each year of the study.

The primary importance of this study is that it took advantage of a unique opportunity to see what happened to children when the quality of their care was improved. Although this study was not a controlled experiment—it did not have a randomly assigned group of centers in which childcare regulations did not change—it did have an advantage over correlational studies because it demonstrated that observed differences in children's behavior were preceded by changes in childcare legislation and quality.

THE NICHD STUDY OF EARLY CHILD CARE AND YOUTH DEVELOPMENT

The third study is the National Institute of Child Health and Human Development (NICHD) Study of Early Child Care. We are most familiar with this study, because we are two of its investigators. In this study, a cohort of children has been studied ever since they were born in 1991. They were selected from twenty-four hospitals in ten data collection sites: Charlottesville, Virginia; Irvine, California; Lawrence, Kansas; Little Rock, Arkansas; Madison, Wisconsin; Morganton, North Carolina; Philadelphia, Pennsylvania; Pittsburgh, Pennsylvania; Seattle, Washington; and Wellesley, Massachusetts. Researchers visited these hospitals at randomly selected times and interviewed all the women who had given birth in the previous twenty-four hours. Of these women about five thousand were eligible for the study: they were at least eighteen years old, spoke English, did not have medical problems, and had healthy, single births. A month later, selected mothers were telephoned and invited to join the study. They were told that it was a study of young children's experiences and development in the early years, not a study of childcare per se, because it was important to include all mothers and not just those who planned to use childcare.

Each week a number of mothers were called. For the first four months of recruitment into the study, these mothers were simply randomly selected from the list of eligible families. For the remaining seven months, specific family characteristics were monitored, and the calling lists were adjusted to increase representation of three subgroups: single mothers, mothers with less than a high school education, and ethnic minority mothers. It was important to recruit more of these groups because they were important minorities to find out about and because they were less likely to join and stay in the study. A total of 1,526 mothers agreed to an interview when their infants were one month old; of these, 1,347 completed the interview and became the study participants, with approximately equal numbers at each of the ten research sites. Of the families, 25 percent belonged to ethnic minorities, 32 percent of the mothers had only a high school education, and 14 percent were unmarried. Half of the mothers planned to work full time during their child's first year of life.

In its initial phase (1991–1994), the study followed the development of these children from birth through age three. Phase II of the study (1995–1999) followed the same children's development through first grade. In Phase III (2000–2004), development through sixth grade was tracked, and a fourth phase to study the children during adolescence is planned.[13] By the end of Phase III there were still one thousand families participating in the study. Assessments of the children and their environments were made when the children were six months, fifteen months, twenty-four months, thirty-six months, and fifty-four months old and then in the first, third, fourth, fifth, and sixth grades. At these assessments, children were observed in their homes; in their primary childcare settings; in university playrooms; and, in the later years, in school. Research assistants from all sites were trained and certified on every procedure to ensure reliable administration and to guard against variability in practices from site to site.

In the childcare assessments, caregivers were asked to provide basic demographic data about themselves, such as their age, education, and ethnic identity, as well as information about the length of time they had been providing childcare and how much training they had received. Caregivers' professionalism was assessed in a brief interview concerning attitudes toward the job, reasons for providing care, plans for the future, and participation in professional activities. They also completed a questionnaire to assess how traditional (strict) or modern (progressive) their attitudes about childrearing were.

The quality of childcare was measured using four different instruments. The Home Observation for Measurement of the Environment Inventory (HOME) was used in all home-based childcare settings (in the child's home or a childcare home) to measure the quality and quantity of stimulation and support.[14] The Profile Assessment for Early Childhood Programs was used to measure health and hygiene practices, safety, organization, and stimulation in the environment.[15] To assess interactions between caregivers and children, the study investigators developed the Observational Record of the Caregiving Environment (ORCE).[16] This instrument provides two types of data: frequency counts of specific caregiver behaviors, and qualitative ratings that take into account the quality of the caregiver's behavior in relation to the child. Observers first code the frequency of caregiver behaviors such as talking affectionately to the child or asking the child a question and then rate the extent to which the caregiver is sensitive and responsive to the child's signals, expresses positive feelings, stimulates the child's cognitive development, and fosters the child's exploration. A composite score based on the average of the qualitative ratings reflects the overall quality of caregiving. At the fifty-four-month assessment, an additional instrument was used: The Classroom Practices Inventory is based on the National Association for the Education of Young Children guidelines for developmentally appropriate practices for four- and five-year-old children.[17] The inventory contains items reflecting the academic-activity focus and the emotional climate of the program. In addition, researchers determined the type of care the children were in (center, childcare home, or in-home care), the number of hours the child spent in each care arrangement, and the number of different childcare arrangements the child had started and stopped.

Information about the parents was collected at each assessment point—income, employment, childrearing attitudes, discipline strategies, quality of interaction with the child, stimulation in the home environment, and physical and mental health—so that these factors could be controlled in statistical analyses, revealing effects of childcare above and beyond the influence of the family.[18] Children's development was also assessed. Social-emotional development included the child's relationships with mother, father, friends, caregivers, and teach-ers; social competence with peers; "internalizing" behavior problems such as depression, anxiety, and withdrawal; and "externalizing" be-havior problems such as aggression, disobedience, and rowdiness. The instruments used to collect this information included Ains-worth's Strange Situation assessment, the classic method of assessing children's attachment to their mothers; Waters' Attachment Q-Set, a way of assessing attachment based on several hours of observation at home; videotaped sessions of the child interacting with parents and with a friend; and the Achenbach Child Behavior Checklist, the stan-dard method in the field for assessing child behavior problems.[19] As-sessed cognitive abilities included overall intellectual functioning, school readiness and literacy, problem solving, memory ability, and language development. The instruments for these assessments were the widely used Bayley Scales of Mental Development, Bracken School Readiness Scale, Reynell Developmental Language Scales, and Woodcock Johnson Achievement and Cognitive Batteries.[20] Chil-dren's growth and health were also evaluated at each age.

This study is important for a number of reasons: It is the first study of childcare to begin at birth and continue into adolescence. It is a national study in that it includes families in diverse geographical locations, from Boston to California. Researchers took pains to re-cruit and maintain a large and diverse sample of families and admin-istered a huge battery of assessments that offered comprehensive evaluation of children's development, childcare quality, and family backgrounds. The study also sent observers and their clipboards into settings that reflected the entire gamut of childcare across the United States, going where no researchers had gone before, into the myriad childcare arrangements families themselves selected.

It should be clear from this brief description of these three exem-plary studies that in today's childcare studies researchers have gone far beyond simple two-group comparisons. Researchers have im-proved their methods of data collection, expanded and extended their research samples, and contextualized their investigation of childcare effects. In the following chapters, we examine the fruits of their labors.

5

EFFECTS OF CARE

Are children in nonparental childcare prepared to succeed in the outside world better than children who stay at home in the parental nest? Are their cognitive and social skills more highly developed, perhaps? Or is the situation just the opposite? Are we socializing saints or breeding bullies? In this chapter we examine the evidence on these issues. We compare the development of children who are in childcare with that of children who are not, in the areas of physical health, language, cognition, social skills, and emotional well-being. We rely on the results of the newer and more sophisticated studies that are available. References to earlier research can be found in the first two editions of this book (*Daycare*).

Physical Health and Development

Children's growth and health may be the least difficult aspects of development to assess. We can at least see and agree about whether the child has a cold or can climb stairs, whether he or she weighs forty pounds or sixty. To find out whether children in childcare differ from children who stay at home with their mothers in these ways, a number of researchers have included in their studies pediatricians', teachers', and mothers' reports of children's physical health and growth, and standard tests of children's motor abilities (walking, jumping, throwing a ball, handling tools). The results of their investigations suggest that there is both good news and bad news associated with being in childcare.

In terms of physical development, being in childcare advances children's motor development and activity, increases height and weight, and decreases the likelihood of pediatric problems—for infants and young children from poor families.[1] However, if children come from families that already provide ample nutrition, adequate health services, and opportunities for exercise and activity, no benefit in physical development accrues from going to a childcare center; there is no advantage in growth or motor skills for middle-class children attending childcare programs.[2]

There may be a difference in health. Children in childcare centers, whatever their family backgrounds, get more diarrhea, flu, rashes, colds, coughs, and ear infections than children at home.[3] Children in childcare catch everything that is going around. On average, they have twice as many gastrointestinal episodes per year as children at home.[4] The explanation most often offered for the higher rates of illness in childcare is that children there are exposed to more pathogens because they are with other children. Children in settings with more children come down with more illnesses.[5] Hand washing and other hygienic measures, such as having different people prepare the food and diaper the children, reduces the incidence of illness. In one experimental study of sixty-six infant-toddler classrooms, for example, staff from randomly selected centers were given training in personal hygiene and environmental sanitation. They increased their hand washing, sanitary food handling, disinfection of diapering areas, use of step cans for diaper disposal, and separation of food preparation and diapering areas. As a result, cases of infant diarrhea were reduced by about twelve incidents per year per child.[6]

The NICHD Study of Early Child Care offered a longitudinal investigation of three common illnesses: gastrointestinal (GI) illnesses, colds, and ear infections.[7] So far NICHD researchers have looked for patterns of illness in the children from infancy to age five, statistically controlling for other factors that might lead to illnesses, such as geographical location; mothers' education, marital status, and life stress; family income and household size; and the child's gender, ethnicity, prematureness at birth, and breast-feeding history. Researchers also compared the incidence of illnesses in different types of childcare. Results indicated that children in childcare centers and childcare homes were more likely to get ear infections and colds than children at home with their mothers over the first two years of life. By age three, however, rates of these illnesses were no longer different. For example, the risk of ear infections associated with being in center care at one year of age was more than twice as high as the risk for children at home, but by age three it was only about one fifth higher, and this difference was not statistically significant. When the children were three to five years old, rates of colds, GI illnesses, and ear infections were higher in childcare arrangements with more than six children. Children were especially likely to get sick if they had just entered care at this age. Those who had been in group care with more than six children since they were infants or toddlers were less likely to get ill than children who entered group care for the first time after age three—but even children in childcare from an early age were still more likely to get sick than children who were in care with fewer children or who were not in childcare at all.

Having experience in large-group care during the first two years of life, therefore, did not protect children against contracting an illness in the preschool period completely. But perhaps such immunity develops later. Findings from the Tucson Children's Recovery Study indicate that children who enter large-group care in infancy have more colds than home-reared children at age three but fewer colds at age six.[8] These children also had a reduced risk of asthma.[9] This last finding is consistent with results from the NICHD study: among the 1,000 children in the study, fifty-eight (5.5 percent) were diagnosed with asthma sometime between four and a half and ten; none of these children was among the 132 children who had experienced large-group care prior to six months.[10]

One important question about childhood illnesses is whether children who experience more of them—because they are in childcare—suffer delayed language and cognitive development. It is not unreasonable to worry that children who have frequent colds and ear infections might suffer in this way. This concern was expressed in the comprehensive review of childcare issues prepared by the National Research Council, *Who Cares for America's Children: Child Care Policy for the 1990s.*[11] There is an urgent need, the panel stated, for prospective studies of the effects of the increased frequency of minor illnesses in infants and young children in childcare. In one such study of thirty-seven children in childcare, chronic ear infections were found to be related to lower verbal ability at age seven.[12] However, in the much larger NICHD study, with other potentially confounding factors controlled, there were no associations between the frequency of communicable illnesses and language competence at age three. Future findings from the NICHD study will clarify whether there are longer-term consequences of early childcare-related illnesses.

The most reasonable conclusion at this point seems to be that for physical health and development, there are both advantages and disadvantages to being in childcare. Childcare offers opportunities for motor development and physical growth that some children would not get at home. But it exposes children to germs and illnesses. This exposure may lead to later immunities, or, if it leads to chronic ear infections, it could possibly lead to later language delays. The key to minimizing children's illnesses appears to be finding a childcare facility with a small number of children and with caregivers who follow strict procedures of physical hygiene.

Intellectual Development

A child's runny nose may be a price working mothers are willing to pay to have their children in a childcare center—especially if most of the nose wiping is done by childcare staff—but what about the child's intellectual growth? Is childcare detrimental to mental development, as some have feared? Or do children in childcare have an advantage; are they readier for school? This question has been a focus of numerous investigations over the past thirty years.

The good news from almost all studies of childcare in the preschool period—in Canada, England, Sweden, Czechoslovakia, Bermuda, and other countries, as well as the United States—is that care in a decent childcare facility seems to have no detrimental effects on children's intellectual development. In only a handful of studies—of very poor care—have researchers found that scores on tests of perception, language, and intelligence were lower for children attending a child-

care center than for children of comparable family backgrounds being cared for by parents at home.[13]

In fact, a number of studies have shown that children in childcare
centers do better intellectually than children who remain at home.[14]
Children in childcare centers did better on tests of verbal fluency,
memory, and comprehension. They copied designs made with blocks;
solved problems; strung beads; wrote their names; and drew circles,
squares, and triangles earlier than children who were not in childcare. The speech of children in childcare was more complex, and they
were able to identify other people's feelings and points of view earlier.
This apparent advantage of childcare attendance occurs most often
for children who attend high-quality, model programs—although
positive results have also been obtained in several studies of children
who attended community preschool programs.[15] In kindergarten and
first grade, as well, children who had been in childcare were more
verbally expressive, had richer vocabularies, asked more questions,
knew more about their environments, and were more ingenious with
materials. Their conversations were more "connected." Their play
was more purposeful, persistent, and creative; they did more school-
related activities, including writing. Their peers and their teachers
thought they had better ideas and did better work. Researchers in
Sweden have found that children who spent more time in childcare
centers scored higher on tests of cognitive abilities at age eight, and in
the United States, boys whose mothers participated in New Chance—
a program for young mothers on welfare who were required to go to
work—significantly increased their "school readiness" after six months
in center care.[16]

Thus it seems that participation in a preschool childcare program
can have benefits for children's intellectual development—especially
if the children come from less-stimulating homes.[17] However, when
researchers in the NICHD Study of Early Child Care removed the effects of family background (by controlling for family income and
mothers' verbal ability and positive parenting in their statistical
analyses), they found that children in childcare were doing no better
or worse than children in exclusive maternal care on measures of

cognitive development. Being in childcare per se is apparently not what makes a difference in children's intellectual abilities.[18] Advantages were found only for children in childcare centers. In this study and others, children in childcare homes or with babysitters did about the same intellectually as children at home with their mothers.[19]

Social Competence

Over the preschool years, as they are learning to count and color, play and paint, children also grow in social skills and develop social relationships. They get better at interacting with their peers. They learn to play complex games, to act out roles, and to participate in cooperative activities in groups. They make friends and acquire "enemies." Childcare researchers have focused on children's relations with their peers, expecting that because these children have daily experience with other children, their social relations with age-mates should be advanced. Researchers have observed children in their childcare settings as they interact with one another; brought pairs of children into play situations in the laboratory and watched their interactions; and tested children on their willingness to cooperate and help one another. The results of their studies suggest that childcare can promote peer skills.[20]

Compared to children not in childcare, children with experience in childcare have been observed to have more complex and mature interactions with their peers.[21] They can sustain their play longer and respond more appropriately and immediately to the other children's behavior, share materials, and behave empathically. They sustain coordinated action at younger ages than is customarily observed.[22] In elementary school, these children have more friends and are more popular.[23] In one fourteen-year longitudinal study, the amount of time children spent in care prior to three years of age shaped their social skills with peers, and these individual differences in social competence remained stable through childhood and early adolescence.[24] Like the differences in intellectual competence, however, differences in social competence with peers appear frequently but not invariably.[25]

Over the early years, children also become socially competent with adults. Children learn how to interact with a stranger, to cooperate, and to behave in public. They learn how to do things on their own without constant adult help and supervision. They learn to take care of themselves, to make decisions, and to follow through on them. Researchers have found that in these ways, too, children who attend childcare may have advantages over those who do not. Children in childcare have been observed to be more self-confident, outgoing, assertive, verbally expressive, and self-sufficient—and less distressed, timid, and fearful in new situations and with strangers.[26] When faced with frustration, they are more likely than children without childcare experience to entertain and soothe themselves and not to depend on their mothers for assistance.[27] In the Chicago Study of Child Care and Development, children who were enrolled in childcare were more comfortable showing a stranger around their homes, getting him or her a glass of water, and showing him or her their toys.[28] These children were better liked by the researchers who were meeting them for the first time. Children in childcare were also more knowledgeable about the social world.

In the NICHD study, children's social competence was assessed in three different ways when the children were two and three years old: mothers and caregivers rated a child's social competence on a questionnaire; the child was observed interacting with peers in childcare; and the child was videotaped playing with a familiar peer.[29] These measures of social competence were then related to children's experience in childcare, controlling for family background factors and child characteristics. Children who had spent more time in childcare settings with other children were more positive and skilled in their peer play in childcare at age three. However, when rated by mothers and caregivers and observed by researchers as a child played with a friend, competence not related to childcare experience. Thus, children with more group childcare experience demonstrated some advantage in social competence, but this advantage did not show up in all assessments. This finding is consistent with other research; differences favoring children in childcare are found in some studies of social competence but not all.

Behavior Problems

But there is another side to the story. Research does not just show improvements in social competence when children attend childcare. Some studies also show that children in childcare tend to be less polite, less agreeable, less compliant with their mothers' or caregivers' demands and requests, less respectful of others' rights, more irritable and rebellious, more likely to use profane language, more likely to be loud and boisterous, and more competitive and aggressive with their peers than children who are not or who have not been in day care.[30] These differences in aggressive and noncompliant behavior appear in tests and natural observations, in the childcare center and on the playground, with adults and with other children, with strangers and with parents, for children from both model and mediocre childcare programs. These differences are more marked for boys and for children from lower-income families, but they also appear for girls and middle-class children.

How can we integrate these negative differences with the differences in positive social behavior? Are children in childcare more socially competent or less? Are they socially skilled but bossy, friendly but aggressive, outgoing but rude? It has been suggested—not totally facetiously—that this profile sounds a lot like a successful CEO. It turns out, however, that it is not the same children who are friendly and bossy. In the NICHD study, the children who were high in social skills were not high in aggressiveness; positive social behavior and negative social behavior were unrelated to each other.[31] Therefore, it seems likely that childcare promotes social advancement in some children and leads to behavior problems in others. In the NICHD study, children who exhibited more positive social behavior with peers scored higher on tests of cognitive ability; children who exhibited more negative social behavior with peers scored lower.[32] More intelligent children, thus, appear to be advanced in the social realm, just as they are in the intellectual realm, and childcare may contribute to their knowledgeability, self-sufficiency, and ability to cooperate. Less intelligent children are more likely to learn that antisocial behavior can get them what they want; they may become determined to get their own way in the group and, without the social skills to achieve this goal smoothly, become aggressive, irritable, and rude as a consequence of being in childcare. Childcare apparently can be a venue for learning social graces *or* a breeding ground for aggression.

Ann Smith and Shanee Barraclough observed two hundred infants and toddlers in childcare centers in New Zealand.[33] Two thirds of these children were involved in a conflict episode within a single twenty-minute observation. Clearly, there are many opportunities for children to learn how to resolve their conflicts—or not. If there is an inherent risk of developing poor interaction patterns in childcare, it may be the result of spending a lot of time in the setting. A full day of care is stressful for young children. This stress is revealed in the child's cortisol levels. Cortisol is a hormone produced by the hypothalamic-pituitary-adrenocortical system, and the hormone level increases when demands exceed the individual's coping resources. Megan Gunnar and her colleagues found that cortisol levels of children in childcare centers were the same as or lower than cortisol levels in children at home in the morning, but by mid-afternoon levels had risen to a significantly higher level for children in childcare than for the children who stayed home; children in half-day preschool programs did not show this increase in cortisol.[34]

Paralleling these differences in cortisol levels, the children who are most likely to exhibit negative behavior are the ones who spend a lot of time in childcare.[35] In the NICHD study, children's negative externalizing behavior—teasing, bullying, hitting, fighting, disobeying, talking back—was observed and rated by mothers, caregivers, and teachers. After controlling for a wide array of possible variables (including geographical location, child's gender and temperament, type and quality of childcare, parents' income and education), researchers found that children who had spent more time in childcare with other children were more aggressive and unsociable in childcare when they were two years of age and had more externalizing behavior problems when they were four.[36] When children spent more hours in care each week, from the time they were three months old to the age of four and a half, they were more likely to destroy things, talk back, argue, get in fights, have temper tantrums, and demand attention—and altogether not be the sort of person you'd like to spend the week with.[37] And the differences didn't disappear when the children left childcare: kindergarten and first grade teachers also noted more aggressive and disobedient behavior in these children.[38] Mothers saw only differences in assertiveness, perhaps because the home situation does not elicit aggression and disobedience to the same extent as childcare or the classroom does.

Although these differences in behavior problems were reliable, they were not extreme. The children who had spent a lot of time in care were not in the "clinical" range of externalizing behavior problems.[39] However, more of these children received "high" scores on the externalizing scale—at least one standard deviation above the mean. When they were four and a half years old, 24 percent of the children who were in care for more than forty-five hours per week received high scores, compared with 15 percent of those in care for ten to forty-five hours and only 2 percent of those in care for less than nine hours. Differences were most marked at the time the children were still in care and became less marked in subsequent years. Other researchers have also found that differences in aggression decrease over the elementary school years.[40]

The finding that children who spend many hours in childcare have more behavior problems is provocative. Presentation of this finding from the NICHD study at a professional meeting in 2001 was greeted with a barrage of media attention. Newspaper articles and television segments were frequent, featuring titles such as "Does Day Care Breed Bullies?"; "Does Day Care Damage Your Child?"; and "Child Aggression Linked to Hours in Day Care."[41] Even humorists took advantage of the finding. For example, one cartoonist pictured a hold up in a liquor store with the caption "I was prepared for deranged crack babies. How was I to know an aggressive daycare kid would do us in?"[42]

The media blitz ratcheted up parents' worries that they were doing damage to their children by having them in childcare. Their concern is not unreasonable. The finding should provide a wake-up call for parents, encouraging them to monitor their child's behavior, particularly if the child is spending many hours in childcare. If children are in care for upwards of forty-five hours every week for the first five years, there is a real chance that they will be more aggressive and disobedient than they would have been if they spent more of their time at home. Parents need to be alert to signs of problem behavior in their children, and, because they may be less likely to pick up on problem behavior than outside observers, they should discuss their concerns with other adults, including the childcare provider. If the child is exhibiting high levels of undesired behavior at home or at childcare, the parents should consider reducing the time the child spends in care. If it is not possible to reduce the time in care because both parents work more than eight hours a day, they should consider changing to a different childcare arrangement. Problem behavior in the NICHD study was more frequent when children spent more time in centers. So, if long hours are necessary, parents might consider not using center care for the entire day but supplementing a part-time center program with a nanny at home. In the NICHD study, children in long hours of center care had more externalizing behavior problems than children in long hours of care that combined center and home arrangements.[43] Of course, it is important to balance the possible advantage of changing or splitting the childcare arrangement with the need for stability. Although the number of childcare arrangements the child had been in was not related to aggression in the NICHD study, in the New Chance Study behavior problems increased with every additional arrangement the child attended.[44]

Relationship with Mother

Another concern about childcare is whether it damages children's relations with their mothers.[45] Many people have worried that when infants are separated from the mother for eight or ten or more hours a day, the mother-child relationship is at risk. Mothers of children in full-time care have less time available to learn their baby's signals and rhythms and might interact less sensitively with their children. Their infants, having fewer opportunities to interact with their mothers, might not form as strong an attachment bond. Fortunately, research has shown that infants whose mothers work full time do form attachments to them.[46] These children go to mother for help, stay close to her, approach her often, interact with her, and rely on her when distressed or bored. In the childcare center they do not greet the teacher in the morning with the same joy as they greet the mother at night. They do not behave as if the caregiver is a substitute mother— nor is this how caregivers perceive themselves.

But the real question is whether the *quality* of the relationship childcare children have with their mothers is as emotionally secure as the relationship of infants who are raised exclusively at home. Putting together data from studies of infants in childcare that included the standard method of measuring children's attachment relationships—Ainsworth's Strange Situation assessment—research reviewers at the end of the 1980s found that infants who were in childcare full time were more likely to be classified as having insecure relationships with their mothers, compared with infants in childcare part time or not at all.[47]

The problem was how to interpret this finding. The Strange Situation assessment had been designed and tested with children who spent much of their time at home with their mothers. Was it adequate for assessing attachment insecurity for children who spent their days in childcare? In the Strange Situation assessment, an infant plays with toys in an unfamiliar room, is left by the mother alone in the room with an unfamiliar woman, plays with and is comforted by that woman in the mother's absence; and then the mother returns and picks up the infant. Some children in this situation cling to their mothers and won't even let them leave the room. Other children ignore their mother's departure; they continue playing with toys or the stranger, and when the mother returns, they actively avoid her. Still other children are ambivalent in their reactions—clinging to the mother one minute and spurning her the next. All of these reactions are signs of insecurity in the mother-child relationship. Most children show a balanced pattern that has been call a "secure" attachment. They are able to leave the mother's side to explore the toys and the room, but they clearly prefer to be with her than with the stranger; they always greet the mother enthusiastically when she returns to the room.

The scenario of the Strange Situation assessment sounds suspiciously similar to the kind of experience infants have in childcare. Could it be that infants who have this kind of experience regularly are less likely to seek physical closeness with their mothers? When other methods of measuring infants' relationships with their mothers were used, it turned out, the differences in children's reactions were not as marked. Studies of children's behavior with their mothers at home in unstructured, natural interaction did not reveal significant differences between children in childcare and children cared for at home.[48] Was the Strange Situation method penalizing children who were more used to separations and reunions with their mothers?

Several researchers have investigated the validity of the Strange Situation method. In one study conducted in the Netherlands, Els Verweij-Tijsterman compared infants who attended a licensed childcare center for at least twenty hours per week with infants reared exclusively at home.[49] She, too, found that in the Strange Situation assessment infants in childcare were more likely to be classified as having an avoidant attachment. But Verweij-Tijsterman also measured the infants' heart rates to determine how stressed they felt during the Strange Situation test. When the infant was alone in the room, Verweij-Tijsterman found, home-reared infants who were classified as avoidant showed major increases in heart rate; they indeed felt stressed. However, the childcare infants who were classified as avoidant showed only small heart rate increases. They apparently experienced only very mild stress, and it seems unlikely that they were avoiding their mothers deliberately during their reunion in order to hide their fear, which, according to attachment theory, is what avoidant infants do. It is more likely, Verweij-Tijsterman suggested, that several childcare infants were erroneously classified as avoidant because their attachment behavior was not activated by Strange Situation assessment and because they did not find the separations from mother sufficiently stressful to cause them to run to mother or cling to her when she returned. In a modified procedure, Verweij-Tijsterman added strange sounds to the episodes preceding reunion with mother to increase the stressfulness for all infants, and, indeed, all of them showed increased heart rates. In this more stressful procedure,

70 percent of the childcare infants who had been classified as avoidant in the original Strange Situation assessment were now classified as secure.

Researchers in another study explored the validity of the Strange Situation method for children in childcare, by devising a new attachment assessment, the California Attachment Procedure.[50] The critical feature of the new procedure was that it did not involve mother-child separations and reunions or comforting by an unfamiliar woman—because these experiences are more common for children who attend childcare regularly. Attachment behavior was elicited by stressful events that are equally familiar for all children whether or not they are in childcare—events that featured a robot, a costumed wizard, and an unseen noise. In this procedure, most of the childcare attendees who were classified as insecure in the Strange Situation assessment were classified as secure.[51] A longitudinal study of children through elementary school further supports the suggestion that the Strange Situation method is not a valid assessment for children in childcare; the study finds that attachment security was related to later positive adaptation only for children in mother care, not for children in childcare.[52]

Meanwhile, studies conducted since 1990 have shown that the link between childcare participation and insecure attachment is less likely to be significant—even in the Strange Situation test—when other child and family variables are statistically controlled.[53] In the NICHD study infants were assessed in the Strange Situation test at fifteen months of age and in a modified Strange Situation assessment with a longer separation at thirty-six months. No significant main effects of being in infant childcare were found at either assessment.[54] Michael Lamb concluded in his review of the research that the available evidence now indicates clearly that childcare, in and of itself, does not harm the infant's attachment to the mother.[55]

Starting Care Early or Late

BEGINNING IN INFANCY

The majority of parents in the United States now enroll their children in childcare early in the first year of life. In the NICHD study,

72 percent of infants were in some form of childcare before they turned one; most (75 percent) entered before the age of four months.[56] So what is the best time to put children in care? Or is there a "best" time? There are many reasons to expect that childcare would have a particularly profound effect on infants' development. Babies require special attention and sensitivity from their caregivers, who must meet all their needs, for food and safety and attention and care, not just for play or education as in the case of older children. Babies need interesting things to look at and hold, safe things to chew and explore. They must not be left in the crib or playpen alone to sleep all day. They need a caregiver who can read their signals and expressions and is concerned enough to do so. The sad fact, however, is that in this country care for infants includes the worst available. Center staff caring for infants have less experience and education than staff caring for older children.[57] Only three states require that childcare facilities have one caregiver for every three infants, the ratio recommended by the National Association for the Education of Young Children; only twenty-seven states require one caregiver for every four infants.[58] Therefore, researchers have been concerned about the effects of starting care this early.

Intellectual Abilities

Some people have feared that children who begin childcare in infancy may be disadvantaged intellectually, but there is little basis for this fear. Jeanne Brooks-Gunn and her associates found that maternal employment in infancy was associated with lower cognitive scores for some children in the National Longitudinal Study of Youth (NLSY) and in the NICHD study.[59] However, other investigators have not replicated their finding.[60] More important for us in this book, Brooks-Gunn found that it was the infants who spent the time their mothers were working in the care of their fathers or their mothers while at work—*not in childcare*—who had the lower scores.[61] Thus, it seems that infants in childcare are not disadvantaged. Researchers in Britain, similarly, have found that there is no detrimental effect on cognitive development if infants are placed in center childcare while their mothers work rather than being with relatives or friends, and, in fact, these children do better than those who don't start childcare until they are three years or older.[62] In another large and nationally representative study in the United States, entry into care in the first year was not related to lower cognitive scores, and, for some children, there were even positive effects.[63] What can we conclude from these studies? The safest conclusion is that there is no consistent negative effect of infant childcare on children's intellectual development.

Social Competence

The same conclusion can be drawn about children's social competence. Some researchers have observed that, compared with children who did not attend childcare or who did not attend until they were older, children who begin care in the first year of life are more socially skilled with peers and have more friends in elementary school—especially if they started care in the first six months.[64] But these effects have not been observed in other studies.[65] Thus, it seems unlikely that beginning childcare in infancy has a negative effect on social competence.

Behavior Problems

But what about behavior problems? Does being in childcare in the first year of life increase the likelihood that children will exhibit problem behavior? As we know, children are more likely to have externalizing problems if they spend more time in care, and one way for them to chalk up hours is to start care in infancy. Indeed, some researchers have found that, compared with children who entered care at older ages or not at all, children who began care in infancy were more likely to have externalizing problems: they were less compliant, acted out more, had less tolerance of frustration, were more aggressive, and were likely to be identified by their peers as children who "hit" and were "mean"?[66] However, these effects are not always found.[67] In the NICHD study, the age of entering care was unrelated to children's behavior problems at two and three years of age, and it was impossible to determine whether the effect of care on externalizing problems at age four was the result of care in infancy or cumulative hours overall.[68] The knotty problem is that, in the real world, starting care early is almost always combined with attending care for more years. In other studies, the apparent effects of childcare in the first year of life disappeared when researchers controlled for the number of different care arrangements children had been in or how much care they attended in the preschool years.[69] Researchers in the second study, conducted by John Bates and his colleagues, concluded that the accumulation of care is what is most important, not care in the first year. For now, this conclusion seems as reasonable as any. There is no proof that being in care in infancy leads to behavior problems down the road.

Relationship with Mother
It has long been suspected that beginning care in infancy leads to impaired infant-mother relations. However, this suspicion turns out to be ill founded. Researchers in Italy observed that, in the third year of life, children who started care in infancy had more difficult reunions with their mothers than children who started care between twelve and eighteen months of age.[70] However, children who started care even later, when they were between eighteen and twenty-four months old, also exhibited difficult reunions. Clearly, infant care was not the culprit.[71] In another study, in which children were randomly assigned to full-time care in a model childcare center, beginning care in the first year was not associated with increased attachment insecurity with mother.[72] And in the NICHD study, no significant effects of age of entry on attachment security were found when children were assessed in the Strange Situation test at one or three years of age.[73] Thus, there is no compelling evidence that beginning care in infancy has detrimental effects on children's relationships with their mothers.

TODDLERS IN CARE
Toddlers are more resilient than infants and can make their wishes known more clearly, so it might be expected that entering care at this age would be better than entering care in infancy. This seems not to be the case. In terms of cognitive learning and social competence, the age of starting childcare doesn't matter much; children can gain in

learning whether they are two or three or four years old.[74] But the emotional issues involved in starting care at age two are just as strong as issues involved in starting earlier—perhaps stronger. When toddlers enter care in their second year, they are just as distressed as infants who enter care in the first year, and their cortisol levels rise over the course of a day in care as much as infants' do.[75] Entry into care in the second year elevates the likelihood that children will develop an ambivalent relationship with their mother.[76] Entering childcare in the second year can also lead to behavior problems. In the NICHD study, children who first entered childcare around their second birthday exhibited more behavior problems in childcare than children who began care earlier.[77] And in other studies, as well, entry into care in the second year has been related to higher levels of behavior problems than entry in the first year.[78] In brief, there is no reason to believe that children who enter care as toddlers do better than children who enter as infants. Research on toddlers shows that they are particularly negatively affected by being in large classes with many children and few caregivers.[79]

CARE FOR PRESCHOOLERS

Preschoolers are much more ready than infants or toddlers to take on the world. They can communicate more easily, and they are ready for a social life with peers. But they have trouble paying attention—to lessons or play—for very long. They still experience elevations in cortisol as the childcare day progresses, although not as much as younger children do.[80] Within the preschool period, there is some evidence that children who start childcare at age three do better than those who start at age four—presumably because they have a longer time to learn the lessons the program offers, to adapt to being in a group, and to develop relationships with other children and the caregivers.[81]

All things considered, the most reasonable conclusion from these studies is that there is no one age for children to start childcare. Children are vulnerable and needy from the time they are born until they go to school, and this neediness is more important to keep in mind than waiting for the "right" age to enroll. Waiting until the child is two doesn't seem to be better than starting care in the first year; waiting until the child is four is apparently not better than starting at three.

Childcare for Different Children

BOYS AND GIRLS

Researchers have documented scientifically what everyone has known all along: boys and girls are different.[82] Even as young as two or three years of age, boys and girls act in ways that foreshadow their adult roles. Boys are more aggressive and competitive (especially with other boys); more physically energetic and assertive; and, given a choice of toys, more likely to go for bicycles, crates, cars, and guns, and to play soccer and bad guys. Girls are more quiet and compliant, cooperative, friendly and compassionate, socially skilled and socially aware; they select dolls, dress up clothes, and domestic toys, and they play house. These differences persist even in the face of parents' conscious efforts to raise more socially responsible sons and self-assertive daughters.

What happens when boys and girls go to childcare? Some people have suggested that attendance in a childcare center should reduce the stereotyped differences between boys and girls. They have predicted that boys attending childcare would be more cooperative and socially aware than boys who do not have this experience and that girls would be more independent and assertive than girls not in childcare. This expectation would be reasonable, as boys in childcare programs have many opportunities to be sociable, and girls have many opportunities to be independent.

Based on the available research, however, what seems to happen is that although boys in childcare do indeed become more sociable than boys at home—and although girls in childcare do increase in autonomy, problem solving, and even belligerence—childcare does not wipe out the differences between the sexes. Childcare does not make boys ladylike or girls macho. Boys in childcare are still more independent and loud and aggressive than girls in childcare, and girls in childcare are still more socially skilled and quiet than boys in childcare. Consequently, gender-stereotyped differences remain in childcare just as at home. Even in childcare it is hard to get away from the gender roles that permeate our society. With their "good" behavior and social skills, girls receive more affection and sensitive and stimulating attention and spend more time in close proximity to teachers; with their "not-so-good" behavior, boys are more likely to require teacher control.[83]

Are there other differences in the effects of childcare on boys and girls? It has frequently been documented that boys are more vulnerable to events in the environment, girls more resilient. From the time of conception until old age in the nursing home, females are less likely to have problems and more likely to survive. Is this difference between males and females reflected in different effects of childcare on boys and girls? Are boys worse off than girls when in childcare? The answer is a weak "maybe." There is some limited evidence that there is a slight disadvantage for boys to be in childcare.

First, boys placed in childcare in infancy have been observed to develop less-secure relationships with their mothers.[84] Second, boys from high-income families have been found to have somewhat slower intellectual development if they are in full-time childcare as infants rather than with their mothers.[85] Third, earlier entry into low-quality care has been associated with problem behavior and anger for boys.[86] However, most research using large samples, including the NLSY, the CQO, and the NICHD studies, have failed to find significantly different effects of childcare for boys and girls.[87] One significant finding in the NICHD study indicating that boys with many hours of care were less likely to be securely attached to their mothers was not replicated at a later assessment or in another study, and an analysis of the effects of childcare on infant-mother relationships for a combined sample from more than twelve different studies found no significant differences overall for boys and girls.[88] If there is a difference in the effect of childcare for boys and girls, therefore, it is small and unreliable.

VULNERABLE CHILDREN

What about children with emotional or physical problems? Do these vulnerabilities create risks for children if they are in childcare? Researchers have pondered these questions. One emotional problem they have studied is temperamental difficulty. Infants with difficult temperaments cry intensely and often, sleep irregularly and briefly, and adapt to change and new situations slowly. Several researchers have studied whether this temperament style makes it harder for children to adjust to being in childcare. They have found that infants with difficult temperaments are indeed disadvantaged when they enter care. Compared with easy infants, difficult ones are less positive in their emotions, receive less attention from caregivers and the other children, and make less progress in their cognitive development during the first year in a childcare center.[89] Their difficult temperaments makes their initial adjustment to childcare—a new and complex situation—difficult. However, eventually, they thrive. Children who are highly anxious, however, may have more persistent problems. In their research on cortisol levels, Gunnar and her associates found that children who were more fearful, shy, and anxious exhibited larger increases in cortisol over the childcare day than their more competent and confident peers.[90] Group care seems to be especially stressful for these children. The length of the day, the need to sustain interactions with many other children, and the need to interact with multiple adults are challenges that tax the emotional resources and coping competencies of these children.

This theme is echoed when children have health problems. Data from the NLSY suggest that childcare provides enriching input that can enhance children's development only if the children are healthy. For children with health problems, childcare does not offer this advantage. In fact, for infant boys with health problems, socioemotional and motor development were most helped by being cared for more extensively by their mothers.[91] One health problem that has received researchers' attention is otitis media (OM, or ear infections). OM is the most frequently diagnosed disease in early childhood, affecting almost all children under the age of three at one time or another. From one-third to one-half of the children in the United States suffer from chronic OM in the first few years. During bouts of this disease their hearing can be affected, with a mild to moderate loss that can last for many months. Children with persistent OM in early childhood have trouble attending to speech.[92] They are at risk for delays in early language development and have lower verbal ability into middle childhood.[93] Childcare environments where the child has little one-to-one interaction with adults, persistent background noise, and caregivers who are not sensitive to the child's hearing loss exacerbate the negative effects of OM on children's language and social development.[94]

The research that we have discussed in this chapter suggests that childcare can have important effects on children's physical growth and health, cognitive and language abilities, and social development and behavior problems. It also suggests that individual differences between children play a part in determining the effects of care. But this is just the beginning of the story, as we go on to consider the infinite variability that childcare comprises. In the next chapter, we talk about some of this variability and describe how differences in childcare settings affect children.

6

What is it about a particular childcare setting that leads to learning new skills or acquiring bad habits? Clearly, not all children who attend childcare programs show advances in cognitive development or exhibit aggression on the playground. We have already pointed out how individual children respond to care differently. The other side of the equation is the childcare environment itself. Childcare ranges in quality from terrible to excellent, and we cannot evaluate childcare without taking into account the nature of the specific caregiving environment. In this chapter, we look at variations in care and see how they affect children's development. First we look at studies of variation in the overall quality of the childcare environment and then delve into three specific aspects of care: the physical space and equipment in the childcare facility, the educational program or curriculum, and the presence of other children.

Overall Quality

WHAT IS GOOD-QUALITY CHILDCARE?

There is consensus among childcare researchers and practitioners about what good-quality childcare is—at least in principle.[1] It involves warm, supportive interactions with caregivers in a safe, healthy, and stimulating environment, where early education and trusting relationships combine to support children's physical, emotional, social, and intellectual development. In high-quality childcare, caregivers have frequent, positive interactions with the children that include smiling, touching, holding, and speaking at the child's eye level; respond promptly to children's questions or requests; encourage children to be actively engaged in a variety of activities; and encourage children to talk about their experiences, feelings, and ideas. Caregivers listen attentively, ask open-ended questions, extend children's actions and verbalizations with more complex ideas or materials, interact with children individually and in small groups instead of exclusively with the group as a whole, use positive guidance techniques, and encourage appropriate independence. Definitions of high quality also include structural features of the program—adequate physical space, a manageable number of children and a sufficient number of adults to supervise them—and a developmentally appropriate curriculum with varied materials and activities.

WAYS OF EVALUATING THE QUALITY OF CARE

It is clear that childcare quality is a complex construct and must be assessed with expert judgment and sensitivity. The best evaluations come from observing children's actual experiences in the care arrangement. This observation is time intensive and requires extensive training. Observers can't just guess or go by their "gut instinct." Earlier we described how quality was assessed in three exemplary studies. These studies used the most widely accepted assessments of overall quality, including the Early Childhood Environment Rating Scale (ECERS) and the Infant/Toddler Environment Rating Scale (ITERS), both of which focus on the furnishings and room arrangement, the planning and scheduling of activities, the amount and accessibility of materials, and the caregiver's behavior with the children. Each item on these scales requires a judgment: for example, to rate caregiver-child interaction, observers must decide whether there is "frequent positive caregiver-child interaction throughout the day." To make this judgment, the observer must spend at least a day in the setting and have a standard of comparison for judging "positive" and "frequent." The ECERS and ITERS require thorough training and extensive experience. Researchers in the NICHD study used a different instrument—the Observational Record of the Caregiving Environment (ORCE)—which involves a behavior checklist and qualitative ratings of the caregiver's interactions with the child. The ORCE, too, requires extensive training so that the observer can evaluate, for example, caregiving qualities such as sensitivity and intrusiveness. These three instruments provide global assessments of the overall quality in childcare settings.

WHAT IS GOOD QUALITY RELATED TO?

Using these global assessments, investigators have found that childcare quality is significantly associated with children's cognitive development.[2] Associations between quality and development have been observed in locations as far-ranging as Bermuda, Sweden, Switzerland, and Singapore, as well as Canada, the United Kingdom, and the United States, and in home childcare settings as well as centers, for children ranging in age from one to four years.[3] The most compelling evidence that childcare quality affects children's cognitive development comes from experimental studies in which children from high-risk families placed in high-quality programs consistently make gains.[4]

Children in higher-quality care are also judged by observers and their caregivers to be more sociable, considerate, compliant, and controlled.[5] They are interested in program activities and well adjusted and have high self-esteem, while children in low-quality care are angry and defiant and have behavior problems.[6] Children in high-quality care have better relationships with their caregivers than children in low-quality care do.[7] Moreover, childcare quality is related to children's cortisol levels.[8] Children who received more attention and stimulation from their caregivers in childcare were less likely to have increased cortisol levels over the course of the day; their cortisol levels looked just like those of children who stayed in the peaceful environment of their own homes.

Perhaps the most thorough and statistically sound examinations of childcare quality are provided by the Cost, Quality and Child Outcomes and the NICHD studies. In the CQO study, overall quality of care in center classrooms was related to children's cognitive and social development; specifically, children in higher-quality classrooms did better on tests of language ability and premath and prereading skills and had more positive views of themselves, better relationships with their teachers, and more advanced social skills.[9] In the NICHD study, after controlling for variables such as family income and geographical location, researchers found that children in higher-quality care in both home-based and center childcare settings received higher scores on tests of cognitive and language abilities, exhibited more positive and skilled interactions with peers in childcare, and were reported by their caregivers to have fewer behavior problems, at ages two and three.[10] At age four, they performed better on a battery of standardized tests that assessed their abilities to read letters and words, do simple math problems, complete words, remember and recite back sentences, and understand and use language.[11] They were less impulsive in a test of attention, and they were rated by their caregivers as being socially skilled and as having few behavior problems than children in poorer quality care.[12] Childcare quality was not related to the child's attachment relationship with the mother or the child's interaction with a good friend, but consistently, across a variety of measures, childcare predicted social and intellectual competence.[13] In fact, children in high-quality childcare performed better than children in full-time maternal care; children in low-quality care performed worse.[14]

HOW LARGE ARE THE EFFECTS?

These associations between childcare quality and children's abilities are statistically significant and consistent, but how large are they in absolute terms? As it turns out, they are not very large. Perhaps this result is not surprising. It is probably unreasonable to expect that the quality of childcare would have a stronger effect than the quality of parenting, and we know from other research that quality of parenting often accounts for less than 10 percent of the variability in child outcomes. Extrapolating from this figure, we might expect that no more than 5 percent of the variability in child outcomes would be accounted for by childcare quality—and this is what was found in the NICHD study.[15] Taking a different approach to estimating the size of childcare effects, other researchers have found that a difference of one point on the ITERS or ECERS measure of childcare quality was related to a difference of six points on the Bayley Scale of Mental Development in a study of African American children from lower-income families.[16] In the CQO study, a one-point increase in quality was related to a two-point increase in language scores.[17] In the NICHD study, a one-standard-deviation increase in childcare quality was associated with increases in cognitive scores of between one-half and two points (the larger increases were for children with lower cognitive skills to begin with).[18] Thus, we see that the effects of childcare quality are modest.

So does this mean that we should not be concerned about childcare quality? Some people have suggested so, but we beg to differ—for two reasons. The first reason is that although studies have not revealed large effects, this result is probably because the researchers have tapped a relatively narrow range of childcare quality. There is undoubtedly poor-quality childcare that has eluded researchers' nets; including a more complete range of quality from the worst to the best would boost the size of obtained associations between quality and development. Researchers have found that when they increased the range of child-care quality by combining data sets from the NICHD study and a study in Israel, for example, associations between quality and child outcomes increased substantially.[19] Perhaps the bulk of childcare in the United States is homogeneous enough that it does not create huge differences in child outcomes, but parents need to be alerted about the importance of recognizing and avoiding really bad-quality care.

The second reason to be concerned about childcare quality is that good quality extends beyond the scores children get on tests and ratings. Childcare quality leads to differences in "quality of life" for the youngsters who spend many hours in childcare every day. We owe it to children to provide them with the best quality of life we can, so that their young lives will be more pleasant, regardless of whether this high quality makes a difference on tests of language fluency or ratings of assertiveness.

HOW LONG DO THE DIFFERENCES LAST?

Another consideration concerns how long childcare quality effects last. Some researchers studying community childcare have found that differences last into the early school years.[20] Childcare quality had a modest long-term effect on children's cognitive and socioemotional development through kindergarten and in some cases through first grade in the CQO study, and through third grade in the NICHD study.[21] (Effects may last even longer, but the data from older ages in the NICHD study have not yet been analyzed.) Model childcare programs have demonstrated more substantial long-term effects. Enrollment in early intervention programs of very high quality has been found to predict long-term outcomes in cognitive and language development, academic attainment, and prevention of delinquency for children from poor families.[22] These advantages have even been tracked into early adulthood, when they show up as higher rates of employment and less criminal activity.[23] Graduates of the Abecedarian Project, a model program at the University of North Carolina, for example, scored significantly higher than children in the control group in reading and knowledge on Woodcock-Johnson Test of Achievement at age twelve and in mathematics and reading at age fifteen.[24] At age twenty-one graduates of the program continued to score higher on tests and were also more likely to still be attending school. Children who participated in the High/Scope Perry Preschool Program in Ypsilanti, Michigan, achieved significantly higher scores than control children in reading, arithmetic, and language on the California Achievement Test while they were in school, and even years later, in their twenties and thirties, they did better in terms of income, high school graduation, and criminal arrests.[25]

The effects of these model programs cannot be generalized to garden-variety childcare. However, they do indicate that long-term effects are possible. Positive long-term consequences are more likely for children from disadvantaged homes who attend high-quality programs, for whom high-quality care supplies missing elements in their lives. The opposite effect is also theoretically possible. If children from excellent home environments spend many hours in dismal childcare, they may suffer long-term negative consequences. For obvious ethical reasons, researchers have not implemented the latter experimental design. Thus, it seems that childcare could have larger and more long-lasting effects, but in most real-world situations, it does not, because contrasts between home and childcare environments are not extreme.

ARE THEY REALLY "EFFECTS"?
There is no question that experimental studies in which children are randomly assigned to high-quality care demonstrate actual causal effects. But these programs are limited in their application to real-

world care, because real-world care seldom reaches the level of excellence of these programs. Observational studies of run-of-the-mill childcare provide less firm ground for determining whether differences in children's behaviors and abilities are a direct result of childcare quality. Correlations do not prove causation.

Researchers try to get around this problem in various ways. One thing they do is to statistically control variables such as family income and parenting quality, which are related to childcare quality. This control provides an estimate of the effect of childcare above and beyond the contribution of the family. A second strategy is to randomly select children from a classroom and look for classroom-level effects; this strategy is another way of eliminating some of the variation due to child and family factors. Researchers also look to see whether childcare quality is related to changes in children's abilities over time, rather than just computing associations at a single point in time. These efforts to look for effects over time generally support the common sense belief that childcare causes observed effects. For example, in the CQO study, childcare quality was related to increases in children's verbal intelligence (PPVT) scores.[26] In the NICHD study, childcare quality predicted cognitive and language performance nine to twelve months later.[27] In both studies, associations with childcare quality remained even with confounding variables controlled. However, definitive evidence of causality—for example, finding an association between the amount of time children spend in high-quality care and the amount they gain in test scores—has not always been found.[28] We are left with our correlations and our common sense to infer that differences in childcare quality probably (but not unequivocally) cause observed differences in children's behavior and abilities.

In the rest of this chapter, we probe these issues further as we discuss a number of specific components of childcare quality: the size, safety and stimulation of the physical setting; the nature of the educational curriculum and organized activities; and the number of children in the childcare setting. Finding links between specific aspects of quality and theoretically related child outcomes provides another piece of evidence supporting the belief that childcare causes differences in children's performance.

Physical Environment

The physical environment is an important part of the childcare arrangement for children. Even years later, adolescents still remember it well. When researchers interviewed children twelve to fifteen years old in one study, many of them remembered the physical layout of their childcare home or center and described it in lengthy and rambling detail.[29] They remembered large playground equipment and specific objects like paintings, beds, couches, and, of course, the sandbox. The experience of childcare is a sensuous one, and we might expect that differences in the physical setting would affect how children behave and what they learn in different childcare programs. Researchers have investigated this question by studying the effects of variation in space, equipment, and materials in childcare settings.

SPACE

The usual measure of space used in childcare research is not simply the total space in the setting but the space per child. In one study of children in classrooms ranging from twenty-seven to fifty-two square feet per child, those in the more crowded classrooms scored lower on a test of functioning cognitive.[30] When the space per child is very limited (less than twenty-five square feet per child), children have been observed to be more physical and aggressive with their peers and more destructive with their toys; they spend more time doing nothing and less time interacting socially.[31] Fortunately, in the United States licensing standards for childcare centers and childcare homes ensure space that exceeds this lower limit (more than thirty-five square feet per child). Therefore, space may not be a major influence on children in most childcare settings, at least those that meet licensing requirements.[32]

ORGANIZATION

The way the space is organized may be more important than square footage. An organization that allows children privacy and quiet and that separates different kinds of activities—loud block play and quiet puzzle play, for example—seems to be more beneficial than simply more square feet of play area.[33] When researchers examined the influence of environmental features in nine childcare centers in Sweden, they found that what mattered most for children's outcomes was how well components of the setting fit and functioned together.[34] This finding is confirmed by a broader body of research showing that orderly, well-defined, predictable environments are important to young children.[35]

MATERIALS

The materials that go into the separate activity areas are also important. Researchers have demonstrated that children act differently in areas with different kinds of materials.[36] Outdoors, children on the vehicle paths play alone. On the slides and swings and climbing equipment, they run, laugh, and enjoy rough-and-tumble play; they are less aggressive and more cooperative; and they play lengthy, complex games with peers and interact less with teachers. Indoors, in the art area, children play in parallel, concentrating on their own drawings and paintings. In the dramatic play area, with dress up clothes and dolls, they talk among themselves and have complex social interactions. The cooking area is more likely to involve adults. In the building-construction area, with blocks and boards, children talk less—except for quarrels—but their play is rich and challenging. In academic areas, with projects and puzzles, children use materials constructively, often accompanied by interaction with the teacher. With materials for "messing around" (sand, clay, buttons, and assorted junk), their activities, often with other children, are creative and experimental but less complex. Small toys also bring out less complex behaviors, as children do what the toys suggest: with toy guns they behave aggressively; with checkers and pickup sticks they interact socially; with gyroscopes and microscopes they play alone.

If few materials are available and if the equipment is fixed, inflexible, or limited, children spend their time watching, waiting, cruising, touching, imitating, chatting, quarreling, and horsing around with peers; their play is of low complexity and little intellectual value. Children do better when varied, age-appropriate, and educational toys, materials, and equipment are available.[37] In the NICHD study, children in settings with more stimulating, varied, and well-organized materials (including materials to stimulate math, movement, music, language, art, and play) received higher scores on tests of language comprehension and short-term memory.[38]

Books, posters, and pencils can have a special role in childcare settings because they promote literacy. In one study, researchers studied the presence and use of these materials in thirty childcare classrooms.[39] Results revealed a situation far removed from best practices. In 30 percent of the classrooms, not a single literacy-related activity was observed during free play. When present, paper and writing materials were used for art, not for writing. In settings that did offer more literacy activities, however, children's language development and verbal intelligence were advanced.

Children do better when they have enough materials to go around; a more plentiful supply of materials leads to more cooperative and constructive participation and less conflict. In one study, pairs of children were videotaped in a painting activity under two conditions: in one, there was only one brush and one piece of paper; in the other, each child had a brush and a piece of paper. When children had to share the brush and paper, more conflict was observed; when each child had his or her own materials, there was more social and task interaction.[40] Similarly, in a case study with a four-year-old who was about to be expelled from his childcare program because he was so aggressive, when researchers increased the number of materials so that there were enough toys for each child, the boy's aggressive behaviors dropped dramatically.[41] In brief, children do better in childcare settings with plenty of materials, and children's development is supported if the materials are varied and stimulating.

A GOOD PLACE TO BE

Space of good physical quality can be found in both homes and in centers, although materials that elicit high-level constructive play (puzzles, block, art) may be more common in centers, and opportunities for free play and tactile exploration (water, sand, dough, pillows) more likely in homes. In either kind of setting, the quality of the physical space affects the adults' behavior as well as the children's.

In physical settings of good quality, caregivers can both allow children freedom to explore and spend their time demonstrating constructive activities with the materials available, rather than supervising and scolding all the time. In the NICHD study, across ages and different types of care—centers, childcare homes, in-home sitters, and grandparents—caregivers consistently provided more sensitive and responsive attention when the physical environment in the setting was safer and more stimulating.[42]

Programs and Activities

Another dimension on which childcare arrangements vary is the activities that make up the program. Childcare arrangements range from strictly care-oriented settings that involve only daily routines and free play to explicitly "educational" orientations that offer a rich diet of intellectual and social stimulation. Activities vary widely from center to center and from centers to homes. How do children's experiences and development differ depending on the activities that are provided?

AN EDUCATIONAL AGENDA

The educational curriculum is the focus of many childcare programs, especially preschool centers, and research suggests that these programs differ from less educationally oriented programs in a number of ways. Programs with an educational curriculum are more likely to offer lessons, guided play sessions, story reading, teaching of specific content, and direct teacher instruction. The children attending these programs spend more time in constructive and complex play with materials, engage in more cognitively challenging tasks, converse more with adults and other children, and score higher on tests of intelligence and achievement.[43] When children spend their time in childcare just playing around with other children or watching television, they experience less "rich" play and are less socially competent.[44] In the NICHD study, children who watched more television while they were in the child-care setting received lower scores on math, vocabulary, and language comprehension.[45] Thus, there is evidence that an educational program promotes more intellectually valuable experiences in the care setting and that these experiences have positive consequences for children. This effect may explain why children in centers often do better intellectually than children in homes with their mother or another caregiver.[46]

A STRUCTURED PROGRAM

Educational curricula can be delivered in a number of ways, which can be organized in terms of how much "structure" the program entails. In a highly structured program, caregivers are clearly in control. They provide children with clear limits and give explicit lessons according to a strict schedule. Caregivers' behavior is consistent and predictable. They make their goals and expectations clear to the children—and their parents. The children engage in activities that are purposeful and task-oriented; however, they lack opportunities to act on their own initiative and to have informal, spontaneous interactions with the caregiver or other children. In an unstructured program, in contrast, caregivers are nonintrusive and indirect. They prepare materials and activities for the children but let them choose which activities to engage in, going at their own pace, following their own interests, and making discoveries about the social and physical world on their own. Caregivers in unstructured programs guide, encourage, and help the children in their activities, but caregivers do not exhort, direct, instruct, or restrict. An unstructured program may be more chaotic than a structured program because the caregiver is not in direct control. The caregiver's behavior and that of the children is more variable. Unstructured programs offer children opportunities for rewarding contact with peers, freedom to explore, and the chance to make choices and decisions. In unstructured classes, children play together more, cooperate, and help each other; their play is more imaginative and physical; they are more likely to persist on a task, talk about it, and ask questions.[47]

But which of these types of program is best? It sounds as if they both have positives—and negatives. Children themselves prefer less-structured programs. In one study, children in eight preschool classrooms were observed and interviewed about their likes and dislikes in childcare.[48] They drew pictures and told stories; they were shown photographs and asked to talk about them. What the children liked most about childcare was unstructured play. Play was the most frequently mentioned and favorite activity of all children in all classrooms—regardless of the quality of care in the classroom. Play is free, fun, noisy, and spontaneous. It is freely chosen, it is free from rules, and it is not work. When activities were required or directed by the teacher, children thought of them as work. The same activities, like art and computer, when chosen by the child, were thought of as fun. Among the children's chief dislikes were circle time, nap time, and time-out—all activities that terminated play. When asked why they didn't like these activities, the children didn't hesitate: "Because you don't get to play." Circle times that focused on rote memorization of letters, numbers, shapes, and rules were, in the children's opinion, boring and stupid and long. Nap time was also long: one child didn't like naptime because "you sleep for ninety hours." Another child made the best of nap time: "I just lie down and rest and whisper playing." All children disliked time-out—even in centers where time-out was never observed.

Teachers and parents are more likely than children to value a structured program. But how much structure is a good idea? Should caregivers rule the roost completely or give the children some freedom to choose how they spend their time? According to research, a moderate amount of structure is best. In an ideal program, the caregiver offers some structured activities and lessons but also gives children opportunities for free play and free choice. In one study that illustrates the benefits of moderate structure, children in highly structured classes expressed more negative emotion, were less compliant, and were more likely to be disciplined than children in moderately structured classes. Children in highly structured classes also showed more evidence of stress—nail biting, frowning, turning away from a task—and had a lower opinion of their own academic competencies.[49] In another study, children's play was more elaborate, complex, and cognitively worthwhile in programs with just two structured educational activities per half-day session, compared with programs that were either more or less structured.[50]

In the most thorough comparison of programs varying in structure, researchers Louise Miller and Jean Dyer set up model preschool programs in four different schools and then observed the behavior of teachers and children and tested the children's abilities throughout the school term and three years later.[51] One program was highly structured. In this program, teachers directed youngsters in small groups of five or six in three twenty-minute lessons on reading, language, and arithmetic every day. The lessons were controlled completely by the teacher, according to a script she was given by the program designers. She modeled, corrected, and rewarded children's responses in a fast-paced, loud, repetitive drill of short questions and answers:

> *Teacher:* This is a wheel (shows picture).
> *Child:* Wheel.
> *Teacher:* Good. It is a wheel. Let's all say it. This is a wheel.
> *Children:* This is a wheel.
> *Teacher:* Again.
> *Children:* This is a wheel.
> *Teacher:* Let's say it one more time.

Children in this program gained rapidly on tests of intelligence, and by the end of the preschool year they scored higher than children in any other program on arithmetic, sentence production, vocabulary, and persistence on a difficult task. Three years later, however, at the end of second grade, these children scored low on tests of IQ, letters, numbers, word meaning, inventiveness, and curiosity. Their preschool gains had completely disappeared. Even years later, in elementary and high school, children who had attended this strictly structured program were less socially skilled and less academically oriented.

Two programs set up by Miller and Dyer were moderately structured. One of these programs included teacher instruction and formal academic lessons, but the lessons were not simply repetitions of verbal patterns; they included playing table games, copying designs, and identifying letters and numbers. There were both formal and informal conversations between children and teachers, often one to one, and children were given free choices as well as prescribed lessons. Children in this program also gained rapidly on IQ tests and tests of arithmetic, vocabulary, sentence production, and persistence, but, unlike the children in the first program, they gained in curiosity, inventiveness, and social participation as well. What is more, the children in this program continued to score high on tests of IQ, inventiveness, curiosity, and verbal-social skills at the end of the second grade.

The other moderately structured program set up by Miller and Dyer was a Montessori class. In this program, the materials were structured but the schedule was not. Children were free to select whatever materials interested them and to work on them at their own pace, with little teacher interference. The teacher introduced the materials at what she thought were appropriate times but gave no lessons in how to use them. Montessori materials themselves are "self-correcting": there is only one right way to build a tower with the Montessori graduated cylinders or to make the staircase with the pink blocks, for example. Children in this program excelled in curiosity and inventiveness at the end of the program school year, and three years later they were not only high in these qualities but also high in IQ, reading, and mathematics, and they were more highly motivated to achieve in school.

The final, unstructured program in Miller and Dyer's study was a traditional nursery school program. This program was child centered and slow paced. Most of the time children engaged in free play, choosing from make-believe, dress ups, physical activities, puzzles, books, and science materials. At other times they had group activities, such as singing, stories, and field trips. The teachers exerted no pressure; they were warm and accepting; the children were free to do whatever interested them. At the end of a year in this program, the children were curious and socially active, but they were also more aggressive and did more poorly on intelligence tests. Three years later, they were still high on verbal-social skills such as cooperation and initiating conversations but, as they were earlier, low in academic achievement.

The results of all these studies are consistent in pointing up the pros and cons of structured instruction. Programs that blend prescribed educational activities with opportunities for free choice and that have some structure but also allow children to explore a rich environment of objects and peers on their own without teacher direction seem to have the most benefits—for constructive activity, for learning academic skills, for later achievement in school, for positive motivation and persistence, for problem solving, and for acquiring social skills. Recently, a national study of preschool care in the United Kingdom confirmed that the most effective preschool programs provided children with both adult-initiated group work and freely chosen yet potentially instructive play activities.[52]

CURRICULAR CONTENT

Childcare programs differ in the area of children's development that they emphasize: physical growth and skills, intellectual and academic development, or social and emotional well-being. Few preschool programs emphasize the first of these. Most preschool children lead sedentary lives—whether or not they are in childcare. Children at home spend their time playing quietly and watching TV; in childcare, children play quietly, read, draw, and listen.[53] As national concerns about children's physical health and obesity grow, however, more emphasis may be placed on incorporating physical goals and exercise into childcare programs.

The most common curricular focus in preschool programs today is intellectual and academic development. There are numerous examples of successful academic curricula. One is the "Books Aloud" program.[54] This program targeted economically disadvantaged children in 330 childcare centers. It flooded the centers with high-quality children's books, at a rate of five books for every child. After the books arrived, literacy interactions almost doubled, as teachers introduced counting, rhyming, and songbooks and engaged children in talking about storybooks. During free play, the children started asking teachers to read to them, or they looked at books and pretended to read. These children also scored higher on early literary measures than children who were not in the program did and these gains were still evident six months later, when the children were in kindergarten. In another literacy program, children were introduced to a new story during group time on the first day of each week.[55] Then, as the week unfolded, they heard the story again and were invited to retell it using the pictures and finally to compose a story of their own in their "big books." When the program began, the children seldom visited the library area or interacted with books or paper, and when they were asked to choose and read a favorite story, they refused. When the program ended, they were spending more time in the library and the writing area and reading to one another. As these two programs illustrate, children in more academically oriented programs are more knowledgeable about words, reading, and telling stories.

However, they may also be more aggressive with their playmates. In one important study, children attending a model, university-based childcare program that focused on promoting children's intellectual development were great at taking intelligence tests but not so good at getting along with other children. When they got to first grade, these children outscored peers who had not been in the preschool program in IQ points but were also thirteen times more aggressive on the playground.[56] They had not developed social skills or learned nonaggressive strategies for solving social problems just by building with blocks and learning their ABCs. When teachers implemented a new curriculum that focused explicitly on teaching social skills, the heightened aggression of children in this childcare program was eliminated.[57] In the case study with the aggressive four-year-old who was about to be expelled from childcare, aggression dropped to almost nothing when the boy was taught specific social skills, such as how to share, make requests, and refuse in an acceptable way and then prompted and reinforced for his use of these skills.[58] A curriculum that explicitly focuses on promoting social skills apparently can be successful in teaching children how to settle conflicts without coming to blows—but this kind of curriculum is not common in contemporary childcare.

Based on these studies, it seems that childcare should offer a balanced menu of academic and social lessons, just as, ideally, childcare should provide a balanced diet of structured and unstructured activities. In fact, researchers in a national study in Britain have just found that when preschool program staff view academic and social development as equally important, children make better all-round progress, advancing in sociability as well as in reading and mathematics.[59]

Peers and Ratios

Implementing a social skills curriculum requires the presence of other children in the childcare arrangement. But what happens when there is no social curriculum? Do children benefit just from interacting with their peers? One reason that many parents send their children to childcare or preschool is for the experience of playing with others children. The children themselves certainly like playing together.[60] But parents also hope and expect that their children will become more socially skilled; will learn to share, cooperate, and make friends; and perhaps will learn more mature behaviors from their peers. The parents' hope is not unreasonable. Advantages in social competence have been observed more often for children in childcare arrangements where there are other children than in arrangements with a caregiver alone.[61] But as we have already mentioned, the result of being with other children is not so simple. Here, we examine research on what happens when children are in childcare arrangements with other children, as we look for answers to questions such as the following: Is it beneficial for the child to be in a childcare arrangement with one other child? Is it better to be in a large class? Is playing with many different kinds of children valuable for the child? Or is being with a crowd of kids stressful and likely to lead to aggression?

ONE GOOD FRIEND

Studies have shown that when young children play with a familiar playmate, their play is more cooperative and connected than when they interact with an unfamiliar child.[62] This observation suggests that having experience with even one other child might benefit children by giving them the opportunity to practice the more-advanced social skills that occur only with friends. In fact, researchers have found that the social skills developed with a friend carry over into interactions with an unfamiliar child. Children who participate in repeated play sessions with another child or who have a regular playmate are more sociable and responsive, have longer interactions, and initiate more games with a new child than children without this experience.[63] Children who remain longer with the same group of children in childcare are more peer oriented and friendlier toward peers in distress than children whose peer groups change frequently.[64] So it seems that repeated opportunities to play with even one other child may be of value for the development of early social competence.

The same observation may be true for intellectual development. Play between pairs of children, researchers have observed, is more complex, intellectually worthwhile, and cognitively challenging than playing alone.[65] Peers can serve as models, tutors, and behavior modifiers, as well as competitive partners and congenial and cooperative playmates. Only with other children can a child do certain things, such as using the teeter-totter, jumping off a platform twenty times, or playing peekaboo under a blanket. Having the chance to play with another child on a regular basis, apparently, is necessary for social development and good for intellectual development.

HOW MANY PLAYMATES? GROUP SIZES AND CHILD-ADULT RATIOS

In most childcare settings, however, children do not play with just one other child; they play with many. In the Chicago Study of Child Care and Development, children in childcare centers and preschools played with an average of ten different children during a two-hour period, whereas children at home played with only two or three—who were usually siblings.[66] Does playing with more children advance children's development beyond the benefit of playing with one other child?

There may be some advantages of being exposed to a number of peers. Children in larger classes in the Chicago study knew more about social rules and expressions and were less shy with unfamiliar peers and adults, and the more different children they played with, the more advanced were their intellectual abilities and social competence. In another study, children in larger childcare groups were more independent in a mildly frustrating situation than children in small groups.[67] When they were presented with a wrapped gift or food and required to wait six minutes before they could have it, children in care with a larger group of children could soothe or distract themselves—they had obviously learned how to wait—but children in care with fewer children asked their mother for assistance or played with the forbidden object—a less mature pattern of behavior.

But does this finding mean that the more children in the class the better? Obviously not. For one thing, we do not know that playing with more children caused children's advanced development. It may be that more advanced children in the Chicago study sought out or attracted more children to play with. For another thing, there are limits on how many children a child can play with. In large classes—classes of more than twenty children—researchers have observed that children are more likely to look apathetic, cry, and act hostile.[68] It seems that there is a maximum number of children in a class, beyond which detrimental effects are likely.

Having too many children for each caregiver to look after can be especially detrimental. Child-caregiver ratios range substantially from one childcare setting to another. In childcare homes, there may only be one or two children for one caregiver. In centers, state-mandated groups for one caregiver range from four to thirteen for toddlers and from seven to twenty for preschoolers. With too many children for one caregiver to attend to, children suffer, and so do the adults—who are worn out before the end of the day. Studies have shown consistently that overall quality of care suffers when child-adult ratios are high.[69] Caregivers in classrooms with high child-staff ratios are less sensitive, responsive, and positive. Children have less contact with the caregiver, spend more of their time playing with other children, and spend less time in intellectual activities; fewer of their questions are answered; their conversations are shorter; and contact with the caregiver is more likely to involve prohibitions, commands, corrections, and routines. These children are less likely to have secure attachment relationships with their caregivers or their mothers, and on tests they receive lower scores for language and communication skills.[70]

The benefits of having low child-caregiver ratios showed up clearly in each of our three exemplary studies: In the Cost, Quality and Child Outcomes Study, lower child-adult ratios were related to better overall quality of care, more caregiver sensitivity, and more effective teaching; children in classes with lower child-teacher ratios also had higher prereading scores.[71] In the Florida Child Care Quality Improvement Study, when child-staff ratios in preschool centers were reduced from 6:1 to 4:1 for infants and from 8:1 to 6:1 for toddlers, overall classrooms quality improved: teachers became more sensitive and responsive and less reliant on negative discipline, and children engaged in more cognitively complex play with other children and classroom materials, gained more in cognitive development, and were more securely attached to their teachers.[72] In the NICHD Study of Early Child Care, the link with child-caregiver ratios was significant even with other aspects of care, such as the quality of the physical setting and the caregiver's professional training, statistically controlled. The child-caregiver ratio was the strongest predictor of positive caregiver behavior with infants. When the ratio of infants to caregivers was 1:1, 38 percent of the caregivers were rated as highly sensitive. When the ratio increased to 2:1, only 17 percent of the caregivers were highly sensitive. With a ratio of 4:1, only 8 percent of the caregivers were highly sensitive.[73] With older children, differences in caregiver behavior were more modest in size but still statistically significant.[74] Children's performance also benefited from low child-caregiver ratios. Children in care arrangements with low child-adult ratios did better on tests of school readiness and language comprehension at age three and on tests of cognitive competence and caregivers' ratings of social competence at age four.[75]

In childcare homes, where there are seldom more than six children for one caregiver, the link with child-caregiver ratio is not as strong—the association may even be in the opposite direction.[76] When caregivers who are taking care of more children provide higher-quality care, however, this result may be because they are more professional than caregivers with few children. In the NICHD study, we found that when caregivers' training and education were controlled, the number of children in the childcare home was not related to the quality of care or child outcomes.[77] In the California Licensing Study, when researchers added two more children to existing childcare homes, they found that the quality of caregiving declined.[78] Thus, it does seem that, all other things being equal, children and caregivers benefit from relatively low child-caregiver ratios.

VARIETY OF PEERS: MIX OR MATCH?
Childcare offers children the opportunity to interact not only with a large number of peers but also with a variety of different kinds of peers. This aspect of childcare may also affect children's learning and relationships. In the Chicago study, for example, children who

interacted with more different kinds of people—with different socioeconomic and ethnic groups, different ages, and both boys and girls—had advanced social and cognitive abilities.[79] These last two sources of variation have received the most attention from researchers. They have observed that children benefit from being in coed and mixed-age playgroups. In terms of gender, boys who play only with other boys are more likely to have behavior problems and poor interactional styles.[80] In terms of age, children in mixed-age groups have more frequent and complex interactions and are more verbal, cooperative, positive, persistent, and flexible; they engage in more imitation and fantasy play and are more knowledgeable in tests of social competence and intelligence.[81] Of course, variation can be taken too far. A range of a couple of years in age may be better than a larger age discrepancy.[82] In general, though, children seem to benefit from exposure to a variety of children.

The issue of the importance of peers in the childcare setting, thus, is a complex one. Experience with one other child seems to be better than experience with none; experience with more different children is probably better than experience with only one; experience with too many children in the same class or at the same time may be detrimental, particularly if the ratio of children to caregivers is large. Experience with a variety of other people appears to be enriching, but with too wide an age spread the advantage may be lost.

What happens within the childcare setting, including the child's experience with peers depends, however, to a large extent on the last critical feature of the childcare environment: the caregiver. The significance of the care provider underlies all three aspects of childcare that we have discussed. Caregivers arrange the physical space and select equipment and materials, they select and administer the educational curriculum, and they divide the children into groups and supervise their interactions. The caregiver is the choreographer of the childcare culture and the key to childcare quality. In the next chapter we discuss this important role.

7

THE CAREGIVER'S ROLE

The research we have just reviewed clearly shows that factors such as the size of the class, the nature of the physical setting, and the presence of educational activities in the program all play important parts in determining the quality and the effects of childcare. But the most important role is reserved for the caregiver. It is she— because the vast majority of caregivers are female, we refer to them in this chapter as "she"—who coordinates the class, the setting, and the educational activities. She is the social glue holding the program together. She provides education, stimulation, affection, and fun. She manages and disciplines the children. She ministers to their bodies, minds, and spirits. Here, we discuss the multifaceted role of the caregiver as teacher, manager, and nurturer. We examine how background factors lead some caregivers to play their role with particular skill and discuss how caregivers' characteristics are related not only to their own behavior but to the behavior of the children in their care.

A Multifaceted Role

THE CAREGIVER AS TEACHER

One key aspect of the caregiver's role is teaching. When actively involved in teaching children and providing them with interesting materials and a moderate number of educational tasks, caregivers promote children's intellectual learning and achievement. The effects of caregivers' teaching begin in infancy. In one study, infants who were given enriched language experiences in their childcare centers were well above norms for verbal and cognitive skills by the time they could be tested; in later years, they developed to gifted levels, excelled academically, and became strongly motivated to acquire multiple interests and competencies.[1] They also enjoyed excellent relations with peers and adults and often became intellectual and social leaders. Other studies have also demonstrated that children whose caregivers offer the children "intellectually valuable" experiences, especially language mastery experiences, have more advanced social and intellectual skills.[2] If the caregiver's lessons focus on social skills, children's cooperation and social behavior with peers may also be enhanced. Children benefit when caregivers mediate their conflicts and use their negative interactions to teach social rules.[3]

Thus, many caregivers serve as teachers of important intellectual and social skills—and they often see it as their role to do so. In the national Profile of Child Care study, one third of the center directors interviewed said that their main goal was to promote children's development or to prepare children for school.[4] Caregivers in childcare centers are more likely than those in home settings to think of themselves as teachers and use more academic teaching methods.[5] They spend a major proportion of their time in curriculum planning and implementation; they plan educational activities and pepper the children with questions.[6] Teaching in family childcare is more informal; children learn through free exploration in the context of "real-life" tasks and situations.

THE CAREGIVER AS MANAGER

Another part of the caregiver's role is to manage the children while they are at childcare and to get them to behave properly. Childcare culture becomes childcare chaos if caregivers are not clearly in charge. This role as manager may be especially important in a setting populated by a large group of children who are close in age. Childcare providers, thus, must be not only teachers but also disciplinarians.

Praise is a tactic caregivers use to manage children and manipulate their behavior. If children are consistently praised for a particular behavior, they will play with a child they would ordinarily ignore, they will be more cooperative or more competitive, and they will persist longer at tasks.[7] The more often caregivers praise the specific kinds of behavior they want to see, the more these behaviors increase. But when teachers simply go around saying positive things all the time, irrespective of what the children are doing, children do not learn. When caregivers do not expect children to behave in particular ways—cooperatively, assertively, persistently, quietly, politely—and consistently praise them for acting in these ways, children do not learn these behaviors.

It is even worse, though, if caregivers are constantly criticizing the children. Neither unconditional acceptance nor heavy-handed criticism are effective styles of discipline. When caregivers are too permissive, children don't learn to follow rules. When caregivers are overly restrictive, children may follow the rules, but when they escape the oppressive regime of the classroom, they go wild and act out aggressively and disobediently. What is more, if children are constantly repressed, restricted, and fearful, they are unlikely to learn anything intellectual in the childcare setting. Their creativity and inquisitiveness will almost certainly suffer as well. Children spend more time working on a task, play at more complex levels, and perform better on tests of intelligence and achievement when their caregivers are less critical and demanding and use positive rather than negative reinforcement.[8] It is important that caregivers enforce rules in the classroom clearly, firmly, consistently, and appropriately. When discipline is lax, children misbehave.[9]

The worst management tactic of all is imposing physical punishment, such as spanking or hitting the children. Not only is this a questionable method of discipline in its own right, but it can lead to physical abuse such as biting, shaking, or spanking the child hard enough to leave bruises. Review of the risk factors associated with child abuse in childcare settings shows that physical abuse most frequently occurs in the form of overly strict discipline and is a response to a prior conflict with the child over fighting, a toilet accident, persistent crying, disobedience, or hyperactivity.[10] Abusive caregivers also hold unrealistic ideas about children, believing, for example, that a toddler could intentionally plan to "defeat" the caregiver.

How caregivers manage and discipline children is directly related to their beliefs about how children should be treated. Some caregivers believe that children should be strictly ruled and regulated; others believe that children should control their own destinies. Caregivers with strict views provide less sensitive, stimulating, and responsive care than caregivers who value children's self-direction. In the NICHD study, caregivers with progressive, child-centered beliefs about how to manage children provided higher-quality care than caregivers with strict, authoritarian beliefs.[11] In Israel, too, caregivers who believed in strict authoritarian control initiated fewer educational activities and provided worse physical environments for the children in their care—and the children, in turn, were less socially competent.[12] In brief, it is important for caregivers to manage children in a way that provides them with clear rules and expectations but to do so with a light hand and an encouraging word. Effective caregivers allow children some control and choice, while at the same time offering them guidance and discipline.

THE CAREGIVER AS NURTURER

It is also part of the caregiver's role to nurture children, to respond to their needs and wishes and provide them with a warm, loving environment. The need for nurturance starts early. It is important for babies to feel loved and to learn that the world is a predictable place. Children are inclined to explore new situations when they know that if they cry, someone comes to comfort or feed them; that when they smile, someone smiles back; and that when they reach for a toy out of their grasp, someone gives it to them. To help infants develop this trust and confidence, adults should respond to their signals and demands appropriately and affectionately. Thus, when infants and young children are spending much of their time with caregivers other than Mom or Dad, it is essential that these caregivers, too, be loving and responsive.

In the Profile of Child Care Settings study and in other research, the majority of caregivers in childcare centers and homes claimed that their main goal was to provide children with warmth and affection.[13] Whether they succeed lingers in children's minds for years. In one study, adolescents were asked to recall their experiences in childcare years earlier and to describe the situations they could remember best.[14] The type of incident they mentioned most was nurturing by the caregiver—the caregiver's tending to a skinned knee, cuddling up to read a story, patting the children's backs at naptime. Being with a warm, nurturing caregiver has positive consequences for children's behavior as well. In a study in Germany, children's reactions to simulated distress was observed when a puppet experienced "pain" and was "frightened" by a popped balloon.[15] Children in childcare with caregivers who were more affectionate expressed more compassionate behavior than children whose caregivers were not as nurturing.

When children experience such nurturant interactions with caregivers, they are likely to form close relationships with them. A growing body of research suggests that children form attachment relationships with their caregivers in childcare, just as they form attachment relationships with their parents at home.[16] Toddlers begin to differentiate between caregivers during their first few days in the childcare setting, and over the next few months they form deeper emotional bonds with the caregivers they prefer.[17] They are more likely to be securely attached to these caregivers if they spend at least twenty hours a week with them and if the children have good relationships with their own mothers.[18] The caregivers that children become attached to are more involved with the children and more sensitive, consistent, and appropriate in their responses; these caregivers comfort the children and respond positively to their behavior.[19] Children with caregivers who are emotionally engaged also display more intense positive affect and less intense negative affect in their activities with these caregivers than children whose caregivers are emotionally detached.[20]

Forming a secure attachment to the caregiver has positive implications for the children's later development. Children who are securely attached to their caregivers are more competent in cognitive play and in their interactions with peers and adults, not just during their childcare years, but in elementary school as well.[21] In the Cost, Quality, and Outcomes Study, the closeness of the child's relationship with the caregiver at age four was related to cognitive and social skills at age eight.[22]

Having a close relationship with the caregiver does not undermine the child's relationship with his or her mother. However, if children do not have a secure relationship with their mother, they benefit from having one with their childcare caregiver; apparently a secure attachment with a childcare provider helps compensate for an insecure relationship with the mother.[23] In fact, in research conducted in Israel and the Netherlands, children's development and well-being were more highly related to having secure attachments to multiple childcare caregivers than to having secure attachments to both parents.[24]

CAREGIVERS WHO HAVE IT ALL TOGETHER

In sum, children are more likely to learn social and intellectual skills when caregivers are good at all three aspects of their role—as teachers, managers, and nurturers. When caregivers are stimulating and educational, responsive and respectful, affectionate and appropriately demanding, children do well.[25] In the Chicago Study of Child Care and Development, the children who did best were those whose caregivers were responsive, affectionate, accepting, and informative and whose caregivers read to them, offered them choices, and gave them gentle suggestions rather than harsh, punitive ultimatums.[26] In the National Day Care Staffing Study, as well, the children who did best had caregivers who were sensitive, responsive, emotionally involved, and less harsh in their discipline.[27] In the NICHD study, children with superior cognitive abilities and social skills had caregivers who provided good teaching (stimulating the child's development), respectful discipline (fostering the child's exploration and not being overly intrusive), and responsive nurturing (responding sensitively to the child's signals, expressing positive feelings, and being emotionally involved).[28]

Who are these caregivers who perform their multifaceted role so effectively? Can we predict the quality of caregiving if we know the caregiver's background? Does it make a difference how much training or education the caregiver has? What about experience, age, and commitment to the child? We examine each of these factors next.

Education and Training

In numerous studies researchers have looked at whether caregivers with high levels of education and specialized training in child development provide better quality care. Not surprisingly, all other things being equal, the best caregivers do have more education and training as childcare professionals than less effective caregivers have.[29]

THE IMPORTANCE OF CAREGIVER TRAINING

Childcare providers with more specialized training in child development are more involved and affectionate with the children in their care.[30] They are less authoritarian—restricting children less and encouraging them more.[31] They implement more developmentally appropriate practices in the classroom and provide richer literacy environments than caregivers with less training do.[32] In our three exemplary studies, links between caregiver training and caregiver behavior were clear. In the Cost, Quality and Child Outcomes Study, caregivers who had formal education in early childhood or who had attended professional development workshops were more responsive to the children and provided higher-quality care, even after researchers adjusted for other caregiver and classroom differences.[33] In the NICHD study, as well, caregivers who had higher levels of specialized training and had received child-related training during the previous year were more responsive, affectionate and stimulating.[34] In the Florida Child Care Quality Improvement Study, when the proportion of staff with specialized training increased from 26 percent to 53 percent, teachers were more responsively involved with the children, and teachers with the most advanced training had the highest scores on classroom quality.[35] In another study in Florida, specialized caregiver training was the best predictor of high-quality care and responsive caregiving—and the associations were remarkably high.[36]

But how much training is enough? Research suggests that although any training is valuable, for the best results a college degree in early childhood education is needed. In one study, Jeffrey Arnett found that caregivers with even a little training (two to four courses) were more positive and less authoritarian than caregivers with no training—but caregivers with college degrees in early childhood education were even more positive and less authoritarian.[37] In another study, Carollee Howes found that teachers with an associate of arts degree in early childhood education or a child development associate (CDA) certificate were more effective than teachers with some college courses in early childhood education or just high school courses and workshops—but teachers with a bachelor of arts in early childhood education were even more responsive.[38] Apparently CDA training gets teachers started toward more positive caregiver behavior—these caregivers were more involved in interactions with the children, more talkative and playful. However, they were not more responsive to the children's particular needs; more-advanced education and training is needed to enhance the caregiver's capacity for individualized care.

DO CAREGIVERS NEED AND WANT TRAINING?

Despite the apparent importance of specialized training, it is by no means universal. The level of training caregivers receive is, to some extent, determined by state requirements, which vary widely. In California, for example, a teacher is required to have twelve postsecondary semester units in early childhood education at a college or university and a CDA certificate or a children's center permit, whereas in Alabama teachers are required only to have a high school degree or general equivalency diploma and at least four hours of job-related training per year. Not surprisingly, then, many caregivers have only very limited training.

As a consequence of their lack of training, most childcare professionals are ignorant about current scientific knowledge of child development. In one study, fifty-three teachers from twenty childcare centers in Delaware were given a test to assess their knowledge of child development.[39] On average they answered only slightly more than half the questions correctly. A survey of childcare center teachers, directors, and family childcare providers found that 60 percent of family providers had never received any training on the subject of children's language and literacy development.[40]

Many childcare professionals apparently believe that obtaining advanced training is unnecessary. As part of a statewide assessment in Missouri, researchers asked childcare providers about what training they thought was necessary for quality caregiving.[41] Three different types of preparation were mentioned: (a) education or training; (b) life experience, such as parenting; and (c) personal attributes, such as patience. Only teachers in childcare centers—that is, caregivers with high levels of education themselves—were likely to say that formal training in child development was necessary. Home care providers tended to view their work as an extension of mothering and dismissed educational aspects of care. When asked directly what level of training and education childcare workers need, only one-third of all the providers said that caregivers needed at least a high school diploma.

WHO SEEKS TRAINING?

In the Family Child Care Training Study, researchers found that the caregivers who sought training were younger, had a higher work commitment, and were more professional than those who did not seek training.[42] Center caregivers with more training are more likely to attend conferences, read professional publications, and seek feedback from other professionals than caregivers in other settings; trained center caregivers also rely on professional resources for information and belong to professional childcare organizations. It may be that one way in which training can improve childcare quality is via childcare workers' increased use of professional resources to evaluate and improve their own performance.[43]

IS MORE TRAINING ALWAYS BETTER?

The association between training and quality of care is consistent, but there is no guarantee that a caregiver with a higher level of training will always provide better care. Although having no training in child development is clearly worse than having some, taking thirty courses is not necessarily better than taking ten. An improvement in quality of care depends on the content, quality, and variety of the courses. There is some suggestion that when teachers take a great many courses in child development, they develop a more academic orientation, which translates into an emphasis on school activities (reading, counting, lessons, learning) in the childcare classroom, to the exclusion of activities that promote children's social and emotional development. In the Chicago study, children whose caregivers had more formal training in child development were advanced intellectually but significantly less competent interacting with an unfamiliar peer. Caregivers with a moderate level of training had children who did well in both social and cognitive realms.[44]

THE IMPORTANCE OF GENERAL EDUCATION

In addition to specialized training in child development, caregivers' general education predicts the quality of their caregiving. Center teachers with college degrees were significantly more sensitive and appropriate in their care, less harsh and emotionally detached than teachers without college degrees, according to the National Child Care Staffing Study.[45] Center teachers with college degrees were more likely to use indirect forms of guidance, such as suggestions and encouragements rather than demands and restrictions, and made more of an effort to develop children's verbal skills, in a study by Laura Berk.[46] In a national survey of preschool teachers, those with higher levels of education were likely to endorse child-centered, individualized activities in their programs, in line with what experts generally consider good practice.[47] When conversations at the center were tape-recorded, researchers found that more educated teachers used more cognitively challenging talk in free play with the children.[48] Finally, in the Cost, Quality, Outcomes Study, childcare quality and caregiver sensitivity were higher in classrooms where teachers had some college education.[49]

In studies of teachers in childcare centers, it is difficult to separate caregivers' general education from their specialized training, because most teachers with college degrees have them in early childhood education or child development. Education and training are more easily separated in home childcare. Researchers have also found that home care providers are more sensitive and responsive and provide higher-quality care when they have higher levels of education.[50] In the NICHD study, quality of care and positive caregiving were related to caregivers' education in both childcare homes and centers, when children were two and three years old, although not when they were younger.[51] Apparently it does not matter for providing infant care if the caregiver has read *Moby Dick* or passed college algebra.

HOW STRONG ARE LINKS BETWEEN TRAINING AND QUALITY?

Despite the consistency and reasonableness of these links between childcare quality and caregivers' education and training, significant associations have not always been found between training and caregivers' sensitivity and harshness, especially for caregivers with younger children.[52] Perhaps these personal qualities are not so easily modified by training or education. Training and education are more likely to be related to overall childcare quality in preschool centers than to styles of caregiving or quality of infant care. In detailed analysis of data from the Cost, Quality, and Outcomes Study, economist David Blau concluded that there is little question that training in early childhood education is related to childcare quality—but the association is not very strong.[53]

DO EXPERIMENTS DEMONSTRATE EFFECTS OF TRAINING?

The studies we have been discussing have mostly relied on observations of childcare naturally occurring in the real world. Studies in which researchers have assessed caregivers' behavior in experiments before and after training yield comparable findings. In one such study, carried out in Ireland, researchers evaluated the effects of a 120-hour preschool training course.[54] Caregivers who completed the course made significant gains, becoming more responsive to the children's needs and more involved in their activities. In another study, participants in the TEACH program made significant gains in the quality of their classrooms, and their ideas became more developmentally appropriate.[55] Childcare home providers who participated in the Family Child Care Training Study improved in global childcare quality and business practices (for example, they were more likely to report their income to the IRS).[56] However, paralleling the results of correlational studies, in this study training did not affect the caregivers' emotional involvement, harshness, and sensitivity. The results of experimental and observational studies are consistent in suggesting that it is easier for caregivers to add stimulating materials, schedule interesting activities, organize the environment, and implement better business practices in their childcare environments than it is to change the nature of their emotional sensitivity through training or education. Education is a long-term project, and reaching a level of increased sensitivity requires more than a short-term course.

DIFFERENT TYPES OF TRAINING

Training is delivered in different forms, ranging from one-shot workshops to extensive course work at community colleges and universities. Short workshops are often offered at childcare conferences by resource and referral agencies or at childcare centers as on-site training for staff. Intensive institutes provide more comprehensive and systematic training, such as teaching caregivers how to implement a certain system like the Perry Preschool/High Scope program. College courses are even more general in scope than institute training and require a more substantial time commitment, and—of course—they are graded. It would not be surprising to find that the more extensive and intensive the training, the more pervasive and comprehensive the effects. Unfortunately, however, researchers have been more intent on developing and evaluating the effects of single training programs than comparing and contrasting the outcomes of different forms of training.

We have already mentioned the effects of three different training programs, and we can compare them. The program in Ireland which was most effective in modifying caregivers' sensitivity and detachment, involved the most substantial training: 90 hours of instruction and 30 hours of observation spread over a period of six months.[57] Topics covered included curriculum development, the needs of children, the value of play, and the developmental function of playgroups. The TEACH program, which led to higher ECERS and ITERS scores and more appropriate beliefs about child development on the part of the caregivers, involved less training (twelve to twenty credit hours of community college course work).[58] The Family Child Care Training program, which improved FDCRS scores and business practices but had no effect on caregivers' sensitivity, required visits to the childcare home and fifteen to twenty-five hours of class time in community-based programs, covering topics such as business practices, local regulations on health and safety, child development, environments to promote learning, methods of discipline, and professional development.[59] This comparison of programs does support the common sense notion that more intensive training leads to more substantial change in caregivers' behavior and quality of care. In another successful training program, caregivers from twenty-seven childcare centers were assigned to experienced early childhood educator "mentors" for four months.[60] The mentors observed the caregivers during the beginning weeks of the program and then gave them specific suggestions about how to improve the quality of their care. Compared with caregivers who had only regular workshop training, these mentored caregivers improved the overall quality of their classrooms and became more sensitive to infants' needs. More intensive training does seem to be consistently more effective than less intensive forms.

Is minitraining ever worthwhile, then? Yes, if it is targeted to a specific goal. In the Books Aloud program, for example, just ten hours of training in strategies for reading was effective in changing the literacy environments of participating childcare centers.[61] In another program, perhaps the briefest training ever, caregivers viewed ten minutes of virtual reality simulating how a toddler experiences care and showing how toddlers have difficulty seeing something from another person's viewpoint, understanding a new place, and understanding why objects appear and disappear.[62] Even this ultrabrief experience led caregivers to adjust their expectations about toddlers' behavior and to think about how the caregivers could change their own behavior—for example, by interacting with children at their own height and moving objects lower.

A brand-new approach to training caregivers makes use of another form of modern technology—the Internet. Childcare providers exposed to information about child development via the Internet did not learn as much as students in regular classrooms in one training program.[63] However, this poor performance resulted from technical difficulties with the Internet. The Internet will undoubtedly become more common and useful as technical difficulties are ironed out. Another use of technology for training purposes is the use of list-servs for childcare providers.[64] This, too, has potential benefits—and problems. In one study, researchers compared the postings from two childcare-related e-mail lists. One list had among its members strong children's advocates who spoke up on behalf of children, educating and challenging the listserv members; the other list permitted hostile caregivers to post messages and encouraged inappropriate venting. Obviously, technology per se is not the solution to the problem of training or supporting childcare providers. Professional trainers are still required to act as informal moderators and mentors if e-mail correspondence is to enhance caregivers' knowledge and commitment. There is no free or even cheap shortcut to satisfactory childcare training.

Researchers in Philadelphia tried to improve childcare quality "on a shoestring" by increasing coordination among organizations that deliver professional resources to childcare providers.[65] Three services were provided: neighborhood resource rooms, which offered materials and technical assistance; training sessions, which helped providers meet state yearly requirement of six hours of training; and traveling teachers, who provided individualized consultation. Although the services were used—by more than two thousand providers—and although caregivers reported gains in their professional knowledge and behavior from using the resources, no long-term effects on the caregivers' behavior, knowledge, or attitudes were observed—even for high users. It appears that it takes more than a modest intervention to produce observable change in childcare quality, or at least it takes longer for effects of low-intensity education to show up.

EFFECTS OF CAREGIVER TRAINING ON CHILDREN

We have been discussing the effects of caregivers' education and training on the quality of the care they provide. Do these effects carry through and affect the children in their care as well? Correlational studies suggest that they do. In a number of studies, children whose caregivers had higher levels of education or specialized training were more involved, cooperative, persistent, and competent in play, and they also learned more.[66] They engaged in more complex play with objects and peers.[67] They did better on standardized tests of cognitive and language development.[68] In one study of low-income African American children in community centers, for example, girls whose teachers had fourteen or more years of education did better on tests of cognitive and receptive language skills than children whose teachers had less education (scoring 114 vs. 104 on the Bayley Scale of Mental Development).[69] In the Cost, Quality, and Child Outcomes Study, children whose teachers had AAs or BAs in early childhood education or reported that they had received training at community workshops had higher scores on a test of receptive language.[70] In the NICHD study, caregiver training was related to higher caregiving quality and this higher quality in turn was related to advanced cognitive and social competence in children.[71] In childcare homes, for example, children with a college-educated caregiver scored seven points higher on the Reynell Developmental Language Scales at age three.[72] Children with college-educated caregivers in centers also displayed advanced school readiness skills and better language comprehension at age three and greater cognitive and social competence at age four.[73] In the Florida Child Care Quality Improvement Study, as the proportion of staff with CDA training increased, children spent more time engaged in learning activities and cognitively complex play and were more securely attached to their teachers.[74]

In studies comparing children's behavior before and after caregiver training programs, too, researchers have found that children make significant gains in complex social and cognitive play and become more securely attached to their caregivers.[75] In brief, the amount and kind of training and education caregivers receive has demonstrable effects on the quality of care they provide and significant consequences for children's behavior and development.

Caregivers' Experience

YEARS IN THE CHILDCARE FIELD

Another factor that is related to childcare quality is the caregiver's previous experience in the childcare field. There is a strong belief among practitioners that experience matters, and, on the face of it, this belief seems logical. The results of research, however, are not so simple.[76] Some studies suggest that more experience is a good thing. In the NICHD study, for example, across all types of care, for children from one to three years, more experienced caregivers were observed to provide more positive caregiving.[77] In other studies, experience appears to have a negative effect, and in yet other studies, experience is unrelated to childcare quality.[78] In the NICHD study, when group size, child-adult ratio, and caregivers' child-rearing beliefs were statistically controlled, caregiver experience was no longer associated with positive caregiving.[79]

Perhaps the explanation of this inconsistency is that caregiver experience is related to childcare quality in a *nonlinear* way. After elementary school teachers get their diplomas, the quality of their instruction increases for the first four or five years—until they reach their potential. The same effect may apply to childcare providers. Indeed there is some evidence that a *moderate* amount of experience is optimal. In the National Day Care Home Study, home-based caregivers whose interactions with the children were most educational had a moderate amount of experience—seven to eleven years in the field.[80] In the Cost, Quality, and Child Outcomes Study, childcare center teachers were more sensitive and offered higher-quality childcare if they had a moderate amount of experience—an average of three years.[81] A moderate amount of experience may be the best predictor of higher-quality caregiving because it falls in a period when caregivers have some on-the-job expertise but are not feeling burned out and are still open to learning. In the Family Child Care Training Study, caregivers who improved in the quality of care they offered had just over five years of experience; those whose quality of care worsened after training had, on average, ten years of experience.[82]

CAREGIVERS' AGE

A related caregiver characteristic is age. Research does not generally indicate that caregivers' age predicts caregiving quality or child outcomes.[83] However, if we push ages downward to include adolescent caregivers or upward to include grandparents and other seniors, there are differences. Adolescents can be effective childcare assistants.

In one study, both children and adults in childcare thought that teenage assistants were effective instructors and related well with the children.[84] On the other hand, adolescents should probably not be left alone to supervise a house full of young children. Child abuse in childcare is not related to the age of the caregiver—until the age drops below fourteen years.[85]

At the other end of the age spectrum, 43 percent of grandmothers help provide childcare on a regular basis, according to the National Survey of Families and Households.[86] Unrelated older adults also work in childcare centers as volunteers and aides. A national study of these older caregivers suggests that the nurturing presence of older adults brings a dimension that complements what younger, trained teachers provide in the classroom.[87] Although their behavior is not always consistent with professional standards for early childhood educators, older adults make a significant contribution that enriches all participants. Older adults see themselves as providing the affection of a grandparent and helping children develop good social skills. These older adults offer encouragement for the children and for teachers, new vocabulary—sometimes in other languages—and a sense of humor. The children seek them out for hugs and cuddles, and the older adults readily reciprocate. Whereas teachers see it as their job to teach children skills, older adults are more likely to help children with their activities. When children misbehave, teachers explain the rules; older adults simply tell the kids to stop. In an aging society like ours, with more elders available, use of grandparent figures as part of the childcare staffing mix is probably good for children and could increase the feelings of efficacy and usefulness for older adults as well. However, this is no substitute for trained younger teachers.

MALE OR FEMALE?

Does the caregiver's gender make a difference in the quality of care? Do women—who traditionally have more experience looking after young children—provide better care? Very little research is available to answer this question, primarily because the overwhelming majority of childcare providers are women. Studies that compare male and female caregivers are needed to answer the question of whether and how the caregiver's gender influences childcare quality. One study suggests that men and women teachers differ in their teaching styles and behaviors: although both male and female teachers in childcare centers were likely to encourage "feminine" behavior such as sitting quietly, reading, painting, or working on puzzles, with both boys and girls male teachers were less likely to do so, and having a male teacher had a positive effect on boys' academic achievement.[88] For various reasons, however, men have been discouraged from entering the childcare field. One reason is that child abuse is more common with male caregivers.[89] Another reason is that women in childcare may not encourage male participation. In one small study, male caregivers were interviewed about the attitudes of children and other staff toward them as male workers.[90] All the men felt that the children in their care treated them in much the same way they treated female workers, but some of the men felt uncomfortable about being the only male worker because of the attitudes of their female co-workers. The lack of men in childcare is unfortunate. It is logical and likely that children can benefit from interactions with both men and women in childcare, as they do at home.

Stability of Care and Caregivers

Another factor that is related to childcare quality is the length of time the caregiver has been in a particular childcare setting with a particular child. Child development experts have decried the rapid turnover of personnel in childcare centers, the alacrity with which home care providers go out of business, and the tendency of babysitters to move on. Stable providers are rare. Turnover rates are among highest of any profession, hovering around 30 percent per year.[91] By comparison, only 7 percent of public school teachers leave their jobs each year.

Experts have been less vocal about the tendency of families themselves to change children's care arrangements, but this kind of instability also occurs with great frequency. Studies that have followed children over time have found that approximately half of them enter a new care arrangement within one year, and one-third within six months.[92] Children are particularly likely to change care arrangements if care is provided by an unrelated, unlicensed sitter who is young, inexperienced, and responsible for only one or two children.[93] Children also experience instability when they are enrolled in more than one arrangement at the same time. In the NICHD study, one-third of the infants in childcare were in at least three different nonparental arrangements.[94]

Stability is a concern because research suggests that care is better if caregivers stay in their jobs longer. In the National Staffing Study, centers with the lowest rates of staff turnover had the highest overall quality.[95] Caregivers who stay in the childcare setting longer have more opportunity to get to know children, read their signals more accurately, and respond appropriately. As they spend more time in a childcare setting, caregivers become more attentive and engaged with the children; caregivers also become more affectionate and responsive and form closer relationships with the children (and possibly the children's mothers).[96]

Instability also affects children's development. In the National Staffing Study, children in centers with the highest rates of staff turnover spent the most time wandering aimlessly and did the worst on intelligence tests.[97] In the NICHD study, children who were in multiple childcare arrangements had more behavior problems at age two than children who did not have multiple arrangements.[98] And in a number of other studies, children who experienced many changes in their childcare arrangements (either because of caregiver turnover or because the parents changed the care arrangement) were less secure in their attachments with their mothers, less competent in their play with adults and peers, and more likely to have behavior problems and cognitive deficits.[99] In contrast, when children spend more time in a childcare setting, they form closer relationships with their caregivers.[100] In one study, for example, 91 percent of the infants who had been with their teacher for more than one year were securely attached to her, compared with 67 percent who had spent nine to twelve months with the caregiver and 50 percent who had spent five to eight months.[101] In another study, toddlers responded more positively to caregivers who had been with them at the center for at least three months; they went to these caregivers when they were distressed, and the caregivers were able to quiet them.[102] But apparently just spending time together is not what cemented the relationship between children and caregivers; relationships are strengthened because children and caregivers are interactively involved when they are together.[103]

So how important is it to keep the child in one childcare arrangement? How important is it to put the child in a facility where caregivers stay for years? Being with the same caregiver clearly has advantages for the child, and in the best of all worlds, children would be placed with caregivers who got to know them well because both caregiver and child stayed in the same setting for a long time. But staying with a poor caregiver—who is insensitive, harsh, or neglectful—is undoubtedly worse for children than shifting to a good one. Some changes are necessary, and stability does not trump other aspects of childcare quality. Being exposed to a *small* variety of caregivers, moreover, can provide enrichment, temper the effects of extreme caregiver styles, and teach the child to adapt to different people. Stability of caregivers within a setting is a different issue. Quality of care may be better when caregivers stay in the setting longer, not only because caregivers get to know the children better, but because the reason caregivers stay is that they have good working conditions, adequate wages, and high staff morale. Care providers who "last" are more satisfied with their jobs, work longer hours, and have more job experience with children.[104] Stability, thus, reflects better quality care.

Commitment to Child and Job

A final factor that may affect childcare quality is the caregiver's commitment. Caregivers who are committed to the children are emotionally closer to them, and the children are more likely to have secure attachments with these caregivers.[105] Who are these committed caregivers? We might expect that caregivers who are biologically related would be more committed to the children in their care. In fact, this seems not to be the case. In one study, children cared for by relatives had less secure relationships with them than children cared for by non-relatives did with their caregivers.[106]

Another kind of commitment is the caregiver's commitment to the work. When caregivers are committed to taking care of children and are doing so from a sense that the work is important and not from a sense that it is the only thing they could find to do, they are more sensitive and responsive toward the children. Home caregivers who are more committed to the job seek out opportunities to learn about children's development and childcare, participate in childcare training, think ahead about what the children are going to do and plan experiences for them, and seek out the company of others who are providing care.[107] They also follow standard business practices and, as a result, charge higher rates.

What, then, makes a caregiver committed to the job? One thing is the money. In 1996, the average hourly wage of childcare workers in the United States was $6.12; for family care providers, it was $3.37.[108] This wage is far lower than that earned by kindergarten teachers ($19.16) and even lower than hourly wages of bus drivers ($11.56) and parking lot attendants ($6.38). Wages were the primary determinant of staff turnover in the National Staffing Study.[109] Teachers who were paid $4.00 per hour or less left at twice the rate of those who earned more than $6.00 per hour. The teachers who left did so to take better-paying jobs, and they were replaced with caregivers who were new to the field, untrained, and poorly educated. Research reveals strong relations between staff wages and quality in both childcare centers and home arrangements. In the Cost, Quality, and Outcomes Study, when teachers received higher wages, childcare quality was higher and the teachers were more responsive—at least if they lacked formal education.[110] Higher-paid center caregivers in a study conducted in Boston, Atlanta, and Virginia also provided higher-quality care.[111] In fact, teachers' wages were the most significant predictor of high-quality classroom processes in that study. The most common suggestion for how to improve childcare quality, made by 90 percent of the teachers interviewed in the National Staffing Study, was to pay caregivers better salaries.[112]

An effort to improve childcare quality for military families is instructive.[113] The U.S. armed services oversee a childcare system that serves more than two hundred thousand children every day at more than three hundred locations worldwide. In 1989, the Military Child Care Act was enacted by Congress in response to reports that detailed extremely poor childcare conditions. This act made pay for childcare workers comparable to that for other jobs on military bases that required similar levels of training, education, and responsibility. It also made advancement and salary increases contingent on caregivers' completing specific training programs, and it added at least one training and curriculum specialist to the staff of every center. As a result, staff turnover dropped from 48 percent to 24 percent.

A second reason that caregivers are committed to the job of providing childcare is their professionalism. Professionalism is particularly an issue for home care providers; most center caregivers have a sense of professionalism—in fact that's why they are called "teachers." Among home childcare providers, however, those caregivers with more professional attitudes have been observed to provide higher-quality care. In the Family Child Care and Relative Care Study, "intentional" providers—who were more committed to caring for children—offered higher-quality, warmer, and more attentive care.[114] Likewise, in the National Day Care Home Study and in a study in Canada, caregivers who participated in family childcare networks—an indication of their professionalism—provided higher-quality care.[115] Childcare home providers in the National Day Care Home Study who considered themselves professionals were more likely to read books on childcare or child development, attend meetings, and take classes in child development; they were observed to talk, help, teach, and play more with the children and to provide better physical environments with more music, dancing, books, and nutritious meals. Caregivers who provided care only because no better job was available or because they reached an informal agreement with friends, neighbors, or relatives were less interactive and stimulating and spent more time on housework.[116] In the NICHD study, quality of home childcare was related to whether the home was licensed—which could be considered another reflection of the caregiver's professional attitude.[117]

This link between licensing and quality has been observed in other studies as well. In the three-state Family and Relative Care Study and in the California Licensing Study, for example, licensed caregivers were observed to provide higher-quality care and to be more sensitive to the needs of the children in their care.[118] Licensed programs in Canada also received higher childcare quality scores than nonlicensed childcare homes.[119]

In sum, caregivers play a multifaceted role in childcare: they are teachers, managers, and nurturers. How well they perform their role depends to some extent on their background: education and training, experience, stability, and commitment. But the explanation of childcare effects does not stop there. The final component in the equation is the family. In the next chapter, we discuss the family's contribution.

8

Childcare providers are neither the first nor the most important of the child's caregivers. Those distinctions go to parents. Even if children spend 40 hours a week in childcare, this leaves 128 hours for them to be at home with their parents—and that time counts. The observations and interviews researchers have used to study parents and children suggest clearly that, even though the parents of children in childcare are not intimately involved in their children's experiences at all times, they do continue to have an influence on their children's development—just as much as if the children were at home. This influence was documented in the NICHD study.[1] Children who spent a lot of time in childcare (thirty or more hours a week) were influenced by their families just as much as children who were in care for less than ten hours a week. Children had better cognitive and language development if their parents were more affluent and well educated and if their mothers were more sensitive and warm—regardless of whether the children were in childcare for many hours. In other words, family influence is not "lost" when children are in care.

Mothers Versus Caregivers

Childcare providers teach and discipline, respond with food and hugs, and guide children's behavior just as mothers do. But a childcare provider is not the same as a mother. Caregivers are not as invested in the children as their parents are, and caregivers do not have the same power to make important decisions. They usually have more training and often more experience taking care of children than parents do; and caregivers are often responsible for a group of children of the same age, not just one child. Given these differences, just how different is the behavior of mothers and childcare providers?

A number of researchers have asked this question. In one study, mothers of children attending childcare centers and teachers in these centers were interviewed and observed interacting with the child on specific tasks.[2] When the adults were asked about their goals and expectations for young children, mothers and teachers agreed on many things: they both valued independence and social skills over academic abilities, for example. But teachers valued children's independence, emotional maturity, and expressiveness even more than mothers did, and mothers thought that politeness, social graces, and school skills were more important than teachers did. These values went along with the disciplinary and management strategies each group favored. Teachers appealed to rational rules and explanations; they were more flexible and permissive than mothers. Their requests were indirect and moderated. ("Please put this block where it belongs." "I wonder how these blocks are alike. I wish you would tell me." "Can you tell my why you put that one there?") Mothers were more direct, demanding, and task-oriented; they made explicit corrections when the child made a mistake and appealed to their own authority rather than abstract rules. ("Put that block there." "Tell me why you put that block there." "No, put the other block there." "Because I'm your mother, that's why.")

Other researchers have observed similar differences in the management styles of mothers and teachers.[3] Researchers have also observed differences in mothers' and teachers' conversational styles. Mothers have more extended and far-ranging conversations with their children—about dos and don'ts and past and future events as well as what's happening at the moment. Children are more equal participants in conversations at home; they ask more questions and give more answers. The different conversational styles of mothers and teachers are illustrated in the excerpts below, taken from transcripts made during observations of one four-year-old, Ann, playing at home and in preschool.[4]

At home:

Ann: Come look at their little bit of hair.

Mother: Love, I'm just looking for Ben's shorts. I don't know what he has done with them.

Ann: Mum, look at his . . . Mum look at his little sch . . . look at his little h . . . Mummy, he's got a little bit hair, so come and have a look.

Mother: Blue hair [*laughs*].

Ann: What's wrong with blue hair?

Mother: Well, I don't know, it can be fair hair, or brown hair, or red hair.

Ann: Don't have red hair [*indignant*].

Mother: Some people do. Know that boy in the park yesterday?

Ann: Yeah.

Mother: With a kite.

Ann: Yeah, Mummy.

Mother: He had what you call red hair, auburn. You know Daddy?

Ann: Mm.

Mother: He used to have red hair before it went grey.

At preschool:

Teacher: What are you going to call your babies?

Teacher: Hm?

Teacher: What are you going to call your twins?

Teacher: Ann?

Ann: Emily and Katy.

Teacher: Emily . . . ?

Ann: And Katy.

Teacher: Katy! Supposing they're boys? You can't call twins that if they're boys, can you? [*Laughs.*]

Although the roles of home childcare providers and mothers have more similarities than those of center teachers and mothers, these caregivers also differ from mothers in their interactions with children. Compared with mothers, childcare home providers are cooler and more emotionally aloof, less playful and stimulating. They don't kiss or caress the children as often and are less tuned in to their individual interests.[5] Both caregivers and parents view physical contact between children and their childcare providers as less appropriate than contact between children and their parents.[6]

Although these generalizations about different patterns of behavior for mothers, teachers, and home childcare providers are based on averages—which hide the enormous diversity found within each category of caregiver—they do suggest that in the child's life different kinds of caregivers are likely to exhibit different styles of behavior. Mothers are likely to be loving, involved, and important; they give the child security, confidence, trust, and affection; they exhibit strong emotions of love, joy, pain, and anger; they give basic socialization training (such as instruction about when and where to go to the toilet) and teach social rules and graces, moral norms and lessons, and conversational skills. Home childcare providers offer discipline and socialization without the emotional investment the parents feel and provide the child with some relief from the intensity of family relationships. Teachers in childcare centers and preschools foster the children's independence, self-sufficiency, and self-direction, providing formal education, intellectual knowledge, and opportunities for positive interaction with other children to increase the child's social competence. Children in childcare can benefit from exposure to different styles of management. As long as the family provides a secure foundation, exposure to other caregivers is an enriching part of these children's early experience.

The Care Parents Select

Another important role of the family is that parents select the childcare arrangement—and they do not do so randomly. Researchers have found a number of ways in which parents are selective about childcare. First, they are choosy about the age at which they enroll the child in care: in several studies, children were enrolled in care earlier if their mothers were more career oriented and better educated, had higher incomes and higher professional status, and expressed more

negative feelings toward motherhood.[7] Second, parents are also selective about the type of care they use: center care is more likely to be
chosen by parents who value education and who have higher levels of
education themselves, who have fewer children, and who believe that
children benefit from being in childcare.[8] Third, parents choose particular caregivers—who are often from their own ethnic group and
who share their child-rearing values and attitudes toward discipline.[9]
Fourth, parents are selective about childcare quality. Mothers in
high-income families and those who work fewer hours are particularly likely to choose a childcare arrangement based on quality.[10] In a
number of studies, including the Cost, Quality, and Outcomes and
NICHD studies, children from more economically advantaged families, with parents who were more sensitive and responsive, were more
likely to be enrolled in high-quality care.[11] Finally, parents select care
with their own child's characteristics in mind. They are more likely to
select center care for preschoolers than for infants, for example.[12] If
their child has special needs, parents also may make choices according to those needs. In one study of infant care, researchers found that
families with difficult children were more likely to choose family care
than center care; they may have recognized that their irritable infants
would adjust to childcare more easily with the personal attention of
caregivers who would not be distracted by the demands of many
children and institutional rules.[13]

Associations between childcare qualities and family characteristics
have not been observed in all studies. Children from more advantaged
families do not always enter care earlier; links with quality of care are
not always found; and, most important, relations with family income
are not necessarily linear.[14] Often it is middle-income families who
receive the poorest-quality care, according to results from the Cost,
Quality, and Outcomes, the NICHD, and the National Child Care
Staffing studies—because parents with high incomes can afford high-
quality care and parents with very low incomes are eligible for subsidized care.[15] Moreover, even when linear associations between childcare
and family characteristics are found, they often are modest in size.[16]

Some researchers, therefore, question just how much choice parents actually have over the type and quality of childcare they select.[17]

Multiple market forces may explain why family selection effects are modest. One market force is parents' ignorance about childcare. Many parents are first-time users of childcare, with little experience and an urgent need for care. They may assume that they have few choices and restrict their search. Moreover, the purchasers of care—the parents—are not the actual recipients of care—the children—and thus parents may not be in the best position to judge the quality of care. Young children are not good informants, and parents are not particularly astute or conscientious observers of quality. In a study of the parents in the Cost, Quality, and Child Outcomes Study, researchers Debby Cryer and Margaret Burchinal found that parents were not well informed about the care their children received.[18] They consistently rated the quality of their children's classes higher than trained observers did. Another market force is the availability of childcare. Availability of care is limited in any given community, for any given family—and so, therefore, are parents' choices. Affordability is another market issue. Less-well-to-do parents cannot really select a form of childcare; instead, they buy what they can afford. Finally, convenience plays a part in the childcare decision: parents with money can pay for high-quality care, but they may not have the time to drive twenty miles to the best center they have heard about. Choosing childcare is not like buying a car or new dishes; you can't just order up what you want and have it delivered.

The issue of links between family selection and childcare quality is a relatively new research topic and one that will be worth pursuing in the future, as market forces shift and childcare availability waxes or wanes. For now, however, there is sufficient evidence suggesting that selection and quality are at least somewhat associated. Therefore, it is important for researchers to consider family factors when they look for the effects of childcare on children's behavior and development.

Controlling for Family Selection of Care

Most contemporary investigators assess background characteristics of the child and family to provide a context for examining childcare effects. Some researchers then deal with these background factors simply by statistically controlling them in their analyses of childcare effects. These researchers identify family characteristics that are significantly related to both childcare experiences and child outcomes and then enter these family characteristics into analyses, along with childcare qualities predicting child outcomes. For example, in the Cost, Quality, and Outcomes and NICHD studies, researchers routinely included mothers' education and parenting quality in their analyses. Of course, it is impossible to control for *all* family effects, but this strategy at least contains the overlap between family and childcare effects by imposing statistical controls. It does not eliminate bias because of family selection entirely, but it does reduce that bias.

When researchers impose these controls, this approach typically reduces the strength of the associations between childcare and child outcomes. In the Cost, Quality, and Outcomes Study, quality of care was related to preschool children's cognitive and socioemotional development, even with parents' income, ethnicity, and education controlled; and in the NICHD study, analyses controlling for child gender, family income, maternal intelligence, and quality of parenting still revealed significant associations between the quality of care and children's cognitive and language outcomes.[19] The reduction in the strength of the associations was substantial, however; correlations were reduced to half.[20] Controlling for maternal insensitivity also reduced the size of the effect of long hours in care on children's externalizing behavior.[21] We do not yet know all the reasons for the links between high-quality childcare and cognitive abilities or between extensive time in care and behavior problems—but parental selection is undoubtedly part of the equation. Parents with higher levels of intelligence may search more extensively to find childcare that will promote their children's cognitive development. Less-sensitive mothers—whose children might be more aggressive regardless of being in childcare—are likely to be heavier users of childcare, and parents with difficult children may choose to leave them in childcare for longer hours because these parents don't look forward to the difficulties that erupt when the child comes home.

Comparing and Combining Family and Childcare

WHO HAS MORE INFLUENCE: PARENTS OR CAREGIVERS?

Rather than simply controlling for family factors, some researchers have included both family and childcare variables in their analyses and compared the relative influence of the two. A number of these investigators have found that family factors predict children's development more strongly than childcare factors. In their studies, family variables such as mothers' education, sensitivity, and stimulation and the quality of the home environment have been found to predict children's cognitive, language, and social development more strongly than whether the child attended childcare, the type of childcare attended, or the quality of the childcare program.[22] In the NICHD study, children's security of attachment to their mothers, self-control, compliance and problem behavior, interactions with peers, and cognitive and social competence were related to maternal sensitivity more strongly and consistently than they were related to childcare quality or the amount of time the child was in childcare.[23] There have been studies in which researchers have found that family variables and childcare variables were equally predictive of children's development.[24] But the problem with these studies is that the researchers did not have comparable measures of childcare and family factors, so they were comparing apples and oranges. Perhaps it is not important to establish that the family wields more influence than childcare; it's not a contest. What is important is that research shows that children's development is related to their experiences *both* at home and in childcare.

EFFECTS OF FAMILY AND CHILDCARE ADD TOGETHER

Rather than controlling or comparing family and childcare predictors, other researchers have taken the strategy of investigating the effects of home and childcare environments on children's development by combining the two sets of predictors in their analyses. These investigators have generally found that predictability is stronger when both sets of variables are included. Optimal development is supported when children receive high-quality care, stimulation, and encouragement in *both* home and childcare settings—or, conversely, children's well-being is most likely to be impaired when children are in poor-quality childcare as well as unstimulating home environments.[25] An example of how children are affected by their experiences at home and in childcare is provided by the NICHD study. As we just mentioned, in that study childcare did not have a direct effect on the security of children's attachment relationships with their mothers. However, when children were in poor-quality care or spent many hours in care each week and also had an insensitive mother at home, this situation led to higher rates of insecure attachment.[26] This finding was replicated in another study: the type, stability, and quality of care and the child's age of entry into care were not related to children's attachment security; but children with less-sensitive mothers using extensive out-of-home care were the least secure six months after care started.[27] Thus, research demonstrates that the effects of parental and nonparental care can be additive.

DOES CHILDCARE COMPENSATE FOR FAMILY DISADVANTAGE?

Another way that family and childcare factors might work together is that childcare could compensate for disadvantages at home. Some children are born into families with problems—money problems, poor health, mental illness in the family, lack of education or parenting skills. When parents are stressed and family resources are limited, it is more difficult to provide good parental care, and children may suffer. This deficit can accrue over the long run, as a result of chronic conditions such as poverty or single parenthood; it can be the result of more acute conditions, such as a parent's bad day at work. In one study, for example, researchers found that mothers responded to job stress by withdrawing from their children—they talked less and expressed less affection—on days when they experienced greater workloads or more interpersonal stress at work.[28] On days like these, it may benefit the child to be in a childcare arrangement for part of the day.

There is indeed some evidence that childcare can compensate for problems at home. In the clearest example, researchers studying three thousand two- and three-year-old children in Canada found that childcare protected youngsters in high-risk families—families in which parents had little education, low socioeconomic status, and

poor psychological functioning—from developing externalizing behavior problems. If children in these high-risk families spent their
days at home with their mothers, 14 percent of them had high levels
of physical aggression; but if they spent their days in childcare, only
3 percent were aggressive. The likelihood of high aggression for the
high-risk children in childcare was about the same as that of children
from low-risk families, who had the same levels of aggression whether
they were in childcare or not.[29] The NICHD study also illustrates
what can happen to children from troubled homes when they are in
childcare.[30] On the down side, children living in poverty were below
norms in language and school readiness—whether or not they attended childcare; childcare did not alter their developmental trajectories. On the up side, however, childcare did offer some protection
against maternal problems. When children were not attending childcare, they did more poorly if their mothers were depressed, unmarried, or very strict; if the children were in full-time childcare, their
development was unaffected by these maternal problems.[31] The most
likely interpretation of this finding is that the negative effect of living in a troubled household is somewhat alleviated by being in childcare.[32] Childcare is not a simple fix for family failure, but it does offer
some relief.

But maybe the compensatory effect of childcare would be stronger
if the children were in high-quality childcare. Run-of-the-mill childcare may not provide enough support to alleviate children's disadvantages, but what about model programs? This idea is the primary
rationale for early intervention programs that provide high-quality
care for children from poor families. These programs, we have seen,
enhance children's behavior and development, perhaps serving as a
buffer against negative family circumstances. In research on community childcare, as well, Albert Hausfather and his colleagues found
that when children were in high-quality centers, stress in their families was not related to children's angry, defiant behavior—as it was
for children in less-adequate childcare.[33]

Researchers have studied this issue of the importance of high-
quality childcare for children from low-quality home environments
by looking for statistical interactions between childcare quality and

family circumstances. If children with more-limited opportunities at home gain more from being in high-quality care than children from more affluent homes, the interaction between childcare quality and family circumstances would be significant. When interactions of family risk factors and childcare quality were examined in the NICHD and CQO studies, the interactions between family factors and quality of care were not significant; childcare quality was related to children's cognitive and social development equally across all levels of maternal education, ethnicity, income, and home environment.[34] However, it is notoriously difficult to find significant interactions in field settings, and in a number of other studies researchers have obtained significant interactions indicating that childcare quality is a stronger predictor of cognitive and language development for children from poor families than for those from more affluent ones.[35]

In the most thorough examination of the issue, Margaret Burchinal and her colleagues gathered data on 1,300 children from the CQO study and two other studies, the North Carolina Head Start Partnership Study and the Public Preschool Evaluation Project.[36] They asked whether poverty, minority ethnic background, and parental beliefs moderated the association between childcare quality and cognitive and social outcomes. Quality of care was related to children's pre-reading abilities, premath skills, and behavior problems for children from all backgrounds equally. Language development was the only outcome for which childcare quality interacted with a risk variable, ethnicity. In this case, quality of care was more important for language development for children of color (primarily African American) than for white, non-Hispanic children. Children of color in this study received language scores of 70 if they were in poor-quality care, 84 if they were in medium-quality care, and 89 if they were in high-quality care, whereas white children received scores of 91, 94, and 97 respectively. Thus, it appears that good-quality care may serve as a protective factor for children from disadvantaged backgrounds, but its effects are not inevitable, nor do they wipe out family disadvantage.

DO CHILDREN FROM ADVANTAGED FAMILIES SUFFER FROM POOR-QUALITY CHILDCARE?

We have discussed what happens when children from poor backgrounds attend high-quality care. What about children from privileged backgrounds? Do children who are born into families with all the advantages—financial, social, psychological—suffer if they are enrolled in poor-quality care? One might expect that children from excellent home environments could be harmed if they were in mediocre childcare and therefore "lost" the resources they would have had if they had been at home. This issue is the other side of the interaction analyses we have just discussed.

In the NICHD study, the lost-resources hypothesis was tested by investigating associations with quality of care for children from different family backgrounds.[37] There was no support for the lost-resources hypothesis, no evidence of significant interactions between childcare (type, quantity, or quality) and parenting quality for children from two to four years of age. Associations between quality of care and child outcomes were equivalent for children receiving better- or worse-quality parenting. When children were divided into groups according to family income, however, stronger associations between quality of care and language abilities were observed for children from the highest income group at age fifteen months. Perhaps if there are effects of lost resources, they occur early on in development rather than after children have absorbed the advantages of their stimulating homes. These issues of whether quality of childcare matters more for children from richer or poorer family backgrounds require further analysis now that researchers collect information about both childcare and family factors in most childcare studies.

Childcare Affects Parents

One final aspect of the family's role is how the family is influenced by childcare. It is possible that parents are affected by childcare, and then they influence their children—so that what appear to be childcare effects are actually indirect effects through the parents.[38] There are a number of ways this indirect influence could happen. For one thing, mothers could observe how caregivers in childcare behave and model their own behavior after these trained professionals, becoming more patient or permissive. For another thing, mothers could act more sensitively with their children because childcare offers parents relief from the constant stress of parenting. A third way that parents could be influenced by childcare is that a mother could act less sensitively because she lacks experience with her child, who is spending much of his or her time in childcare. Fourth, children in higher-quality care could develop skills that would elicit better parenting, which in turn would feed back to promote the child's further development. Finally, children in lower-quality care could develop more obnoxious behaviors in care and be viewed as more difficult by their parents, who would then interact with their children less sensitively. Researchers are just beginning to study whether and how childcare experiences influence parenting beliefs and practices.

To study the influence of childcare on parenting, Lynne Vernon-Feagans and her associates tracked children from the time they entered childcare in their first year until they were four years of age.[39] Some children were in high-quality care, others in poor-quality care. When the children were four years old, their mothers were observed reading them picture books that contained two questions on each page. When children gave the wrong answers to the questions, mothers whose children were in low-quality childcare prodded more—repeating the question and saying things like, "Come on, you know this!" Mothers whose children were in high-quality care, in contrast, restructured the question: they asked the question in another way or made it simpler. This study suggests that mothers absorb ideas and emulate childcare staff, whose behavior is less directive and authoritarian. In another study, Margaret Burchinal and Lauren Nelson created an index of parenting quality based on observations of mothers interacting with their children at home and during videotaped play sessions. Correlations across time suggested that children with better parenting in the first year were in childcare of higher quality in the second year; children with better-quality childcare in the second year received better parenting in the third year. Thus, this study suggests that there are both direct and indirect effects of childcare and that these effects form a complex feedback loop over time.

Researchers have not done as much to document the effects of good childcare on family functioning as they have to demonstrate the effects of good childcare on child functioning, but these efforts are beginning. Research now confirms that when children are in good-quality care, their parents are happier and more satisfied.[40] In an e-mail to one of the NICHD study researchers, one satisfied mother describes her experience visiting her son in his childcare center, unannounced.[41]

> today i paid a surprise visit to the infants room at st. james. i had a no-show appointment not too far away and popped over to visit henry. i walked in and spied him in the lap of another woman! shannon was holding him on her lap and talking with him while chrissy, another "teacher" was bending over kissing him and they were all laughing and giggling together. henry was beaming from ear to ear and cooing like a little dove while his little dimples lit up the room. it did my heart good. sometimes, paranoid mom that i am, i think that they must, when they know I'm coming, stage little scenes like this to keep me coming back as a paying customer. but today, i know for sure this is a place i feel good about leaving my baby. there's a lot of love at st. james and it begins to feel like an extension of family. i've learned so much about mom-stuff by watching the staff interact with the kids. and i've been given the opportunity to appreciate my child through the eyes of a group of women who care about him very much. i feel so lucky. this kind of place is priceless. i think i would choose to work just so that my kids could go here! and THAT gives me a feeling of great joy.

Unfortunately, most mothers using childcare do not share this warm glow. According to one survey, most working parents with preschool children in this country believe they would do a better job looking after their youngsters than any nonparental caregiver.[42] Only 40 percent of the parents surveyed by Public Agenda agreed that a "top-notch" center could provide a child with care as good as a stay-at-home parent. Most parents expressed strong concern that children could suffer abuse in childcare and said that childcare should be the option of last resort. On the other hand, the Cost, Quality and Child

Outcomes Study found that parents with children in childcare tended to rate the quality of their selected childcare facility highly, much more highly than the more objective trained professionals did, perhaps out of the parents' defensive need to believe that they had made the right decision.

The tensions expressed by these parents—who are using childcare and worrying about it—suggest that researchers need to communicate better about the positive effects of care on children's development and family well-being. Parents need to feel assured that they are doing well by their children, that childcare can be a positive experience, and that both they and their children can benefit from it. Parents also need to feel empowered to evaluate childcare facilities accurately with an eye to those factors that make a difference in the quality of their children's experience (e.g., staff ratios, curriculum, hygiene, staff training, adequate space, and good deployment of play materials). And, finally, parents should appreciate that the quality of a child's home life is still likely to be the most important factor in his or her development, even for children who spend many hours in childcare each week.

PART THREE

LOOKING TO THE FUTURE

In my eight years of trying out different options for the working mom, I have learned above all else that nothing is perfect, mostly because life keeps changing, and that to keep your sanity you have to be adaptable. My husband has a more time-demanding, higher-paying job than mine, so I have always been the parent who makes the bigger career sacrifices and have taken on the de facto role of CEO of our family's childcare decisions.

I had my first child, Alex, as I was starting my first real job. I worked full time and left my son at a friend's house with a sitter and my friend's two children. It was a nice, intimate setting for a baby. The biggest stress at the start was, and still is, trying to fit it all in. I was trying to get my-self and the baby packed up and ready for work and childcare, commute thirty minutes to and from work, work a ten-hour day and still be back by 6 P.M. to relieve the exhausted sitter.

I got pregnant with my second child, Cameron, before Alex was a year old. Six months later my husband got a job in another state, so we packed up and moved four hours away from family and friends—and of course the babysitter. The adjustment was difficult, but I rolled with the punches and landed on my feet, with a great new job and a chance to work just four days a week. With the new jobs we were now able to af-ford to have a sitter come to our house, a big luxury when I compared it to those snowy winter days of old, when I bundled my little one up at 7 A.M. to schlep him over to my friend's house! Our sitter, Maureen, was a woman in her twenties who turned out to be a wonderful match for our family, a real once-in-a-lifetime find. She watched the boys, took them to and from school, organized play dates, helped with laundry, started dinner some nights, and best of all loved my children as if they were her own. She was like a sister to me. Life was running so smoothly that we decided to have a third child. Trevor was born when Cameron was four and Alex was five and a half years old. Maureen stayed with me through my maternity leave, and I went back to work when Trev was just eight weeks old. Life was good.

Then it was all turned upside down again. My husband decided he had to make another job change—this time it was eight hours away to a small town in eastern North Carolina. Besides moving away from friends again, I lost two important things in my life with that move: my irreplaceable sitter and my career. Maureen, who had been with us for four years, could not make that sacrifice to move with us—it was too far away and too small a town. As far as my career, there were jobs I could take but not exactly in the same field and not at the level I had been. To make the transition easier, I took a year off. Ironically, it was probably the hardest thing I have ever done! My career has always been as big a part of my identity as being a wife and a mother, and without a job I felt less than whole. It was the first time in my adult life that I didn't get a paycheck. It was a year of revelations for me—about myself, about motherhood, about childcare. Although I think I am a wonderful mother, I am not a very good full-time mom. I need to feel appreciated and successful, and I did not get enough of that from mothering. I also discovered that raising kids essentially by yourself is really, really hard work! My husband was working long hours as always, but now all of a sudden I had to take care of the kids and the household on my own, without our beloved Maureen to help out. In retrospect I began to wonder if we would have had that third child if we had stopped to consider that Maureen might not always be there to help.

I decided that in order to be a better mother and wife, I needed to make some new adjustments yet again. So I went back to work part time, just three half days a week, which is where we are now. We have a sitter who watches Trevor a few hours a week when he is not in preschool. It was hard to find someone who could live up to Maureen, but I found a very acceptable alternative. I compromised on the job I took as well. I am no longer on the same career path, but I know that can hap-

pen later in my life. With a part-time job I can do better quality and quantity mothering than in either previous situation. I am with the boys after school and am available two days a week during school hours, so I can share their school experience. I volunteer in the classroom and am on the school's mothers' committee. I have two mornings a week when I can do things for me, like getting a haircut or working out a little. I still make far less money, and I struggle with trying to feel like a career woman during work hours and a stay-at-home mom the other times. But I get enough of the pieces I need to feel whole again. Our situation will undoubtedly change again as the boys become teenagers; I again will struggle with what to do but will hopefully continue to try different options until I find what works best for me and our family.

—Maria, age 37

"A journey of a thousand miles begins with a single step"—but who knew that the voyage would not be at all linear, destination oriented, or systematic—or anything I thought characterized me?

I began this journey a budding professional—I'd worked hard for my advanced professional degree, and I happily spent long hours in a research position I had felt lucky to get. I thought that I was launching an academic career—a life devoted to teaching and scholarship. Adding a child to the tableau would alter little, I thought—nannies, day care, things would take care of themselves. I really should have spent more time babysitting in my youth.

My daughter was born ten weeks before Christmas. I had expected to feel happy and devoted but found that I had vastly underestimated the intensity of those emotions. I was utterly besotted. When Christmas arrived, I suddenly understood the enthralling magic of that story. My decision to stay home was thus less a reasoned response to the circumstances than a natural manifestation of my desires. I wanted to be with my child.

It's been almost ten and a half years now and I still feel an overpowering wish to be my daughter's "primary caregiver," in the parlance of the childcare professionals. It hasn't been at all easy—it has required every kind of sacrifice and the most profound cognitive restructuring imaginable. I have learned to spend apparently directionless hours do-

ing nothing in particular, with nothing to show for it at the end of the day—week—month—year. I have learned to tolerate feeling unproductive and out of step with my peers. I even cook (if you can call it that). I wouldn't have done it, nor would I keep doing it, if the rewards did not far exceed the losses. I'm not sure I can categorize or list what makes our time together so precious. On the most fundamental level, I am glad that I do not have to suppress or sublimate my innate desire to care for my child because of other demands. I am also glad that I am not forced to compress her childhood into my spare time. But what really sustains me is all the fun—the sheer joy of sharing everything I love with her. So we read, and read, and read, and sing, and swim, and tell riddles, and do puzzles, and play cards. And then there are the delights to which she has introduced me—she fell in love with ballet, and suddenly I was no longer falling asleep during The Nutcracker; *she discovered* Calvin and Hobbes, *and now I laugh out loud at the comics; she learned to play recorder and flute, and now I get to listen to her lyrical, lovely improvisations. I even surf (if you can call it that).*

Occasionally I will go to a conference or interview for a job in my field, experiencing a pulse of enthusiasm for my profession. But when I perform the thought experiment of imagining what my days would be like should I return to work—how my opposing responsibilities would inevitably compete for my time and attention—I always gently set aside the old ambitions so that I can experience the offer-good-today-only moment of mothering my child.

So the journey turned out to be more of a random stroll, but over the loveliest terrain imaginable. "And that has made all the difference."

—Ellen, age 44

9

MAKING BETTER
CHILDCARE CHOICES

Whether a mother *wants* to work or *has* to work, central to her satisfaction and success is the kind of arrangement she has made for the care of her children while she is away. If a mother cannot be assured that her children are safe in her absence, she can neither concentrate on her work nor feel she is doing right by her family. Finding the right childcare fit for her child and her family is perhaps one of the most challenging yet important tasks she will ever face as a mother.

But where to begin? It is difficult to know what care arrangement to make, in part because of the wide variety of types that are available. Childcare may occur in the child's home or someone else's, in a home setting or a center, with an unpaid relative or a paid care provider, with a friendly neighbor or a professional nanny. The child may be in a setting with one other child or many; of about the same age or mixed ages; in a facility run by a church, a community organization, the government, or the school district; in a program that stresses academic success or school readiness, social skills, or play. Research on different types of childcare settings has failed to yield a single answer or recommendation about the best type of care. How can parents know what type of arrangement is best for their own child and family?

Part of the difficulty in being able to declare a certain type of childcare "the best" is that within each type of care there is an enormous range in the quality of care offered. Childcare quality ranges from merely custodial, with minimal or subadequate standards of care and safety, to perfectly wonderful, with frequent and fond attention from adult caregivers, a safe and stimulating physical environment, and the opportunity to play with other children in a program of enriching educational experiences. How can parents assess the quality of the childcare arrangement? How can they be sure that the quality of the care they find is adequate?

A third challenge in choosing a childcare arrangement is that, for a variety of reasons, the choices are in reality often limited for any given family. Although a variety of types of care are generally available nationwide, not all are available in every community or neighborhood, and not all that is available to a family will fit into their budget, match their schedule, and be open to their child. Unfortunately, as we have described, in general the overall quality of childcare in the United States is minimally adequate at best. Few parents can find "model" childcare programs for their children—or afford them. The most affluent families can afford excellent care and are more likely to find it. The poorest families are eligible for the few slots in government-subsidized centers. But all the families in between—the vast majority of families—can neither afford nor find care of such high quality.[1] They must find an acceptable childcare facility, get their child into it, monitor it, pay for it, all the while worrying whether their children will be happy and safe there. Childcare is as necessary for most families as an automobile and a microwave oven, but infinitely harder to find and more expensive to buy. And there is no *Consumer Reports* rating to refer to in assessing the quality of that care.

In this chapter we discuss the various decisions parents face in selecting the right childcare for their children, and we offer practical advice on how to tackle the search.

Full-time or Part-time Care

For many working mothers, the issue of part-time vs. full-time care is not a decision at all; they simply must work full time to stay out of poverty or to avoid an unacceptably stressful decline in the family's accustomed standard of living. However, for those who have the luxury of choice, part-time work and therefore part-time childcare is a solution many women gravitate toward as a way to have the best of both worlds—maintaining a foothold on the career path, earning a little extra income, having a little break from the children, getting a sense of personal fulfillment, enjoying a little adult conversation and still being able to take the baby to the park or be a chaperone for the school field trip.

But part-time childcare is not for everyone. Many children, especially younger infants and toddlers and more sensitive preschoolers, find it difficult to adjust to a part-time schedule; if too much time elapses between trips to the childcare arrangement, the young child has difficulty understanding the pattern, knowing what to expect next, or getting fully comfortable with the care setting and the caregiver. In fact, some childcare centers do not even offer part-time care, particularly a Tuesday-Thursday schedule, for infants and toddlers because it has simply proven too difficult to help the child adjust: with a five-day lapse between visits to the center, for some children it is as if they are starting anew every week.

An added challenge of finding part-time care is being able to find an arrangement that matches the working mother's childcare needs. If her work schedule is not flexible, she must find a care arrangement that fits in with a predetermined time frame. Childcare centers and some family childcare providers have a certain number of "slots" available for children. If a child is to occupy a slot for only part of the time, some childcare providers either require that the parent pay for the full-time slot or give preference to a parent whose schedule dovetails with that of another family such that together the two children fill the slot by attending on opposite days or times.

Type of Childcare Setting

The next decision is what type of setting the parent desires. Most parents have a sense of what they prefer for their child—care with a relative or a nonrelative, care in their own home, care in a homelike setting, or care in a more formal setting.

CARE BY THE FATHER OR OTHER ADULT RELATIVE

A small but growing number of mothers who work are able to coordinate their schedules with their partners' so that the father can take care of the children while the mother is at work. This type of arrangement is most commonly preferred by parents when their children are very young. It has many obvious advantages: the child is in the safe, loving care of his or her own father, and the father has a wonderful opportunity to spend one-on-one time with his baby, getting to know him or her and maybe coming to appreciate his wife's parenting challenges and efforts all the more. And a significant benefit of such an arrangement is that it is free. As we have discussed, childcare costs can level a devastating blow to the family budget. However, as ideal as this arrangement is in some ways, it does not come without a cost. Simple mathematics suggest that if each parent is working a full-time job, once commuting is factored in (not to mention sleeping), there is precious little time left in a twenty-four-hour period for the partners to spend with each other. Shared childcare can therefore run the risk of exerting a toll on the quality of the marital relationship.

Another popular option, especially for very young children, is care by another adult relative, such as a grandmother or aunt. Similar to shared parental care, this type of arrangement has the obvious advantage of allowing the child to spend time in the doting, attentive care of a loved one, usually for no cost or at most for a very modest stipend. And indeed, this type of arrangement can be ideal for infants and toddlers, especially if there are only one or two children in the setting. There is not likely to be any kind of "curriculum" per se, but children this age hardly need flashcards, and the sensitive, responsive care of someone who genuinely loves and cares for them may outweigh the lack of formal lessons. One of the primary drawbacks of this kind of care is that, because it is completely informal, there is no working agreement or contract, making it a less stable, less dependable arrangement. In addition, parents might find themselves in conflict with the adult relative caregiver over matters of childrearing or discipline; it is easier to tell a hired, nonrelative caregiver how you would like to have various childcare situations handled than to tell your own mother, who may believe her way is better, and by the way, it worked just fine with you when *you* were a child.

NONRELATIVE CARE IN THE CHILD'S OWN HOME

A very small minority of parents can afford to hire an adult to come to their home to care for their children. This kind of arrangement, though often difficult to find, is popular among more affluent families, who can afford such an arrangement. It also becomes more popular as the family grows in size, when in-home care becomes more economical. In-home care offers many advantages. The hours are flexible; there is no need for the child to travel to the care arrangement; the child remains in a familiar, secure place; and the mother, to some extent, is able to monitor the behavior of a caregiver who, though unrelated, becomes like one of the family. In-home care keeps siblings together, and the caregiver can provide each child with individual attention.

On the other hand, the arrangement also has disadvantages. The caregiver is usually untrained and unlicensed and may or may not provide good care. And this form of nonrelative care is the least stable. Frequently having to replace caregivers is a frustrating drawback to in-home care. There is also a disadvantage for the child because educational or group activities with peers are less likely in in-home care than in other kinds of childcare. Beyond these obvious advantages and disadvantages, childcare in the child's home is an unknown commodity of infinite variety: we have no solid assessment of its quality.

CHILDCARE HOMES

Childcare homes are the cheapest, most numerous, and most elastic childcare arrangement. There is no need for construction of a facility (although some basic modifications are often necessary to meet safety regulations) and no need to set up a complex administrative structure. Childcare homes are usually located near the child's home; therefore, they are easy to get to and are in a familiar neighborhood, where people are likely to share the parents' values and circumstances. The mother has more control over what happens to her child in a childcare home than she would in a childcare center because she can give instructions to a childcare home provider that she would not be able to give a childcare center teacher, who must attend to a large number of children and follow guidelines set up by the center. Studies show that parents using family childcare are more likely to have a close personal relationship with the care provider than are parents using center care. They talk to the care provider more and say that they intend to "keep in touch" with her after the child leaves the childcare home.[2] A childcare home provider is usually flexible about taking children of different ages and in adjusting her hours to the mother's schedule. For a family with one or two children, a childcare home is also a relatively economical form of care.

For children, a childcare home offers the advantages of providing new experiences they wouldn't have at home and fostering relationships with people outside the family, while at the same time providing continuity with the kind of family care the child is used to, in a home, with a "mother figure." Family childcare offers the child the opportunity to interact with a handful of other children of different ages, rather than overwhelming the child with a large group of agemates. A childcare home provider, like an in-home caregiver, can devote individual attention to the children she is looking after. If the provider is licensed or participates in a training and support network, a childcare home is relatively stable and adheres to health and safety standards. If the care provider is in a network, she is likely to be given training in childcare and to have regular consultation with child development professionals. The network may be affiliated with a school, university, or childcare center.

But this kind of childcare has disadvantages as well. A major disadvantage is that a childcare home provider is the least accountable to parents for her actions. Childcare homes are private and not open for public inspection. After the mother drops off her children—although she may instruct the care provider about how she wants the child taken care of—she has no knowledge of what really happens. Babies cannot report to their mothers what happened during the day. The vast majority of childcare home providers are not trained or licensed and are unaffiliated with a support network. They are unlikely to offer the children organized educational activities, and the physical equipment they have is not as plentiful or as varied as in most childcare centers.

CHILDCARE CENTERS

Centers, too, have their pros and cons. For the most part, they are relatively stable, keep predictable hours, and are publicly accountable
and easily monitored by parents. Childcare centers don't quit or get
sick or go on vacation. Caregivers usually have some training in child
development and are likely to offer children educational opportunities and the chance to play with other children in a child-oriented,
child-sized, safe environment that is rich in materials and equipment.

On the other hand, childcare centers often are located at some dis-
tance from the child's home, have less flexible hours, do not offer care
for sick children, are more expensive, and are less available because of
strict eligibility criteria. All other things being equal, the majority of
parents prefer centers for their preschool children. Parents like centers because they are convenient, because they offer the child learning experiences and social contacts, and because the children's daily
experiences are carefully planned by a caregiver who has received
professional training to know what activities are age appropriate,
safe, stimulating, and fun.

WHICH IS BEST?

In general terms, there are clear differences among the types of care
arrangements available to parents. Many researchers have attempted
to detail differences in the "ecology" of center-based vs. home-based
care. On average, the physical conditions (space, ventilation, light,
toilets, cleanliness, toys, safety, nutrition, and immunization) are better in childcare centers, whereas childcare homes rank higher in social-
personal conditions (fewer children per adult, more interaction with
the caregiver, more conversation, more socialization attempts, more
emotional input, and more sensitive approaches to the child by the
caregiver).[3] Centers typically have more structured educational activities than childcare homes, and children's play in centers is more
complex.[4] Children in childcare centers typically spend more of their
time in adult-directed creative activities and instruction. In contrast,
children in family childcare homes spend more time playing with
peers.[5]

This difference in program emphasis may be related to child outcomes. In a number of studies, children in center childcare have been observed to do better than children in home childcare on tests of ability.[6] In the Chicago Study of Child Care and Development, two- to four-year-old children in community childcare arrangements were tested on their abilities to understand sentences; name colors, fruits, and animals; remember numbers; identify photographs of objects; use play materials; solve problems; label pictures of emotions; copy designs made with blocks; visualize how things would look to another person; and communicate a message.[7] On all these measures of intellectual competence, children in centers were, on the average, six to nine months advanced over children cared for by in-home or childcare-home providers. The differences appeared for children of all family backgrounds, for both boys and girls, after as little as six months in childcare. In a study of young children whose mothers had been on welfare, researchers found that lower-performing children who entered center programs displayed significantly stronger gains in cognitive skills and school readiness, moving about three months ahead of the children who remained in home childcare settings.[8] This association was significantly stronger for children who attended higher-quality centers. In the NICHD study, children who had more experience in center care did better on tests of preacademic skills and language performance at age four than children in home childcare (even with parenting quality, family income, ethnicity, parents' education, and quality of care controlled).[9] In a study of preschool children whose mothers entered welfare-to-work programs in 1998, the ones who were in center care made more progress in developing school readiness than the ones who were in home childcare settings.[10]

Of course, it should be noted that an educational program can also be implemented in home settings and that this kind of enrichment levels the playing field. Differences between children in childcare centers and childcare homes are less pronounced when the childcare homes are of high quality. For example, in one study, although children in unlicensed childcare homes were not as competent as children in centers, children in regulated homes were.[11] In another study, when childcare homes were enriched with an educational curriculum, children's intellectual performance improved to the level of children in childcare centers.[12] A third study demonstrated that when the Head Start curriculum was imported into childcare homes, these homes were like Head Start centers in terms of their program dynamics; the only differences were that centers were more likely to display children's artwork and use child-sized furniture.[13] Children who were randomly assigned to attend the Head Start homes performed just as well as those assigned to Head Start centers on cognitive and language tests at the end of the year; the next year, when the children were in kindergarten, they performed as well on measures of cognition, social-emotional well-being, and physical outcomes.

In brief, children attending center programs often do better on tests of their intelligence and competence, but when home-based childcare programs include the educational activities that are most commonly found in centers, care setting is not a concern. But research is based on statistical probabilities, not absolute truths; it is based on averages, not individuals. Results apply to groups of children, not specific ones. If a statistically significant difference is found between children in childcare centers and those in childcare homes, it means that children in centers are more likely than children in childcare homes to behave this way; it does not mean that *every* child in center childcare will behave this way. Just as the weatherman can predict only a 60 percent chance of rain on a particular day, so research can predict only that, other things being equal, there is a greater probability that a child will behave in a certain way if he or she is in a certain type of childcare setting. Just as, after hearing the weather forecast, each person has to decide whether to take an umbrella, each parent has to make a value judgment about which type of childcare to select for her or his own child.

To some extent, then, the choice of type of care should be based on a combination of the unique characteristics of the individual setting and parental preference. One approach parents might use in deciding which type of care is best for their family is to consider the unique needs and characteristics of the child. For example, children who are very sociable and independent and those who are very active or need a lot of stimulation or a predictable schedule might thrive in a child-care center. By contrast, those children who tend to get overwhelmed in large groups, are slow to warm up to new people, and thrive on in-dividual attention might be better off in in-home care or a family childcare home. The parents' own preferences might also be consid-ered. For example, some parents feel more comfortable leaving their children in the care of someone with similar values or ethnic back-grounds, while others welcome the chance to expose their children to different backgrounds and beliefs. Last, parents who would enjoy the opportunity to have the childcare arrangement become a part of the family's extended social network might prefer a home-based arrange-ment, where the interpersonal relationships with the caregiver, and per-haps with the parents of the other children as well, tend to be closer.

A WORD ABOUT CENTER AUSPICES

Although there is immense variation across childcare settings and, thus, no way to make absolute definitive statements about one kind or another, one factor that has been shown to predictably discriminate among centers is the center auspice. Whether a center is run for profit often makes a significant difference in the kind of care it is likely to provide.[14] On average, nonprofit childcare centers, especially those supported by public, government funds, are more likely to have a trained and experienced staff, to offer a comprehensive program with a child development component, and to adhere to a higher set of li-censing standards than for-profit centers. The teachers in a nonprofit center are more likely to offer the children developmentally appropri-ate activities. These centers also offer more services: screening, testing, immunization, transportation, social work, referral to other agencies or professionals. They pay their teachers higher wages than for-profit centers do. Although these typical differences are not guarantees, they can be of some help in searching for the best available childcare.

Aside from the for-profit vs. nonprofit distinction, some parents prefer certain kinds of centers because they match the parents' values or are particularly convenient. For example, some parents gravitate toward large, franchised childcare centers because of the "brand recognition"—as they do with McDonald's, parents derive a sense of comfort and security with a setting that has corporate muscle behind it, with a familiar logo that they may have seen on television or in other neighborhoods around town. Other parents prefer a church-based setting because they hope for religious instruction for their child, and they feel comforted by knowing that their children are being cared for in a spiritual, wholesome setting. A few very lucky parents have access to on-site childcare at their place of work; this type of care tends to be of very high quality and is eminently convenient for the parent, who does not have to make an extra stop at a childcare setting on the way to work. Having the child nearby also affords the parent the opportunity to visit during the day, nurse a baby, or have lunch with a preschooler. Another lucky few parents have access to university-based childcare; although in principle these settings often offer spots for children from the community, in practice the coveted spots are usually taken up by university-affiliated employees and students. And for those fortunate families, the care offered in such settings is typically of very high quality, reflecting the latest thinking on optimal childcare practice.

Evaluating and Monitoring Quality

As we have tried to emphasize throughout this book, there is tremendous variability in the quality of care found in all kinds of childcare settings. For that reason, regardless of the choices parents might make about part-time or full-time care, center-based or home-based care, relative or nonrelative caregivers, the single most important job of the parent in choosing a childcare setting is to evaluate the quality of care delivered in that setting. Most parents have a common sense notion of what constitutes high-quality childcare; but they can also rely on three decades of childcare research to tell them the kinds of specific features that tend to indicate high quality.

To some extent, states take a first pass at screening for quality by setting licensing standards for childcare centers and homes. But as we have discussed, there is wide variation in the levels of standards set in different states; some standards are as stringent as those recommended by childcare experts, but many are not. In addition, as we have also discussed, the preponderance of childcare arrangements used in the United States today are not regulated by state licensing, either because they are legally exempt or because they are operating illegally. Beyond state licensing, then, another screening tool parents can use is whether the center is accredited by NAEYC and meets standards, based on the most current wisdom on childcare "best practices." NAEYC accreditation is growing in popularity among center directors: in 1990 only about one thousand centers had been accredited, but by 2004 that figure had jumped to nearly eight thousand.[15] Still, this figure, though encouraging, represents less than 10 percent of all existing childcare programs. In addition, although NAEYC accreditation is a good benchmark parents can use to identify high quality—research studies have shown that centers that meet these kinds of higher standards generally provide higher quality care, and the children in that care are better off—it is still not an unqualified *guarantee* of high quality.[16] For all these reasons, the task of identifying a childcare arrangement of high quality falls largely to the individual parent. There are several key elements to look for, as we will discuss. Some are more applicable to large, formal childcare centers than to smaller, less formal home-based childcare arrangements, but many of the same basic principles apply in both kinds of settings.

STRUCTURAL CHARACTERISTICS

As a first level of screening, the parent can simply call the childcare center or family childcare provider to ask about a handful of structural characteristics that researchers have consistently found to be related to high-quality childcare. These questions should include the following: How many children are cared for in the group at any one time? How many adults supervise the children? What are the qualifications (education, training, and experience) of the caregiver(s)? The savvy consumer will then follow up these basic questions with more probing ones to get the true, definitive answer, as these numbers are sometimes "fudged" a bit. For example, there may be certain times of the day when a much larger number of children are present than the "usual" daily number first reported by the director or caregiver, either because older children are present before or after school hours or because groups of children are combined at certain times of the day (e.g., in the morning or during outside time). Similarly, the reported count of adults might include people who are not usually around on a continual basis (e.g., a volunteer who helps out in the setting on occasion but is not really a "regular," or a music teacher who comes only once a week). These kinds of questions may help narrow the list of settings that the parent will consider further. In general, of course, the fewer children per regular adult caregiver, the more likely it is that children will receive individualized attention. And the smaller the total size of the group, the less likely it is that the setting will feel noisy and chaotic and that individual children's needs or crises will get lost in the confusion. As a general rule, the younger the child, the more caregivers there should be per child and the smaller the total group size. Childcare experts recommend no more than about three or four infants and toddlers to each adult, with a maximum group size of six to eight children; five to seven older toddlers per adult, with a maximum group size of ten to fourteen; and ten preschoolers (age three to five) per adult, with a maximum group size of twenty.

CAREGIVER BEHAVIOR

But these simple head counts are only a quick-and-dirty first step in evaluating childcare quality. The next, perhaps most crucial step is for the parent to visit and observe in the setting for an extended period of time. This kind of observation does not mean taking a guided walking tour of the facility, briefly glancing at the areas where children play, sleep, eat, and are diapered. It means sitting down on the floor, at the child's eye level, and simply watching what goes on in the setting, fly-on-the-wall style, for several hours.

One of the primary focal points of such an observation should be the behavior of the caregiver in the setting, as the ultimate quality of the childcare experience often hinges on the behavior of that very central figure. Indeed, as one childcare expert recently noted, "Picking the people who will care for your child is as important as picking your spouse."[17] Indeed, the caregiver might very well be spending as much of the child's weekday waking hours with the child as his or her own parents do; the caregiver is likely to become a very important person in the child's life and, in optimal circumstances, a partner with the parent in the child's development. Unfortunately, the marriage analogy is all too accurate, and as the startlingly high divorce rate might indicate, choosing that perfect partner is usually easier said than done. An extended visit in the childcare setting, and perhaps a separate chance to chat with the caregiver when she is not preoccupied seeing to the needs of the children, can help the parent get a sense of what kind of person the caregiver is and whether the fit is right, not just between the caregiver and the child, but between the caregiver and the parent. Research findings showing positive links between caregiver behavior and positive child developmental outcomes can provide parents with a specific set of criteria to look for when evaluating observed caregiver behavior, as we describe next.

One of the most important things to look for is whether the caregiver is warm and nurturing. Does she—remember that we refer to the caregiver as "she" because in practice most caregivers are female—seem to enjoy talking and playing with the children? Does she squat or sit at children's eye level to talk with them? Is she cheerful and patient? Responsive and attentive? Does she monitor the activities of all the children, responding appropriately to their overtures or bids for attention? Does she provide individualized care, responding appropriately to the unique characteristics of different children and situational demands? Does she genuinely seem to feel affection for the children in her care, sharing in their triumphs with a hug or a "high five," comforting them in their disappointments with a well-timed snuggle, and worrying about their safety and well-being? Does she share the wealth, behaving in the same warm manner to all the children in her care without singling out a favorite child?

But warmth and physical affection are not the only important things to look for. A good caregiver will also engage the children in interesting and developmentally appropriate conversations and activities. Does the caregiver have back-and-forth conversations with the children, chatting with them, answering their questions, asking them questions, and listening to their responses? Does she read to them, label objects, extend conversations by following up on children's comments? Is she actively involved in activities with the children, not just supervising from afar? Does she provide interesting materials and gently encourage children to be involved? Does she provide more structured opportunities for learning as well as free play? Does she avoid using the television as a babysitter?

Of course, the skilled caregiver must do all of these things while at the same time maintaining control of the environment. To that end, does the caregiver have some sort of schedule for the activities of the day so that children have at least a general idea of what to expect? Does that schedule include a variety of activities—indoor and out-door play, rest and active play, quiet and boisterous time, structured and free play? Does the caregiver use praise and encouragement and avoid orders, threats, criticism, or punishment to get children to comply? Does she help children resolve conflicts rather than leaving them to fend for themselves? Does she use such inevitable conflicts to teach social problem-solving skills? These are just some of the many skills a talented caregiver will possess.

Often, the caregiver's behavior will tell parents everything they need to know about how good a childcare setting is. But a nice, long visit will also allow the parent to get a feel for what that setting is like, a sort of intangible sense of the quality of the environment. For example, a setting where children wander aimlessly and seem disengaged or un-interested is usually a sure indicator of low quality. By contrast, a place where the children seem happy and involved, share smiles with the caregiver and with peers, and move through the setting in a re-laxed and confident manner is probably a high-quality arrangement. Similarly, a care setting that is too quiet may indicate not enough ac-tivity or too much adult control. A place that is too noisy, on the other hand, may mean that the caregiver has difficulty maintaining control.

An important part of this exercise in getting a feel for the emo-tional climate of a childcare setting is to imagine one's own child in that setting, fending for him- or herself as it were. It is a good idea to think about the unique characteristics of the child to decide if the setting is matched to his or her style. For example, a slow-to-warm-up child might benefit from an unpressured, supportive atmosphere; children who sometimes have difficulty controlling their behavior might benefit from a setting with more structure and consistency; and shy or withdrawn children might thrive best in a smaller setting with ample opportunity to develop a warm, intimate relationship with the caregiver and a few playmates.

The caregiver's observed behavior in the setting is an excellent indicator of the quality of care delivered in that setting. But the parent might also inquire as to the level and type of training and experience in childcare the adult has. It is important to recall that research studies have shown how specialized training in childcare and early childhood education is often an excellent predictor of how good a person will be at caring for children. Some parents might be inclined to dismiss this factor as unimportant; after all, what more is childcare essentially than "mothering," a task that countless people have mastered across the ages without stepping foot into a classroom or cracking a book on the subject? But, of course, the crucial difference is that in a childcare setting the caregiver is being asked to care for children in whom she does not have a biological investment (as she does with her own children); in addition, she is faced with the challenge of caring for a group of children often much larger and closer in age than the typical family grouping. Specialized training can help her to handle the unique demands of such a situation, as she assists children, for example, in conflicts over toys or helps a sad child understand that mommy will return soon enough. Training and experience, then, should not be overlooked as an indicator of quality.

PHYSICAL SETTING

Although finding the perfect caregiver is a key to quality, the parent must also evaluate the quality of the physical context for that care. And as with caregiver behavior, the research we reviewed in detail earlier in this book can be used to give parents a specific set of quality criteria to look for in the physical setting. First and foremost in this category, of course, is health and safety. The setting should be one in which reasonable measures have been taken to protect children from harm: For example, is there some method for controlling who can enter the setting? Is the physical setting generally in good repair? Are dangerous items such as medicines or household cleaners locked away out of children's reach? Do the caregivers wash hands before handling food and after diapering? Are toys and equipment in good repair, with no sharp edges, splinters, or loose parts? Is the out-door play area fenced in and safe, with age-appropriate play struc-tures anchored firmly over shock-absorbing surfaces such as sand or wood chips? Are all areas of the outdoor space visible from one loca-tion? Do the caregivers have an emergency exit plan? Do they have emergency contact information handy?

Beyond a safe environment, parents should look for a physical set-ting that is organized, uncluttered, large enough for the number of children in the setting, and stimulating to children's play and learn-ing. To that end, is there a wide variety of toys and materials that are stored in labeled containers or shelves within the child's reach? Are there enough materials so that children will not be in constant con-flict over a few coveted objects and will not have to wait more than a few minutes to have a turn playing with something? Are there mate-rials available for building and construction (e.g., blocks, Legos), art and music (paints, musical instruments), manipulative play (sand, buttons, water, clay), pretend play (dolls, dress ups), and active play (slides, swings, tricycles)? Is the space organized into interest areas, with, for example, a dramatic play area, a cozy corner for relaxing or reading books, etc.? Is there adequate space for napping, eating, dia-pering or toileting, and storing the child's personal belongings? Is there also adequate space for free play, outdoor play, and structured activities? This is not an exhaustive list, but it is a general idea of the kinds of things to look for in a good physical setting.

PARENT-CAREGIVER RELATIONSHIP

Another indicator of quality is the caregiver's willingness to enter into a partnership with the parent in looking after the best interests of the child. Research indicates that parent-caregiver communica-tion is valued by parents and childcare providers, but its frequency is uneven.[18] Communication is more common in high-quality centers. In one study of twelve childcare centers, for example, researchers found that in centers with high overall quality scores, there was more frequent two-way communication between the school and the par-ents.[19] In another study, which included informal care arrangements as well as centers, more communication between mothers and caregivers about the child, as reported by both mothers and caregivers, was significantly related to better-quality care.[20] Moreover, in a national study in the Netherlands, children felt more at ease in the childcare setting if the quality of communication between parents and caregivers was better.[21]

From the time of the initial screening process, the caregiver should be friendly and open, interested in answering the parent's questions, and willing to view these questions as a positive sign that the parent is vigilant and invested rather than as a threatening interrogation. In the best partnership, caregivers and parents are willing to listen to each other's ideas and perspectives on child rearing and on the management of the individual child, and they are able to reach agreement on matters of discipline and developmental goals. Once the child starts attending the childcare setting, parents should be welcome to visit at any time, and in fact caregivers might encourage parents to do so, with parents perhaps signing up on occasion to lead a special activity (such as reading a special story, making banana bread, assisting in a holiday party). Caregivers should make themselves available to chat informally with parents at drop off or pick up time, communicate openly with the parent about the child's day, and even schedule more formal time to talk about the child's progress during a time when children are not present. Parents, in return, should also share information about the child's behavior and events at home. Parents should be suspicious of a setting that discourages them from dropping in or that welcomes parents only at certain times of the day with advance notice; these childcare settings should be avoided.

CONSUMER ENDORSEMENTS

In the best of worlds, the childcare setting the parent selects will include many if not all of these features of high quality, and as we have emphasized, nothing can take the place of actually visiting any potential childcare arrangement to observe what goes on and chat with the caregivers. But one approach parents often use to narrow down the list of potential care arrangements is to seek word-of-mouth recommendations from friends, neighbors, trusted co-workers, and loved ones. It can be reassuring to know (at least indirectly) other parents who have used a childcare arrangement for their own children. But parents need to ask these other parents specific questions: "What is it you like about this place? Is there anything you do not like?" It is important for prospective childcare consumers to know specifically what others like about the arrangement so that they can decide if these are factors that are also important for them personally and appropriate for their own child. Keep in mind also that people generally rate their own childcare arrangements as high in quality; they are unlikely to leave their children somewhere that they judge to be a terrible place. For that reason, word-of-mouth recommendations can be a good starting place in the search for childcare, but they cannot replace a thorough personal screening of the arrangement.

BACKGROUND CHECKS

Last but far from least, a critical step in any childcare search is to conduct a background check of the potential caregiver. Perhaps because of high staff turnover and the need to constantly fill positions, ex-convicts abound in childcare. Indeed, in one survey of the childcare used in the state of California, one in twenty children in childcare were being cared for by someone who had been convicted of a crime.[22] Often, background checks—when they are made at all—are cursory, and evaluators often miss or ignore information about a person's past. Databases are incomplete. The law in California generally prohibits people with criminal records from working in childcare and requires that every childcare worker be fingerprinted and go through a criminal background check. But the California Department of Social Services is required by law to allow people convicted of certain crimes to show they have been rehabilitated and to earn a waiver (although some crimes, such as child molestation and murder, automatically ban the person from childcare for life). As of March 2002, in California parents can learn whether a person with a criminal waiver works at a particular childcare center or home, but still the state won't release the nature of the crimes and will only give out information about waivers granted since 1994. The message here is that it is basically up to parents to search and find an acceptable, safe, and stimulating childcare arrangement for their most vulnerable family member.

Ensuring Continued Quality

Enrolling a child in childcare is not like parking a car in a garage: parents need to stay in touch and be involved. Selecting the setting, even after extensive assessment and careful deliberation, is only the first step in ensuring childcare quality. The parents' task is not yet done, and further steps are necessary to make sure that what looked like high-quality childcare when the parent visited really is. The parent also can take steps to create a positive experience for the child. The skills and interests of parents and childcare providers should be complementary. They need to think of themselves as partners in the childcare arrangement.

PREPARING CHILDREN FOR CHILDCARE

Before enrolling or leaving children in the childcare facility, parents should spend some time preparing children for the new arrangement. Plunking children down in a center, with no warning or preparation, and leaving them there for eight hours on the first day is not a good idea. The immediate effects of leaving the child in the childcare setting can be especially distressing for very young children. "Separation anxiety"—for both children and their parents—is normal. From as early as seven months of age, it is likely that children will be upset at being left in an unfamiliar setting with strange people. When mothers first leave children in childcare, the children's cortisol–that hormone that shows how stressed they are feeling—rises to twice the level it is at home.[23] Their distress can be lessened, however, if parents take precautions to ease the child into care.

For one thing, parents could give the child experience with other children in a playgroup or church school, before childcare commences. Parents could also "practice" separating by leaving the child with a babysitter occasionally. Then, before the first day of "class," parents and children should visit the childcare setting together, and parents should stay with the child until the setting and caregiver are familiar. Letting the child keep a "security blanket" or favorite toy at childcare is sometimes a help, as is having another family member (father, grandmother, sibling) or friend stay with the child in childcare for a while. Telling the child when the parent will be back and encouraging the caregiver to remind the child of this fact until the parent returns are also good ideas.[24] After the child is used to the care setting, transitions are easier if parents say good-bye and leave rather than hovering anxiously around the door or peeking in the window to see how the child is doing. Parents can call later to check in and make sure things are going smoothly. Older children may not be so distressed at the separation as younger ones, but they also need reassurance, especially if they are shy or slow to warm up. Also, this is not a time to try out new things at home—getting a dog, taking in a boarder, or buying new furniture. It will be easier for the child to adjust to starting childcare if things at home continue to be familiar and stable.

MONITORING QUALITY

Parents also have a responsibility to monitor the quality of childcare on an ongoing basis—another reason not to park the child and leave for work. Even though the caregiver has "passed the test" of giving good care to other children before the parents chose the childcare setting, parents need to watch carefully to see how the caregiver behaves toward their own child. Are caregivers friendly, gentle, welcoming, playful? Are they sensitive and responsive to a child's needs and behavior? It is important to recall that, in a study of parents by the Cost, Quality, and Child Outcomes team, researchers Cryer and Burchinal found that parents were not well informed about the care their children were receiving; parents also rated the quality of their children's classes higher than trained observers did.[25] Parents' average rating on the ECERS-ITERS seven-point scale was a 6, whereas the average rating given by trained observers was only a 4.

Parents may give these inflated ratings because they are not trained to observe childcare quality, because they haven't spent enough time in the center to know if the child is receiving quality care, or because it is in the parents' own best interest to believe that their children are receiving excellent care. If parents spent more time in the setting, were more informed about the indicators of quality, and were more critical consumers of care, this monitoring of quality could benefit the childcare field. Monitoring would also benefit the child.

Practical Considerations

This laundry list of steps for choosing the perfect childcare arrangement is in some sense a "best of all worlds" scenario. But, of course,
these steps must also be juxtaposed against a number of practical
considerations. Chief among these is cost: parents need to think
about what they can reasonably afford to pay for childcare on a
monthly basis; unfortunately, the family budget is often a major lim-
iting factor in allowing them to select the best care available. Second,
parents must factor in matters of convenience: Is the setting close to
the parents' home or workplace? Does the setting offer care during
the hours needed? Is breakfast or lunch offered? What are the expectations regarding parental involvement in the setting? Can the parent
meet those expectations? In selecting the best care arrangement, parents must include these kinds of issues in the equation. For example,
if the best childcare setting happens to be on the other side of town,
a daily hour-long rush through traffic to get to work on time in the
morning and to pick up the child on time in the afternoon is likely to
diminish the value of that arrangement if everyone is tired, cranky,
and frazzled by the end of the day.

In summary, parents are at the core of any hope of better childcare
for the future. More than anyone else—policy makers, researchers,
providers—they know their children best, understand their unique
needs and characteristics, and must be their children's strongest advocates. For those reasons, all parents must become educated consumers and demand reasonable childcare for their children. To make
educated demands, they must understand the various choices, learn
how to identify high-quality childcare, take the time to monitor its
quality, and reject suboptimal care. Only then will parents be able to
make the best of childcare. One tool for making such choices is to
rely upon sound, well-designed research. In the next chapter we turn
our attention to the future of such research.

10 PLANNING BETTER
CHILDCARE RESEARCH

The future of childcare in the United States must include an increasingly sophisticated research agenda. As we chronicled in Part II of this book, the first attempts to study the effects of childcare on children's development consisted of comparisons between children at home and in childcare. Realizing these studies were overly simplistic, researchers then began to look at variations within the childcare setting and to link these variations to differences in child outcomes. Soon they began to analyze multiple aspects of care at the same time, constructing flow charts, with some aspects of childcare having a direct influence on the child and others having indirect effects. In the most recent and most complex studies, researchers have incorporated family factors into their diagrams, recognizing that childcare factors alone do not paint a complete picture of the effects of caregiving experiences on children's development. This latest wave of childcare research, with its more sophisticated design and more comprehensive focus on child and family development, has allowed us to begin to understand the effects of childcare on children's development in a more complete way than ever before. What happens in the next decade will help us gain an even clearer understanding of the effects of childcare experience not only on young children but on their families as well. Here, we discuss some of the research directions that will be most helpful in advancing our knowledge.[1]

Valid and Comprehensive Assessments

COMPLETE AND ACCURATE EVALUATIONS

One of the important requirements of future research is that studies include a comprehensive range of evaluations, with each construct being assessed accurately and reliably. It is critical to have reliable assessments because the extent to which associations between childcare and child outcomes can be detected in any study depends on that reliability; without accurate assessment, researchers won't even know what their results mean. One limitation of most studies (including the CQO and NICHD studies) is that researchers have relied on caregivers' self-reports of their own background characteristics. On the face of it, this approach is sensible: who would know better about caregivers' training, education, experience, and attitudes? However, even without any deliberate efforts to deceive, caregivers are, unfortunately, not always accurate reporters. For example, in the CQO study, when center staff were asked about the kinds of training they had, many of them did not even include the training sessions the researchers had provided. What is needed to assess caregiver training are detailed and specific questionnaires concerning every possible training opportunity—from workshops to courses—with information gathered about how intensive the training was and what content it covered; open-ended interviews are not the way to gather accurate information about caregivers' backgrounds.

It is also important to conduct on-site observations of childcare quality. In this regard, two suggestions for future research seem worth making. First, there is value in probing into specific aspects of the caregiver's behavior (how she talks to or disciplines the children, for example) rather than relying on global evaluations of overall quality. Although all good things in childcare may go together, it would be helpful to identify those that are more amenable to intervention. Second, there is value in going beyond evaluations based on individual observers' judgments. Videotaping care settings would allow observers to probe and reprobe classroom dynamics; would allow multiple investigators, with different experiences and views, to express their opinions about those dynamics; and would allow researchers to retrace their steps later, going back to examine childcare quality and classroom dynamics—after they find out how children fared.

Although videotaped observations of minute-to-minute interactions between caregivers and children are key indicators of good-quality care, in the future researchers should also extend their search for quality beyond these interactions. Certain aspects of the childcare setting that have not previously been included in most research may in fact play important roles (for example, the leadership style of the director may play a role in high-quality care).[2]

DEFINING AND MEASURING QUALITY

Most researchers have developed or used measures of childcare quality that are difficult to describe and complex and expensive to use. They are also redundant, containing many similar, overlapping, or identical items. When researchers have boiled these measures down, they have been surprised to find that much smaller sets of items are adequate to represent each measure. The most commonly used measures, the ITERS and ECERS and their cousin the FDCRS, can be reduced to a single factor that requires no more than twelve randomly selected items (rather than the thirty-seven items they each contain).[3] The Profile Assessment for Early Childhood Programs, another widely used instrument, can also be reduced to a single factor with far fewer than the 150 items it contains.

In the future, it would be helpful if researchers could devise measures of quality that are easier to collect and less expensive to use. In the field of health care, "proxy measures," such as the percentage of children who receive immunizations on schedule or the percentage of children with ear infections who are treated with the correct antibiotics, have been used to monitor quality. Proxy measures that would serve as indicators of *childcare* quality could also be found, and these measures would be valuable not only for reducing costs for researchers on tight budgets but for communicating with parents, helping childcare providers improve quality, and providing childcare regulators with guidelines beyond the number and size of toilets. Structural measures, such as child-caregiver ratios, caregiver training, education, wages, and turnover, are one kind of proxy for childcare quality, but they have their limitations. Future researchers should exercise creativity and ingenuity in devising other easy-to-use assessments.

One effort to come up with a simple measure of childcare quality in the NICHD study revealed that simply counting the number of minute-long observation intervals in which a caregiver spoke to a child without yelling or criticizing was a proxy for the more complex rating of overall caregiving quality.[4] NICHD researchers divided the rating of overall quality of caregiving into four levels: poor, fair, good, and excellent. They then related these levels to the number of minute-long intervals in which the caregiver spoke to a particular child. In one hour of observation, caregivers who were judged by the trained observers to provide poor-quality caregiving talked to the child in fewer than fifteen minute-long intervals; caregivers providing fair-quality care talked to the child in sixteen to twenty intervals; good-quality caregivers talked to the child in twenty-one to thirty intervals; and excellent caregivers talked in more than thirty intervals. This is an example of a simple behavior count that could be used as a proxy to index quality.

Another team of researchers found that a proxy for childcare quality could be obtained from a telephone interview with the provider.[5] Observations were conducted in eighty-nine childcare homes and ninety-two centers using the FDCRS and the ECERS. A twenty-five-item telephone interview with home providers accurately predicted quality in 92 percent of the homes, and a twenty-two-item interview with center staff accurately predicted quality in 89 percent of the centers, in terms of three levels: "poor," "mediocre," and "developmentally appropriate." The most predictive item for centers was "Does the center require staff with less than an associate's degree to continue their formal education?" For homes, the most predictive item was whether the caregiver used varied materials for art and drama every day. Shorter forms of the telephone interviews (twelve items for homes and thirteen items for centers) also demonstrated predictive capability.

These are just two suggestions of proxy measures—one a behavior checklist, the other a brief phone interview—to get researchers thinking about streamlining their assessments and making them available to nonspecialists.

EXPANDED CHILD OUTCOMES

Not only is it important in future research to refine measures of childcare *inputs,* it is important to develop and refine assessments of child *outcomes.* One critical need is for clinically sensitive evaluation of children's psychological problems; another is for tools that measure school readiness. Recently, it has been suggested that a common set of outcome indicators should be developed and that desired outcomes at the national, state, and program levels should be identified. There is now a move toward establishing performance standards at the state level. For example, in California "desired results for children" include personal and social confidence, effective learning, and physical coordination. Uniform outcomes will be useful for evaluating programs and helping childcare staff monitor children's progress toward desired results.[6] But it will take a lot of work to get to the point of agreeing on what those outcomes should be and determining how they should be defined and measured. Then, after the performance measures are in place, further research will be necessary to determine whether the standards and measures are appropriate for the community and to suggest improvements when policies and programs are not working well. Developing and refining outcome measures will keep childcare researchers busy for the foreseeable future.

Large and Representative Samples

SELECTING AND KEEPING PARTICIPANTS

Another important advance that must be made by future researchers is improved sampling. Most studies to date have one feature that limits their conclusions—their samples are small, nonrandom, and nonrepresentative of the population. Even in the largest studies, such as the CQO and NICHD studies, although samples are relatively large, they are not nationally representative and, therefore, cannot be used to make generalizations about the overall state of childcare in the United States. The CQO is often cited as proof that childcare at most centers in the United States is poor to mediocre, but this study involved centers in only four states, not a national sample. Although CQO researchers represented a range of standards, the states studied were those where the researchers lived rather than a systematic representation of licensing standards across the country (the same was true in the NICHD study, although it includes ten sites).

Another sampling concern is the underrepresentation of low-quality childcare. Samples in childcare research are usually truncated because staff in lower-quality childcare facilities are less likely to consent to participate in research, and at-risk families are less likely to complete questionnaires and submit to observations.[7] To study the effect of this underrepresentation, two researchers artificially truncated the lower end of the childcare quality distribution in the CQO data set.[8] They randomly deleted 30 percent of the classrooms in which quality was at least one standard deviation below the mean, 20 percent of the classrooms in which it was between the mean and one standard deviation below, and 10 percent of the classrooms in which it was above the mean. There were marked decreases in the strength of the associations between quality and outcomes in this doctored sample. In future research, it is important to make more determined efforts to include extremes of quality at both ends of the continuum. To conclude that quality matters little or not at all, based on a sample of homogeneously moderate care, is clearly unreasonable; yet this conclusion is not out of line with the results of many studies.

Another sampling limitation that must be considered in future research is the limitation imposed by childcare providers' and parents' unwillingness to participate or remain in research studies. In the CQO study, for example, only 52 percent of the eligible center directors agreed to participate in the observation phase of the study, only 45 percent of directors agreed to participate in the child outcomes component, and only 64 percent of the eligible parents agreed to participate.[9] Therefore, the cumulative response rate for the core of this exemplary study was only 15 percent; 85 percent of the eligible sample was never seen. And this percentage of participation was even lower once participants started dropping out of the study. Because of sample attrition, only 47 percent of the children assessed in childcare were still in the sample at second grade. As these figures make abundantly clear, future researchers must put more effort into recruiting participants and preventing attrition. In the past, most childcare researchers were content to study effects of childcare in the preschool years. Now they have begun to look for consequences in the school years. The issues of recruitment, retention, representativeness, and sample size will become increasingly critical in longitudinal research probing long-lasting effects of care. Unfortunately, these issues are typically among the most expensive problems to address for research with real-world samples. Perhaps new technologies and advances in methods will help to improve sampling and design without radically increasing the cost of research.

LARGE DATA SETS FOR SECONDARY ANALYSES

One way to sidestep the challenge of recruiting and maintaining a large and representative sample is to let someone else do the work for you. A number of large-scale, longitudinal data sets will be available for secondary data analyses in the near future, providing information on the quality, type, and extensiveness of childcare.[10] The Project on Human Development in Chicago Neighborhoods is a longitudinal study of more than six thousand children in seven cohorts from before birth to age eighteen. So far, the first three cohorts have entered the study. In each cohort, childcare providers and parents are interviewed about childcare; childcare observations are made for a subsample of the children; and child outcomes, including IQ, achievement, behavior problems, physical health, conflict with parents, depression, anxiety, and delinquency, are assessed. Other data sets that will soon be available or that are already available include the following:

- The Early Head Start Research and Evaluation Project is a seven-year national study with a randomized design, in which children are observed in childcare and their caregivers are interviewed.
- Welfare Reform in Three Cities is a four-year study of 3,600 low-income families in Boston, Chicago, and San Antonio. Children's physical, social, and emotional development and

achievement are assessed, and childcare providers and parents are interviewed.

- The Panel Study of Income Dynamics Child Development Supplement is a longitudinal study of 3,563 children from birth to twelve. Data on childcare characteristics were collected in 1997, and a follow-up was carried out in 2001. Assessments of the children include standardized tests of achievement, grades, literacy, behavior problems, self-esteem, and physical health.
- The National Study of Child Care for Low-Income Families is a study of a random sample about five thousand low-income families with working parents and at least one child under age thirteen, in seventeen states.
- The JOBS Study is a welfare-to-work study with over three thousand families with young children.
- The Early Childhood Longitudinal Study is a national sample of over twelve thousand children born in 2000, who will be assessed when they are nine months, eighteen months, thirty months, and forty-eight months old and again when they are in kindergarten and first grade, to get information about their participation in childcare and their physical, language, cognitive, social, and emotional development.
- Data from the NICHD study of Early Child Care and Youth Development is available for secondary analyses through first grade and later phases of data will become available in the future.

All these data sets include large samples of low-income families and multiple ethnic groups. They include assessments of childcare in states that vary in generosity of childcare subsidies and in stringency of childcare requirements. Some data sets also include a large number of family-level characteristics, such as parents' mental health, employment patterns, income and income sources, child-parent interactions, and community characteristics, all of which may be entered into analyses to lessen the possibility of childcare effects being due to selection bias. Future researchers will be able to take advantage of these impressive samples.

Control by Design

ANALYSIS STRATEGIES

The important issue in trying to determine whether there are childcare effects—no matter how large and adequate the sample—is to take account of factors in the child and family that bias the selection of care. As we have noted, most contemporary researchers assess family background variables for this purpose and include them in their analyses. Differences of opinion abound, however, about which and how many of these "control" variables should be included for different kinds of analysis. Some argue that research has not been sufficiently controlled for various important family and selection factors.[11] These critics say, and researchers all agree, that studies should control for more than mother's education, child's gender, and family's ethnicity. But when researchers use regression analyses to control for family background factors that may be affected by childcare–such as family income and parents' attitudes toward childcare—other experts argue that this constitutes "over control" and washes out genuine childcare effects.[12] Such over control may lead to misleading conclusions because it statistically removes the effects of variables that cannot be removed in real life.

An alternative to using regression analysis to control family variables is to use structural equation modeling to examine family variables. Such analyses can incorporate a variety of childcare and family factors into an overall model of the effects of these variables on real lives, but these analyses may miss important nonlinear effects. Another type of analysis involves "instrumental variables"—variables that are completely independent of the family but are related to childcare quality, such as state childcare regulations and availability of childcare arrangements in the community. These variables are used to create a latent variable representing childcare quality, which is then related to child outcomes. The problem with this approach is that these variables are not really very good indexes of childcare quality. It will be important in future research for childcare researchers to craft sensitive and reasonable analysis models that incorporate the positive elements of each of these methods to provide greater assurance that observed associations between childcare and child outcomes are unbiased.

EXPERIMENTS, EXPERIMENTS, EXPERIMENTS

For developmental psychologists, experiments are the gold standard in research design. They believe it is not possible to infer cause and effect from observational studies. A correlation is not a cause, and although everyone assumes that quality of care causes better child outcomes, the association may run in the other direction: more competent children may evoke higher-quality caregiving from their care providers. Experimental studies of childcare have been rare, however. There are both ethical and practical problems in carrying out experiments on childcare. Is it ethical to randomly assign children to childcare of varying quality that includes poor quality? Will parents allow researchers to randomly assign their children to varying amounts of care? In only a handful of studies have children been randomly assigned to attend childcare or stay home or to attend different early childhood education programs. These studies have provided useful information and demonstrated significant long-term effects of programs on children's cognitive, academic, and social performance. However, the programs in these studies were outstanding, and the children participating were from poverty backgrounds. We need to conduct rigorous experimental research to find out whether high-quality care leads to improved child outcomes and whether low-quality care causes deficits across a broader range of childcare settings and more diverse families. Experiments should not all be "show projects" in which lavish resources are allocated to severely deprived children, for whom almost anything would be an improvement over their home circumstances.

Future researchers should conduct experimental studies with the sorts of childcare that ordinary parents actually use. Researchers need to test the limits of the usual fare of American childcare, not just model programs. They need to study effects of childcare on more privileged children as well as disadvantaged ones. We do not know how poor the quality of childcare must be to produce detrimental effects on children or how excellent it must be to change the performance of children from advantaged families. These issues should be probed experimentally.

It may be too difficult or expensive to experimentally study the effects of childcare vs. parent care if it means paying salaries so that working mothers can stay home (although it should be noted that the price tag on large-scale observational studies is gigantic). But if research on this scale is not possible, researchers can use experimental designs to probe specific aspects of childcare. In the 1970s, researchers in the National Day Care Study randomly assigned a group of children in daycare centers to classrooms with different staff-child ratios. Their study indicated that ratio had no consistent effect on the quality of care for preschool children—but perhaps the differences were not extreme enough or perhaps this variable is not critical to childcare quality. What is important for future researchers is that the powerful design of the National Day Care Study has not been replicated—and it should be.

There is a plethora of worthy hypotheses to investigate. Experimental designs will allow researchers to answer questions like the following: How much difference does a particular increase in quality make for child outcomes? Which aspects of quality matter most—caregiver stimulation or ample materials, caregiver attention or a limited number of peers . . . ? Are different aspects of quality important at different ages? How does the impact of a high-quality childcare intervention compare with the impact of a high-quality parenting intervention? What effect does a specific training module have? What are efficient methods of providing training? Can a curriculum designed to teach children to solve their problems nonviolently counteract the apparent effect of long hours of care on children's aggressive behavior problems? Does a combination of center care in the morning and home care in the afternoon reduce the incidence of aggressive behavior (and the rise in cortisol)? What is the minimal amount of cognitive stimulation that will support children's preacademic achievement and make them "school ready"? What are the thresholds or limits for child-staff ratios that predict decreased or enhanced child performance?

Policy Research

Childcare is not an academic issue; it is a real-life concern, and researchers should conduct studies that are relevant for childcare policy. There have been some attempts to do this. For example, data from the NICHD study were used to determine what happens when childcare centers meet recommended standards for caregiver training and staff-child ratios, and cost-benefit analyses of early intervention programs have been conducted.[13] Policy research will continue to be an important focus in the future.

PARTNERING WITH POLICY MAKERS

The best way to conduct policy-relevant childcare research is for researchers to partner with policy makers and practitioners. Research like the Florida Child Care Quality Improvement Study illustrates such a partnership. It also illustrates the messy nature of field research. Although centers were mandated to increase caregivers' training and decrease the number of children per caregiver, not all of the centers complied. The proportion of trained staff increased but still did not reach the level mandated by the state. In fact, center directors did not think that the new ratios improved quality—just that they were more expensive—and many did not even expect the new regulations to be enforced.[14] Though the payoff for policy makers is large, doing policy relevant research in the real world will be a daunting challenge for future researchers.

STUDYING POLICY ISSUES

Moving into the policy arena involves a certain change of orientation for many academic researchers. Size of effects, practical recommendations, and cost-effectiveness are not necessarily the primary concern of "ivory tower" research scientists. Research may need to adapt somewhat to the types of questions that are of interest in the real world.

First, associations between childcare quality and child outcomes may be statistically significant, but how large do they have to be to justify a change in policy?[15] Is the association between caregivers' backgrounds and caregiving behavior strong enough that concerned citizens and legislators should try to promulgate new regulations? Decisions about whether the government should invest resources in improving adult-child ratios or training caregivers in childcare centers must be based, in part, on the magnitude of associations between these factors and childcare quality and child outcomes. Yet research by developmental psychologists and economists has led to different conclusions about the magnitude of quality effects, in part, because these experts use different conceptual and analytic models. In the future, researchers must focus on and come to consensus about effect sizes.

A second concern for policy studies is cost. Researchers have to be concerned about the costs of the policies they recommend. There are real implications of advocating better child-staff ratios or providing caregiver training or increasing teachers' wages, the last of which some researchers have suggested might be the best way to improve childcare quality.[16] Policies like these come with price tags. The question policy researchers must wrestle with is how best to invest limited resources to enhance or ensure childcare quality. To answer this question, researchers need to conduct rigorous research on the costs and benefits of increasing childcare quality. Policy makers need more information about the levels of quality needed to produce positive child outcomes as well as the cost associated with achieving those levels of quality. How much does a given increase in quality cost, and how much does it improve child outcomes? Where is the "sweet spot" between efficacy and cost for child-adult ratios and childcare quality? Are the benefits of early, high-quality care sufficiently great that shifting resources from care for older children to high-quality care for younger children would result in better outcomes? Can similar trade-offs be made by shifting resources from children in part-time care to those in full-time care? Are there thresholds such that increases from low quality to fair quality may be more cost-effective than increases from good quality to excellent quality? Would policy makers get more bang for the buck by targeting the worst-quality care and children with the lowest ability levels? Can public funds currently dedicated to childcare be distributed more efficiently and equitably? These are important questions for policy-oriented researchers in the future.

A third concern of policy studies is the regulation of care. Researchers need to determine which of the potentially regulable dimensions of quality (ratio, group size, caregiver training, and so on) is most critical and how these dimensions can be successfully regulated. This determination can be accomplished only with research designs that sample programs from multiple states or assess the quality of care before and after a regulatory change. Careful examination of this question requires experimental designs.

INFORMATION TO THE PEOPLE

Researchers have not done a good job of communicating information to those who need a clearer picture of what is good or bad about childcare: policymakers, practitioners, and parents. In the future, researchers should design and test a comprehensive initiative to address information problems in the childcare market. This initiative could include aggressive outreach efforts to provide parents with information on the links between childcare quality and child outcomes, potential benefits of high-quality care, and ways of evaluating the quality of care that specific providers offer. This initiative could also include the dissemination of comparable information to childcare practitioners. This information intervention should then be rigorously tested to determine the extent to which it could improve the childcare market.

Broader Contexts

One final suggestion for future research is that researchers should broaden their investigations of childcare. They should do this in two ways. One is by examining the role of societal and cultural values in the childcare realm. Israeli researcher Miriam Rosenthal notes that, up to this point, childcare researchers have typically adopted European American values and ideologies regarding childhood, child development, and the role of the family.[17] Researchers need to step outside this box and take cultural and societal values into account when considering the effects of childcare on child and family development.[18] As a first step, they could talk to parents from many backgrounds about their experiences with childcare and their goals for their children. Researchers could interview parents about why they selected the arrangements they did and whether they deliberately chose them because of certain characteristics of the child or certain desired outcomes. In this era of diversity, it is no longer appropriate for researchers to impose their values and assumptions on families.

Researchers should also broaden the study of childcare by considering childcare in the context of the sum total of children's experiences. Rather than focusing on childcare alone, they should examine it within the context of all the experiences that make children better off. Progress in this direction has already been made. Parental care, health care, and community factors, as well as childcare, all contribute to children's well-being. What is left for the future is the development of theory and research that integrates these diverse influences on children's development by specifying direct, indirect, proximal, and distal factors and going beyond a focus on either parental care or childcare to illuminate the larger and more complex ecology of children's lives.

11 | IMPLEMENTING BETTER CHILDCARE SOLUTIONS

We began this book by looking backward at the history of childcare in this country; we end it by looking forward to childcare's possible future. It seems clear that childcare and maternal employment are now a mainstay of the American way of life, with no evidence of a reversal of this trend in sight. Players in the policy arena have been slow in responding, but within the last fifteen years there appears to have been some acceptance of the fact that childcare is here to stay. Policy makers have begun to play a more prominent role in assisting families with their childcare needs. We have seen that government is becoming more involved in childcare issues (by increasing funding for provision of childcare to lower-income families, for example, and by providing tax breaks for middle-income families). Industry, too, is beginning to respond to its workers' needs with employee benefits such as paid or unpaid parental leave, childcare resource and referral lines, flextime, and other "family friendly" policies. A quick glance at the childcare policies and programs of other industrialized nations, however, reveals that the United States still lags far behind its peers in supporting families' childcare needs; other countries have tackled the issues of maternal employment and childcare with a multipronged variety of solutions, such as extended parental leaves; subsidized childcare; national preschool; and high-quality, carefully regulated childcare.[1] What might we do in the United States to make parents' lives easier and childcare better in the coming years? In this final chapter we offer some suggestions for the future of childcare and maternal employment.

Reduced Dependence on Childcare

One way to alleviate the childcare crunch in the United States is to reduce the need for childcare in the first place, by making adjustments that reduce women's need to participate in the paid labor force, at least while their children are young. To that end, several different kinds of solutions have been proposed and, in fact, have gained in popularity over the last several years. In this section we outline some of those solutions.

INNOVATIVE WORK SCHEDULES

One way to reduce women's participation in the labor force is to introduce greater flexibility into traditional work schedules. For example, some women can manage to meet their financial needs and career aspirations by working part time for a few years while their children are young. In other countries, such as Britain, part-time work is the norm for mothers of preschool children. And indeed, as early as 1981 employees in one survey responded that part-time work with full-time benefits would help "a great deal" in reducing the tensions caused by balancing work and family obligations.[2] However, this "solution" is not without its costs. Part-time workers, especially when they retain the same job they once held full time, often struggle with disproportionate work loads; many full-time jobs cannot simply be cut in half and managed successfully in twenty hours per week. In addition, part-time workers are usually at a disadvantage compared to their full-time counterparts when it comes to issues of professional advancement. From a financial standpoint, many part-time positions do not include employee benefits such as health insurance. It is for reasons such as these that many have argued that part-time jobs must actually be reconceptualized rather than merely split in half if part-time work is to become a viable solution for working mothers' childcare concerns.[3] In response to these concerns, some have argued that perhaps a "four-thirds solution" might achieve the goal of reducing children's time away from parents but not disproportionately penalize a mother seeking financial independence or career mobility. In the four-thirds solution, each parent works two-thirds time at their paid employment, freeing up time for family and thereby reducing the strains of balancing work and family.[4]

A second way in which parents' dependency on childcare might be decreased is through flexible work schedules for one or both parents. "Flextime," as it has come to be known, allows employees to tailor their work schedules around their family schedules. Employees must maintain certain core hours at the job, but they can arrive and depart at different times, arriving extra early, for example, and therefore completing an eight-hour work day by early afternoon. This option has become increasingly available in recent years, in part as a function of an increasingly global economy, where multiple time zones mean that the people a company might be doing regular business with are in the middle of their workdays when most Americans are sound asleep in their beds.

A third way in which the need for extended childcare might be reduced is through telecommuting. The rapid rise of technology over the past several years has meant that many employees have ever-increasing flexibility to conduct their work from virtually any location; high-speed Internet connections, laptop computers, e-mail, voice mail, and cell phones have made it possible for the employee to stay connected to the workplace even when not physically present in the office building. Telecommuting offers parents the advantages of being able to avoid long commutes that add to the length of the childcare day or to work on a more flexible schedule. This flexibility allows parents to finish an important task after the children go to bed at night or to take a couple of hours off during the day to attend the preschool Halloween parade. Telecommuting also allows parents to be nearby to keep tabs on how things are going during the child's day. In addition, telecommuting can be beneficial to employers, who save the overhead cost of providing work space for the employee. However, like part-time work, telecommuting carries the disadvantage of less time for networking and, in some cases, of loss of professional status.

PARENTAL LEAVE

Another way of reducing the need for childcare, at least for the youngest infants, is to provide extended paid maternity leave following the birth of an infant. As we described in Chapter 2, some strides have been made in the United States over the last several years in this area. The Family and Medical Leave Act of 1993 guarantees employees in covered firms twelve weeks of unpaid leave. However, FMLA applies to only a fraction of American workers, and for those covered, even fewer can actually afford to go the full twelve weeks without pay. By contrast, countries large and small around the world offer much more generous leaves to new parents. Italy provides an excellent example of government policy being responsive to its citizens' needs. Italy was concerned, as many other countries are, that early and extensive separations from the parent could be detrimental to the very young child's development. The Italian government responded to this concern by enacting a generous national parental leave policy that allows mothers to stay home with their infants at full salary for the first five months of the child's life and at half salary for six additional months.[5] Infants in Italy are therefore rarely placed in center care before the age of six months.[6]

Further behind in our evolving thoughts on work and family is the notion of fathers being entitled to parental leave following the birth of a baby, primarily because of the firmly entrenched American notion that matters relating to the family, and especially to young infants, are the mother's sole responsibility. Indeed, in one survey, 63 percent of large employers thought it was inappropriate for men to take any paternity leave at all; 17 percent responded that a maximum of two weeks leave was acceptable.[7] By contrast, other countries have recognized that fathers are also important in the infant's earliest weeks. For example, in Sweden, a country that has long been regarded as the model social services of all kinds and that is often cited as having the most progressive views on the role of fathers, both men and women are entitled to paid leave following the birth of a child. Parents are entitled to a total of 450 days of leave, to be divided between mother and father, with at least 30 days reserved for each parent. As a result, most Swedish children (84 percent) do not enter nonparental child care before about age seventeen months.[8]

Increased Accessibility of Childcare

Decreasing our nation's dependency on early and extended childcare is a goal many believe to be the optimal solution to the childcare crisis, particularly from the standpoint of the best interests of the young child. But the kinds of employee benefits we have described are not typically available to all workers, and the workers most likely to need work-family benefits—women, minorities, and low-wage workers—are also those least likely to hold jobs providing these benefits.[9] Thus, even though solutions such as the ones we have suggested might work for some, they will not work for all. In the following sections we focus then on solutions aimed at increasing the availability, accessibility, affordability, and quality of childcare.

INCREASED FUNDING

The past ten to fifteen years have indisputably seen generous increases in government spending on childcare for American families. But further investment is still needed. Indeed, economists estimate that an initial investment in early childhood programs would actually result in net savings on future costs (e.g., remedial education, welfare benefits) within the span of about seventeen years.[10] As we have noted, one of the greatest challenges facing American families today is being able to afford high-quality childcare. Recent estimates suggest that high-quality childcare costs about $10,000 per year to provide; but the average American family can afford only about two-thirds of that.[11] The public investment in childcare and early childhood education has recently been estimated to be about $600 per child in the United States, compared with anywhere from $3,000 to $4,500 in virtually all countries of Europe.[12] In these other countries, parents themselves are expected to cover only a fraction of real childcare costs; the bulk of the cost is covered by a combination of funding mechanisms such as subsidies, tax benefits, and employer contributions.[13]

One of the most innovative if relatively small-scale examples of cost sharing that the U.S. federal government has taken on in recent years is the military childcare program. The Military Child Care Act of 1989 allowed for the creation of high-quality childcare centers for families of military personnel. The estimated expenditures on this program in fiscal year 2000 were $352 million.[14] The care offered in these facilities is of uniformly good quality; caregivers are well trained, wages are higher than at most civilian childcare facilities, and all centers are NAEYC accredited. The estimated cost of such care is $7,700 per child, half of which is financed by the federal government. This bright spot in government involvement in childcare has been held up as a model that state and local governments might emulate.

INCREASED CHILDCARE ACCESSIBILITY

As we have noted, parents today are faced with the daunting task of not only being able to pay for childcare but also being able even to find good-quality childcare in the first place. In recent years, great progress has been made in increasing childcare accessibility, primarily through the development and expansion of childcare resource and referral (R and R) services. These services can be provided by city governments, by private individuals, or by corporations. In fact, this was the fastest-growing corporate childcare initiative in the 1980s, as companies realized that R and R was a low-cost employment benefit; by 1997 about 20 percent of all American workers had access to R and R services through their employee benefits.[15] Many more individuals have gained access to such services through community development of similar services. Resource and referral services offer counseling to help parents make childcare choices and may also provide money or resources to increase the quantity or improve the quality of childcare. Parents phone or visit an R and R service when they are first thinking about childcare. They are interviewed about the kind, location, and cost of childcare desired. Then the R and R staff provides a list of options that fit the parents' criteria. R and R staff members do not recommend one program over another, but they may give parents guidelines for making a choice. Resource and referral services often provide an invaluable first step in helping new parents find childcare for their children.

CORPORATE INVOLVEMENT

After years of dragging their feet, larger corporations are finally beginning to appreciate the benefits of providing childcare and family-
related benefits to their employees. In fact, many companies now
clamor to be named on the annual list of "most family-friendly employers" put out by *Working Mother Magazine.* Of course, savvy business people consider every move in terms of the bottom line—and as
it turns out, more and more of them are understanding that it is cost-
effective to provide such benefits. In a recent survey of over one
thousand companies, more than two-thirds of employers reported
that the benefits from childcare programs were greater than or equal
to the costs, in terms of reduced employee absenteeism, increased retention of trained employees, and greater staff morale.[16]

Childcare benefits are becoming more and more popular in employee benefits packages: for example, in the span of just two years
(from 1995 to 1997), the number of employees in medium or large
businesses receiving childcare benefits increased from 8 percent to
10 percent, a modest overall number but nevertheless a 25 percent
increase.[17] A golden nugget among such benefits is provision of on-
site childcare. Though relatively few companies offer such a perk, the
number is growing: in 1998, more than eight thousand on-site childcare centers were in operation around the United States.[18] Employers
report that this benefit improves their employees' morale, attracts
talented employees, and serves as good public relations. It also reduces
employee turnover and thus improves the company's productivity.[19]

UNIVERSAL PRESCHOOL AND EXTENDED PRIMARY SCHOOL

Another potential solution to the childcare crisis might lie in an expansion of the current American public school system. The current
nine-month school year was designed to fit the needs of an agrarian
society; many have argued that it is time to revamp the school calen-
dar to fit the needs of modern American working families. Adjustments might include year-round school and extended school days in
which before- and after-school care is provided in a safe, educational
environment. In addition, many states have implemented or are ex-

ploring the possibility of universal preschool, that is, extending the public educational system to include four-year-olds. Universal preschool is already a feature of many national early childhood education programs in countries throughout Europe. Such programs, although voluntary, are immensely popular; in France and Italy, for example, about 95 percent of all three- to five-year-olds are enrolled in state-sponsored preschool.[20]

There are many advantages to using schools for childcare. For one thing, schools are the most reliable, permanent, and stable institutions in our society. Their existence is not contingent on finding new funding from year to year. For another thing, schools could offer equal access to childcare for all children who need it, because public schools are open to all children. Additionally, schools have as their goal the optimal development of children, not the more controversial goal of allowing parents to work or the goal of helping the needy. As part of the school system, childcare would be a "right" for all citizens rather than a service for the poor or a luxury for the affluent. Finally, tying childcare to the schools could upgrade its quality. Teachers are better paid than childcare workers and childcare workers in school-based childcare programs are the most highly educated and well paid in the field. Having childcare in the schools could lead to upgrading childcare as a profession and improving the salaries of childcare workers.

Despite these advantages of tying childcare to schools, critics point to a number of disadvantages as well. Teachers themselves, in one study, expressed some reservations about expanding school services to include childcare.[21] In addition, schools are stretched to the limit finding physical space to house school-age children and would find it difficult if not impossible to come up with additional space to house younger children during regular school hours. Further, as we have discussed, most parents prefer home-based childcare settings for their infants and toddlers and shy away from more institutional settings. For reasons such as these, schools are likely a promising solution for before- and after-school childcare for school-age children rather than for other kinds of childcare needs.

Childcare Quality

Of course, merely making more childcare available to families is only half the challenge. Efforts must be made to make sure that new care is of adequate quality and to get the existing care up to reasonable quality standards. In this final section we suggest some future solutions for accomplishing these lofty but necessary goals.

QUALITY REGULATION

Noticeably absent in the United States is a national-level effort at assuring that the childcare available to children and families is of adequate quality—despite over thirty years' worth of research that all converges on one clear fact: childcare quality matters for children's development. And even though the effect of childcare quality on children's development is relatively small, it seems more than reasonable to make an effort to ensure that the places our children spend their days are at least pleasant places to be, above and beyond whether they raise children's IQs two or three points.

Researchers in the field of child development have repeatedly shown which kinds of childcare settings are supportive of children's development, as well as which are potentially detrimental. As an outgrowth of this body of research, standards have been developed to define thresholds of childcare quality that are believed to ensure adequate care (such as the NAEYC accreditation standards). The challenge for policy makers in the United States is to recognize that, just as so many other industries in this country are carefully regulated, the childcare industry should be subjected to the same level of quality regulation.

Although the United States continues to resist federal regulation of childcare, in recent years many states have begun to respond to the urgings of childcare and child development researchers to improve their childcare quality regulations, thanks to research such as the Florida Quality Improvement Study.[22] Positive findings from that study have been used to encourage other states to follow suit in improving their quality standards. Just fifteen years ago, for example, some states allowed a single caregiver to look after as many as twelve infants in a center classroom, and one state did not even regulate teacher-child ratios. Today, ratios are much more in line with those recommended by NAEYC and less disparity exists across the country.[23]

Government regulation cannot create or guarantee high-quality care. But research shows that unregulated childcare is of lower quality than regulated care and that childcare quality is higher in states with more stringent regulations.[24] This research does seem to suggest that regulation could help eliminate low-quality care. Setting a floor for quality that all states could agree with could only help ensure better and more equitable childcare. Government regulation could establish minimal adult-child ratios of 1:4 for infants and 1:10 for preschoolers and minimal levels of training for caregivers, and this regulation would do much to improve the quality of existing care and lower the chances that children would find themselves spending their days in care arrangements that researchers have rated as potentially harmful to development.

Some policy makers have expressed concern, however, that government regulation would increase childcare costs. They worry particularly about the cost of home childcare, which is all many families can afford. But government regulation need not increase the cost of care provided by friends or neighbors. Childcare providers who offer cheap home childcare are not in the childcare business to make a lot of money. Therefore, if childcare were regulated so that the home care provider took in fewer children, or increased the safety of the childcare home by turning in the pot handles and barricading the stairs, or learned a bit more about how to play with young children, or found out how to reduce children's aggression by teaching them social skills, regulation would not increase the cost to the parents or the government. Regulations that required expensive physical changes to childcare homes or enrollment in community college courses could be eliminated to keep childcare costs down. Training of care providers could be accomplished economically by means of community telecourses or coordination with organized childcare networks or playground programs. If the purpose of regulation is to identify a reasonable *floor* of quality and to eliminate or modify care that falls below that floor, the enforcement of regulations may be more

feasible and childcare costs would not increase. Government regulation could at least serve to prevent the warehousing of large groups of
children in unsafe and unstimulating facilities.

FAMILY CHILDCARE SUPPORTS

A quick survey of the changes in state childcare regulations over the
last several years suggests that the strides toward improvement that
are being made are most likely to be found in center settings. This
finding has resulted partly because centers are less slippery to define;
as we have seen, so many different combinations of care arrangements might be found in a childcare home that it has proven difficult
for states to agree on which specific combinations of factors should
make a childcare home subject to licensing. Yet, because so many
American children are cared for in precisely these kinds of settings,
further efforts need to be invested in providing supports to improve
the quality of care offered in childcare homes. Toward that end, one
idea that gained momentum in the 1990s was to organize childcare
homes into networks. The services provided by networks include re-
ferrals, caregiver training, toy lending libraries, technical assistance,
shared activities, drop-in centers, and emergency backup caregivers.
Childcare providers in networks have been observed to offer higher-
quality care than licensed care providers who are not in networks.

This idea, too, has roots in the practices found in other countries.
In Israel, for example, family childcare homes are an integral part of
the national childcare system subsidized by the government. In a typical childcare home, one adult cares for five children. The care
provider typically has not completed specialized training or earned
an advanced degree of any type, but he or she is supervised by a local
social worker or early childhood education professional. In research
comparing the quality of care received in family daycare homes to
the famous, highly regarded Israeli kibbutzim, the quality of care received in family childcare homes was comparable to that received in
the kibbutzim.[25] Similarly, in Sweden, family childcare homes supplement childcare centers as part of the national childcare system.[26]
Care providers receive small equipment grants from the government
to stock their homes with toys and materials for the children. In some

communities, groups of four to six caregivers and their children get together at a community center or other public area on a regular basis and conduct larger group activities with the children. Programs such as these provide support, decrease caregiver isolation, and enhance the care provider's sense of professionalism and job commitment. As such, they point to a golden opportunity to improve the quality of a large share of childcare used in the United States today.

PARENT EDUCATION

Another means of improving childcare quality in the United States is by educating young parents, the primary consumers of this service, about the importance of good-quality childcare and the ways to find and monitor the quality of such care. In the last several years parents have been targeted on multiple fronts to try to get the word out—through educational materials distributed in hospitals and pediatrician's offices, employee assistance programs, resource and referral agencies, and the like. In the 1990s brown bags at the local Target store were printed with a checklist of things to look for when evaluating the quality of a childcare facility. A trip to the local bookstore or library yields entire shelves of resource books offering support to working parents, with titles like *The Anxious Parent's Guide to Quality Child Care, The Child Care Sourcebook,* and *The Working Parents' Handbook,* to name but a few. With the explosion of the Internet as a virtual library available in many homes, libraries, and workplaces around the country, parents now have at their fingertips a seemingly endless array of childcare information resources. Dozens of organizations, such as the I Am Your Child Foundation, Zero to Three, the National Association of Child Care Resource and Referral Agencies, and the National Network for Child Care, offer everything from checklists for rating childcare quality, to work sheets on how to select the best care to suit a family's individual needs, to "childcare finder" search engines that allow parents to enter their desired zip code to find providers in their area within a specified radius. Grassroots organizations such as the Child Care Now Action Campaign organize parents and care providers alike to lobby for better childcare and family-friendly policies. With parents demanding a better product, modest progress has been made in the quest for minimally adequate childcare for all. By continuing to get the word out to even more parents, childcare advocates are likely to achieve a net result of higher overall quality offered in our nation's various childcare settings.

A Final Word

We close as we began—noting that when the book *Daycare* appeared in 1982, we never thought we would still be talking about childcare as a major issue requiring major solutions in the twenty-first century. The intervening quarter century has seen progress: more government funding, greater acceptance of childcare and maternal employment as a fact of everyday life, strides toward improvement in childcare quality. But the goals are far from accomplished: childcare continues to be a restrictively pricey commodity for all but the most affluent families; loud and powerful conservative voices continue to blame "selfish, myopic" working mothers and bemoan the future of America's "childcare generation"; and poor-quality care that compromises children's development is far too widespread. In closing this book, we have outlined some ways that parents' plight in choosing childcare and the quality of childcare *could* improve. This improvement is unlikely to happen without a great deal of effort. Making that effort, however, will be worthwhile in the end. Only then will our children receive the kind of care they—and we—need and deserve. We should make the effort.

PREFACE

1. A. Clarke-Stewart, *Daycare* (Cambridge, Mass.: Harvard University Press 1982).

INTRODUCTION

1. Descriptions of the Kaiser Shipyards childcare centers are taken from S. Cleary and K. Altares, "An Investment Opportunity that Yields Predictably High Returns," Education Policy and Issues Center, *To the Point* 3 (2003), M. Crawford, "The Struggle for Public Housing," *Blueprints: The Journal of the National Building Museum* 12 (1994), 5–6, www.nbm.org/blueprints; D. K. Goodwin, "The Way We Won: America's Economic Breakthrough During World War II," *The American Prospect* 3 (1992), www.prospect.org; S. Weinstein, "If We Are United, We Cannot Lose!" *Socialist Viewpoint* 1 (2001), www.socialistviewpoint.org.

1. MAKING THE BEST OF DIFFICULT CHOICES

1. J. P. Lecanuet, C. Granier-Deferre, and M.-C. Busnel, "Prenatal Familiarization," in G. Pieraut-Le Bonniec and M. Dolitsky, eds., *Language Bases . . . Discourse Bases* (Amsterdam: John Benjamins, 1991), 31–45; C. Moon and W. P. Fifer, "Syllables as Signals for 2-Day-Old Infants," *Infant Behavior and Development* 13 (1990), 377–390; M. J. Spence and A. J. DeCasper, "Prenatal Experience with Low-Frequency Maternal-Voice Sounds Influence Neonatal Perception of Maternal Voice Samples," *Infant Behavior and Development* 10 (1987), 133–142.

2. P. G. Hepper, D. Scott, and S. Shahidullah, "Newborn and Fetal Response to Maternal Voice," *Journal of Reproductive and Infant Psychology* 11 (1993), 147–153; J. R. H. Porter and J. Winberg, "Unique Salience of

Maternal Breast Odors for Newborn Infants," *Neuroscience and Biobehavioral Reviews* 23 (1999), 439–449; M. J. Russell, "Human Olfactory Communication," *Nature* 260 (1976), 520–522.

3. I. W. Bushnell, "Mother's Face Recognition in Newborn Infants: Learning and Memory," *Infant and Child Development* 10 (2001), 67–74.

4. J. P. Rushton, R. J. H. Russell, and P. A. Wells, "Genetic Similarity Theory: Beyond Kin Selection," *Behavior Genetics* 14 (1984), 179–193.

5. D. G. Freedman, *Human Sociobiology* (New York: Free Press, 1979); D. M. Brodzinsky and E. Pinderhughes, "Parenting and Child Development in Adoptive Families," in M. Bornstein, ed., *Handbook of Parenting*, vol. 1 (Hillsdale, N.J.: Lawrence Erlbaum, 2002), 279–311; E. M. Hetherington and M. Stanley-Hagan, "Parenting in Divorced and Remarried Families," in M. Bornstein, ed., *Handbook of Parenting*, vol. 3 (Hillsdale, N.J.: Lawrence Erlbaum, 2002), 287–315.

6. J. Bowlby, *Attachment and Loss*, vol. 1 (New York: Basic Books, 1969).

7. M. E. Lamb, R. A. Thompson, W. Gardner, and E. L. Charnov, *Infant-Mother Attachment: The Origins and Developmental Significance of Individual Differences in Strange Situation Behavior* (Hillsdale, N.J.: Lawrence Erlbaum, 1985).

8. L. A. Sroufe, "Infant-Caregiver Attachment and Patterns of Adaptation in Preschool: The Roots of Maladaptation and Competence," in M. Perlmutter, ed., *Minnesota Symposium in Child Psychology*, vol. 16 (Hillsdale, N.J.: Lawrence Erlbaum, 1983), 41–83.

9. For a discussion of the anxiety mothers feel about being apart from their children, a feeling imposed upon them in part by societal views of the mother-child bond, see J. M. Smith, *A Potent Spell: Mother Love and the Power of Fear* (Boston: Houghton Mifflin, 2003).

10. For a discussion of the role the media plays in sensationalizing risks to children, see F. Furedi, *Paranoid Parenting* (Chicago: Chicago Review Press, 2003).

11. See, for example, D. Rapoport and J. Levy, "The Conditions of Life for an Infant Without a Family: The Possibilities and Limitations of a Study in a Day Nursery," *Revue de Neuropsychiatre Infantile et d'Hygiene Mentale de l'Enfance* 25 (1977), 103–116; E. Habinakova, "Mental Development of Children Brought up in Collective Institutions of Socialist Countries," *Psychologia a Patopsychologia Dietata* 9 (1974), 229–240.

12. B. M. Caldwell and H. W. Boyd, "Effective Marketing of Quality Child Care," *Journal of Children in Contemporary Society* 17 (1984),

25–39; for research on maternal deprivation, see J. Bowlby, *Maternal Care and Mental Health* (Geneva: World Health Organization, 1951); R. A. Spitz, "Hospitalism: An Inquiry Into the Genesis of Psychiatric Conditions in Early Childhood," *Psychoanalytic Studies of the Child* 1 (1945), 53–74.

13. A. Crittenden, *The Price of Motherhood: Why the Most Important Job in the World is Still the Least Valued* (New York: Metropolitan Books, 2001).

14. For a more general discussion about American parents' apparent obsession with parenting advice from the "experts," see A. Hulbert, *Raising America: Experts, Parents and a Century of Advice About Children* (New York: Knopf, 2003).

15. J. Belsky, "Emanuel Miller Lecture: Developmental Risks (Still) Associated with Early Child Care," *Journal of Child Psychology and Psychiatry and Allied Disciplines* 42 (2001), 845–859.

16. M. E. Lamb, "Nonparental Child Care," in M. E. Lamb, ed., *Parenting and Child Development in "Nontraditional" Families* (Mahwah, N.J.: Lawrence Erlbaum, 1999), 39–55; see also M. Burchinal, J. Roberts, L. Nabors, and D. Bryant, "Quality of Center Child Care and Infant Cognitive and Language Development," *Child Development* 67 (1996), 606–620; S. Scarr, D. Phillips, and K. McCartney, "Working Mothers and Their Families," *American Psychologist* 44 (1989), 1402–1409.

17. K. McCartney and R. Rosenthal, "Effect Size, Practical Importance, and Social Policy for Children," *Child Development* 71 (2000), 173–180.

18. NICHD Early Child Care Research Network, "Maternal Reasons for Employment, Going to School, or Doing Neither: 1, 6 and 15 Months," *Child Care Data Report* 47 (1994).

19. S. Farkas, A. Duffett, and J. Johnson, *Necessary Compromises: How Parents, Employers, and Children's Advocates View Child Care Today* (New York: Public Agenda, 2000); N. Hellmich, "Never Enough Time for Women's Work," *USA Today,* May 11, 1995, D4; B. C. Robertson, *Forced Labor: What's Wrong with Balancing Work and Family* (Dallas, Tex.: Spence, 2002); NICHD Early Child Care Research Network, "Satisfaction with Employment/School Decisions: 1, 6 and 15 Months," *Child Care Data Report* 36 (1994). In this NICHD study over two-thirds of full-time–employed mothers of six month-old infants indicated that their "ideal situation" would be to work part time (48 percent) or not at all (24 percent).

20. W. B. Fay, "The Great Time Famine," *Demographic and Social Change* 4, n3 (1992), 50; S. M. Bianchi, "Setting the Stage: Work and Family Lives of Americans," in E. Appelbaum, ed., *Balancing Acts: Easing the Burdens and Improving the Options for Working Families* (Washington, DC: Economic Policy Institute, 2000), 13–24; A. E. Winkler, "Earnings of Husbands and Wives in Dual Earner Families," *Monthly Labor Review* vol. 121, no. 4 (April 1998).

21. The conceptualization of working mothers' household responsibilities constituting in effect a second job has been widely discussed, but see, for example, A. Hochschild, *The Second Shift: Working Parents and the Revolution at Home* (New York: Viking, 1989).

22. Hochschild, *The Second Shift.*

23. L. E. Tetrick, R. L. Miles, L. Marcil, and C. M. van Dosen, "Child-Care Difficulties and the Impact on Concentration, Stress and Productivity Among Single and Nonsingle Mothers and Fathers," in G. P. Keita and J. J. Hurrell, eds., *Job Stress in a Changing Workforce: Investigating Gender, Diversity, and Family Issues* (Washington D.C.: American Psychological Association, 1994), 229–239.

24. J. T. Bond, C. Thompson, E. Galinsky, and D. Prottas, *Highlights of the 2002 National Study of the Changing Workforce* (New York: Families and Work Institute, 2002).

25. C. L. Booth, K. A. Clarke-Stewart, D. L. Vandell, K. McCartney, and M. T. Owen, "Child-Care Usage and Mother-Infant 'Quality Time,'" *Journal of Marriage and Family* 64 (2002), 16–26.

26. L. W. Hoffman, L. M. Youngblade, R. L. Coley, A. S. Fuligni, and D. D. Kovacs, *Mothers at Work: Effects on Children's Well Being* (New York: Cambridge University Press, 1999).

27. L. Ahnert, H. Rickert, and M. Lamb, "Shared Caregiving: Comparisons Between Home and Child-Care Settings," *Developmental Psychology* 36 (2000), 339–351.

28. M. J. Zaslow, F. A. Pedersen, J. T. D. Suwalsky, R. L. Cain, and M. Fivel, "The Early Resumption of Employment by Mothers: Implications for Parent-Infant Interaction," *Journal of Applied Developmental Psychology* 6 (1985), 1–16.

29. D. Caruso, "Maternal Employment Status, Mother-Infant Interaction, and Infant Development in Day Care and Non–Day Care Groups," *Child and Youth Care Forum* 25 (1996), 125–134; E. Hock, "Working and Nonworking Mothers and Their Infants: A Comparative Study of Maternal Caregiving Characteristics and Infant Social Behavior," *Merrill-*

Palmer Quarterly 26 (1980), 79–102; J. B. Schubert, S. Bradley-Johnson, and J. Nuttall, "Mother-Infant Communication and Maternal Employment," *Child Development* 51 (1980), 246–249.

30. NICHD Early Child Care Research Network, "Child Care and Mother-Child Interaction in the First Three Years of Life," *Developmental Psychology* 35 (1999), 1399–1413.

31. S. M. Bianchi, "Setting the Stage: Work and Family Lives of Americans," in E. Appelbaum, ed., *Balancing Acts: Easing the Burdens and Improving the Options for Working Families* (Washington, DC: Economic Policy Institute, 2000), 13–24.

32. Booth et al., "Child-Care Usage and Mother-Infant 'Quality Time,' "; Hoffman et al., *Mothers at Work*; F. M. Deutsch, J. L. Lozy, and S. Saxon, "Taking Credit: Couples' Reports of Contributions to Child Care," *Journal of Family Issues* 14 (1993), 421–437; NICHD Early Child Care Research Network, "Factors Associated with Fathers' Caregiving Activities and Sensitivity with Young Children," *Journal of Family Psychology* 14 (2000), 200–219.

33. J. T. Bond, C. Thompson, E. Galinsky, and D. Prottas, *Highlights of the 2002 National Study of the Changing Workforce* (New York: Families and Work Institute, 2002).

34. H. H. Bohen and A. Viveros-Long, *Balancing Jobs and Family Life* (Philadelphia: Temple University Press, 1981).

35. F. M. Deutsch and S. E. Saxon, "The Double Standard of Praise and Criticism for Mothers and Fathers," *Psychology of Women Quarterly* 22 (1998), 665–683; P. Moen, "Women, Work and Family: A Sociological Perspective on Changing Roles," in M. W. Riley, R. L. Kahn, A. Foner, and K. A. Mack, *Age and Structural Lag: Society's Failure to Provide Meaningful Opportunities in Work, Family, and Leisure* (New York: John Wiley, 1994), 151–170.

36. T. A. Whelen and C. M. E. Lally, "Paternal Commitment and Father's Quality of Life," *Journal of Family Studies* 8 (2002), 181–196.

37. Bond et al., *Highlights of the 2002 National Study of the Changing Workforce*.

38. G. Ranson, "Men at Work: Change—or No Change?—In the Era of the 'New Father,' " *Men and Masculinities* 4 (2001), 3–26.

39. E. Sorensen and C. Zibman, "To What Extent Do Children Benefit from Child Support?" (discussion paper 99–11, The Urban Institute, Washington, D.C., 2000), www.urban.org.

40. S. Hofferth and K. G. Anderson, "Are All Dads Equal? Biology Ver-

sus Marriage as a Basis for Paternal Investment," *Journal of Marriage and the Family* 65 (2003), 213–232.

41. M. Weinraub, E. Jaeger, and L. Hoffman, "Predicting Infant Outcome in Families of Employed and Nonemployed Mothers," special issue, *Early Childhood Research Quarterly* 3 (1988), 361–378.

42. NICHD Early Child Care Research Network, "Chronicity of Maternal Depressive Symptoms, Maternal Sensitivity, and Child Functioning at 36 Months," *Developmental Psychology* 35 (1999), 1297–1310; M. A. Pett, B. Vaughan-Cole, and B. E. Wampold, "Maternal Employment and Perceived Stress: Their Impact on Children's Adjustment and Mother-Child Interaction in Young Divorced and Married Families," *Family Relations: Interdisciplinary Journal of Applied Family Studies* 43 (1994), 151–158.

43. M. K. McKim, K. M. Cramer, B. Stuart, and D. L. O'Connor, "Infant Care Decisions and Attachment Security: The Canadian Transition to Child Care Study," *Canadian Journal of Behavioural Science* 31 (1999), 92–106.

44. E. Hock and J. B. Clinger, "Behavior Toward Mother and Stranger of Infants Who Have Experienced Group Day Care, Individual Day Care, or Exclusive Maternal Care," *Journal of Genetic Psychology* 137 (1980), 49–61.

45. J. B. Schubert, S. Bradley-Johnson, and J. Nuttall, "Mother-Infant Communication and Maternal Employment," *Child Development* 51 (1980), 246–249.

46. NICHD Early Child Care Research Network, "Relations Between Family Predictors and Child Outcomes: Are They Weaker for Children in Child Care?," *Developmental Psychology* 34 (1998), 1119–1128.

47. K. McCartney, S. Scarr, A. Rocheleau, D. Phillips, M. Abbott-Shim, M. Eisenberg, N. Keefe, S. Rosenthal, and J. Ruh, "Teacher-Child Interaction and Child-Care Auspices as Predictors of Social Outcomes in Infants, Toddlers, and Preschoolers," *Merrill-Palmer Quarterly* 43 (1997), 426–450.

48. L. W. Hoffman, "Maternal Employment and the Young Child," in M. Perlmutter, ed., *Parent-Child Interaction and Parent-Child Relations in Child Development* (Hillsdale, N.J.: Lawrence Erlbaum, 1984).

49. A. M. Farel, "Effects of Preferred Maternal Roles, Maternal Employment and Sociodemographic Status on School Adjustment and Competence," *Child Development* 51 (1980), 1179–1186.

50. Bond et al., *Highlights of the 2002 National Study of the Changing Workforce.*

51. For example, Hoffman, "Maternal Employment and the Young Child."

52. Hoffman et al., *Mothers at Work.*

53. M. Milkie and P. Peltola, "Playing All the Roles: Gender and the Work-Family Balancing Act," *Journal of Marriage and the Family* 61 (1999), 476–490.

54. Crittenden, *The Price of Motherhood.*

55. E. McCrate, "Working Mothers in a Double Bind" (Economic Policy Institute Briefing Paper #124, May 2002).

56. K. Keniston and the Carnegie Council on Children, *All Our Children* (New York: Harcourt, Brace, Jovanovich, 1977).

57. Milkie and Peltola, "Playing All the Roles: Gender and the Work-Family Balancing Act."

2. THE EVOLUTION OF CHILDCARE IN THE UNITED STATES

1. For more detail on the history of childcare in the United States, see the following sources, from which our description was gleaned. G. Youcha, *Minding the Children: Child Care in America from Colonial Times to the Present* (New York: Scribner, 1995); V. C. Lascarides and B. F. Hinitz, *History of Early Childhood Education* (New York: Falmer Press, 2000); E. D. Cahan and J. Bromer, "Trends in the History of Child Care and Family Support: 1940–2000," in R. P. Weissberg, H. J. Walberg, M. O'Brien and C. Kuster, eds., *Long-Term Trends in the Well-Being of Children and Youth: Issues in Children's and Families Lives* (Washington, D.C.: Child Welfare League of America, 2003), 207–228; S. L. Kagan and M. J. Neuman, "Early Care and Education: Current Issues and Future Strategies," in J. P. Shonkoff and S. J. Meisels, eds., *Handbook of Early Childhood Intervention,* 2nd ed. (New York: Cambridge University Press, 2000), 339–360; E. F. Zigler and E. Gilman, "Not Just Any Care: Shaping a Coherent Child Care Policy," in E. F. Zigler, S. L. Kagan, and N. W. Hall, eds., *Children, Families, and Government: Preparing for the Twenty-First Century* (New York: Cambridge University Press, 1996), 94–116; V. L. Getis and M. A. Vinovskis, "History of Child Care in the United States Before 1950," in M. E. Lamb, K. J. Sternberg, C.-P. Hwang and A. G. Broberg, eds., *Child Care in Context: Cross-Cultural Perspectives* (Hillsdale, N.J.: Lawrence Erlbaum, 1992), 157–302; M. E. Lamb, K. J. Sternberg, and R. D. Ketterlinus, "Child Care in the United States: The Modern Era," in M. E. Lamb, et al., *Child Care in Context: Cross-Cultural Perspectives,* 157–302; G. Miller, "The Expanding Federal Role in Child Care," in S. S. Chehrazi, ed., *Psychosocial Issues in Day Care* (Washington, D.C.: Ameri-

can Psychiatric Association, 1990), 257–273; E. D. Cahan, *Past Caring: A History of U.S. Preschool Care and Education for the Poor, 1820–1965* (New York: National Center for Children in Poverty, 1989); S. Scarr and R. A. Weinberg, "The Early Childhood Enterprise: Care and Education of the Young," special issue, *American Psychologist* 41 (1986), 1140–1146.

2. U.S. Department of Education, National Center for Education Statistics, Preprimary Enrollment (Washington, D.C., various years); U.S. Bureau of the Census, Current Population Survey (Washington, D.C., October 2002), table 43; enrollment of three-, four-, and five-year-old children in preprimary programs, by level and control of program and by attendance status [in thousands], October 1965 to October 2001, http://nces.ed.gov.

3. C. Etaugh, "Effects of Nonmaternal Care on Children: Research Evidence and Popular Views," *Annual Progress in Child Psychiatry and Child Development* (1981), 392–411.

4. K. Smith, "Who's Minding the Kids? Child Care Arrangements: Spring 1997," *Current Population Reports* (Washington, D.C.: U.S. Census Bureau, 2002), 70–86.

5. U.S. Bureau of the Census, *Child Care Arrangements for Preschoolers by Family Characteristics and Employment Status of Mother: Spring 1999: Percentages* (Washington, D.C., 2003).

6. The prediction of a two-thirds childcare participation rate by 2000 has been widely quoted, but see, for example, S. Hofferth, and D. Phillips, "Child Care in the United States: 1970 to 1995," *Journal of Marriage and the Family* 49 (1987), 559–571; W. B. Johnston and A. H. Packer, "Work and Workers for the 21st Century," *Workforce 2000* (Indianapolis: Indiana Hudson Institute, 1987), HI-3796-RR.

7. U.S. General Accounting Office, *Early Childhood Programs: Multiple Programs and Overlapping Target Groups* (Washington, D.C., 1995).

8. U.S. General Accounting Office, *Child Care Funding* (Washington, D.C., 2001), GAO-01-293.

9. W. S. Barnett, "Long-Term Effects of Early Childhood Programs on Cognitive and School Outcomes," *The Future of Children* 5, (1995), 25–50; N. Zill, G. Resnick, R. H. McKey, C. Clark, D. Connell, J. Swartz, R. O'Brien, and M. D'Elio, *Head Start Program Performance Measures: Second Progress Report* (Washington, D.C.: U.S. Department of Health and Human Services, 1998).

10. Calculations by the Children's Defense Fund using data from the U.S. Department of Health and Human Services, Head Start Bureau on

Head Start enrollment in FY2000, and U.S. Census Bureau on poverty rates by single year of age for 1999.

11. S. E. Rosenkoetter and N. E. Cohen, "The Family Supportiveness of Federal Early Care and Education Policy," in C. J. Dunst and M. Wolery, eds., *Family Policy and Practice in Early Child Care* (Greenwich, Conn.: JAI Press, 1997), 11–39; U.S. Administration for Children and Families, press release, "Early Head Start Shows Significant Results for Low-Income Children and Families," www.acf.dhhs.gov/news (accessed 1/12/01).

12. For a more comprehensive review of federal initiatives in financing childcare in the United States, see data provided by the Administration for Children and Families, Department of Health and Human Services, www.acf.hhs.gov; House Committee on Ways and Means, *Child Care: The 2000 Green Book* (Washington, D.C., 2000).

13. U.S. Department of Health and Human Services, Administration for Children and Families, *Child Care and Development Fund (CCDF) Report to Congress-Fiscal Year 2001* (Washington, D.C., 2001).

14. K. Moore, M. Zaslow, M. Coiro, S. Miller, Child Trends, and E. Magenheim, *The JOBS Evaluation: How Well Are They Faring? AFDC Families with Preschool-Aged Children in Atlanta at the Outset of the JOBS Evaluation* (Washington, D.C., U.S. Department of Health and Human Services, 1995).

15. U.S. House Committee on Ways and Means, *Overview of Entitlement Programs: The 1996 Green Book* (Washington, D.C., 1996).

16. U.S. House Committee on Ways and Means, *Overview of Entitlement Programs: The 1998 Green Book* (Washington, D.C., 1998).

17. Moore et al., *The JOBS Evaluation: How Well are They Faring?*

18. Data are based on state regulations as of August 2003. A state by state listing of childcare licensing requirements can be obtained from the National Child Care Information Center, www.nccic.org (accessed August 2003).

19. G. Morgan and S. L. Azer, *What's in a Name? Family Child Care Definitions* (Boston, Mass.: Wheelock College Center for Career Development in Early Care and Education, 2000).

20. A state by state listing of licensing thresholds can be found in Morgan and Azer, *What's in a Name?*

21. S. LeMoine, "Definition of Licensed Family Child Care Homes," National Child Care Information Center (NCCIC), http://nccic.org/pubs/definition-fcc.html (August 2003).

22. S. LeMoine, *Child Care Licensing Requirements: Minimum Early Childhood Education (ECE) Preservice Qualifications, Orientation/Initial Licensure, and Annual Ongoing Training Hours for Family Child Care Providers,* National Child Care Information Center (NCCIC), http://nccic. org (August 2003).

23. K. A. Clarke-Stewart, "Day Care in the U.S.A.," in P. Moss and E. Melhuish, eds., *Current Issues in Day Care for Young Children: Research and Policy Implications* (London: Her Majesty's Stationery Office, 1991), 35–60.

24. K. A. Clarke-Stewart, D. L. Vandell, M. Burchinal, M. O'Brien, and K. McCartney, "Do Regulable Features of Child-Care Homes Affect Children's Development?" *Early Childhood Research Quarterly* 17 (2002), 52–86.

3. CHILDCARE IN THE UNITED STATES TODAY

1. For example, see K. Smith, "Who's Minding the Kids? Child Care Arrangements: Spring 1997," *Current Population Reports* (Washington, D.C.: U.S. Bureau of the Census, 2002), 70–86; Urban Institute, *Primary Child Care Arrangements of Employed Parents: Findings from the 1999 National Survey of America's Families* (Washington, D.C.: Urban Institute Press, 2002); Federal Interagency Forum on Child and Family Statistics, *America's Children: Key National Indicators of Well-Being* (Washington, D.C., 2002); Urban Institute, *Child Care Arrangements for Children Under Five: Variation Across States* (Washington, D.C.: Urban Institute Press, 2002).

2. Federal Interagency Forum on Child and Family Statistics, *America's Children: Key National Indicators of Well-Being,* 73, table POP50, http://childstats.gov; U.S. Bureau of the Census, "America's Families and Living Arrangements," March 2000 and March 2002 Supplement, *Current Population Reports* (Washington, D.C., 2002).

3. B. D. Whitehead and D. Popenoe, *The State of Our Unions: The Social Health of Marriage in America, 2001* (New Brunswick, N.J.: National Marriage Project at Rutgers University, 2001); http://marriage. rutgers.edu.

4. J. C. Day, "Projections of the Number of Households and Families in the United States, 1995 to 2010," *Current Population Reports* (Washington, D.C.: U.S. Bureau of the Census, 1996), 25–1129.

5. A more complete discussion of the welfare reform initiatives of the 1990s can be found in Chapter 2.

6. J. R. Goldstein, "The Leveling of Divorce in the United States," *Demography* 36 (1999), 409–414; R. M. Kreider and J. M. Fields, "Number, Timing and Duration of Marriages and Divorces: 1996," *Current Population Reports* (Washington, D.C.: U.S. Bureau of the Census, 2002), 70–80.

7. A. Thornton, "Changing Attitudes Toward Family Issues in the United States," *Journal of Marriage and the Family* 53 (1989), 873–893.

8. The General Social Survey, conducted by the National Opinion Research Center (University of Chicago, 1994).

9. Whitehead and Popenoe, *The State of Our Unions;* Federal Interagency Forum on Child and Family Statistics, *America's Children: Key National Indicators of Well-Being,* 73, table POP5.

10. Whitehead and Popenoe, *The State of Our Unions.*

11. S. J. Ventura, "Births to Unmarried Mothers: United States, 1980–92," *Vital and Health Statistics Series* 21, no. 53 (Washington, D.C.: U.S. Department of Health and Human Services, 1995).

12. National Center for Health Statistics, 1990–2000 Natality Data Set CD, Series 21, nos. 2–9, 11–12, and 14 (Hyattsville, Md.: 2000; S. J. Ventura and C. A. Bachrach, "Nonmarital Childbearing in the United States, 1940–99," *National Vital Statistics Reports* 48, no. 16 (2000).

13. Survey Research Center, University of Michigan, "Monitoring the Future," in Whitehead and Popenoe, eds., *The State of Our Unions.*

14. Whitehead and Popenoe, *The State of Our Unions.*

15. Population Reference Bureau, analysis of data from U.S. Bureau of the Census, Census Summary File 3, 2002, tables PCT70A-G and P46.

16. U.S. Bureau of the Census, *Median Income of Families by Type of Family in Current and Constant (1998) Dollars, 1970 to 1998,* Statistical Abstract of the United States (Washington, D.C., 2000). Median family income for married couples with only the husband in the paid labor force was $36,720 in 1970 (adjusted for constant 1998 dollars) and $37,161 in 1998.

17. S. M. Bianchi, "Setting the Stage: Work and Family Lives of Americans," in E. Appelbaum, ed., *Balancing Acts: Easing the Burdens and Improving the Options for Working Families* (Washington, D.C.: Economic Policy Institute, 2000), 13–24; A. E. Winkler, "Earnings of Husbands and Wives in Dual Earner Families," *Monthly Labor Review* 121 (1998), 42–48.

18. P. Cattan, "The Effect of Working Wives on the Incidence of Poverty," *Monthly Labor Review* 121 (1998), 22–29; T. W. Hale, *A Profile of the Working Poor, 1995* (Washington, D.C.: U.S. Bureau of Labor, 1997).

19. NICHD Early Child Care Research Network, "Nonmaternal Care and Family Factors in Early Development: An Overview of the NICHD Study of Early Child Care," *Applied Developmental Psychology* 22 (2001), 457–492.

20. B. Bluestone and S. Rose, "Overworked and Underemployed: Unraveling an Economic Enigma," *The American Prospect* 8, (1997), www.prospect.org.

21. U.S. Bureau of the Census, *Married-Couple Families with Wives' Earnings Greater Than Husbands' Earnings, 1981 to 2001* (selected years), www.census.gov (accessed 9/30/02).

22. International Labour Organization statistics, *Gender: Equality Between Men and Women,* www.ilo.org.

23. S. Burggraf, *The Feminine Economy and Economic Man: Reviving the Role of Family in the Post-Industrial Age* (Reading, Mass.: Addison-Wesley, 1997).

24. J. Waldfogel, "Understanding the 'Family Gap' in Pay for Women with Children," *Journal of Economic Perspectives* 12 (1998), 137–156; J. Waldfogel, "The Family Gap for Young Women in the United States and Britain," *Journal of Labor Economics* 11 (1998), 505–519.

25. J. Jacobsen and L. Levin, "The Effects of Intermittent Labor Force Attachment on Women's Earnings," *Monthly Labor Review* 118, no. 9 (1995), 14–19; R. G. Wood, M. E. Corcoran, and P. N. Courant, "Pay Differentials Among the Highly Paid: The Male-Female Earnings Gap in Lawyers' Salaries," *Journal of Labor Economics* 2 (1993), 417–441.

26. International Labour Organization, "Maternity Leave Around the World," www.ilo.org, a list of the maternity leave policies of countries around the world, is available at www.womenz.org.

27. K. Smith, B. Downs, and M. O'Connell, "Maternity Leave and Employment Patterns: 1961–1995," *Current Population Reports* (Washington, D.C.: U.S. Bureau of the Census, 2001), 70–79.

28. Commission on Family and Medical Leave, *A Workable Balance: Report to Congress on Family Medical Leave Policies* (Washington D.C.: U.S. Department of Labor, 1996).

29. D. Cantor, J. Kerwin, K. Levin, S. Heltemes, and D. Becher, *The Impact of the Family and Medical Leave Act: A Survey of Employers* (Rockville, Md.: Westat, 1995).

30. F. Goldscheider, D. Hogan, S. Short, and B. Miller, *The Growing Isolation of Parenthood in the Life Course and in the Family, 1880–1990* (Chicago, Ill.: American Sociological Association, 2002); see also R. A.

Levine, S. Dixon, S. LeVine, A. Richman, P. Leiderman, C. Keefer, and T. B. Brazelton, *Child Care and Cultures: Lessons From Africa* (New York: Cambridge University Press, 1994).

31. See, for example, E. L. Schor, "Early Brain Development and Child Care," *Healthy Child Care America* 1, 3 (1999), 5–8; R. Shore, *Rethinking the Brain: New Insights Into Early Development* (New York: Families and Work Institute, 1997).

32. U.S. Department of Education, National Center for Education Statistics, Preprimary Enrollment, various years (Washington, D.C.); and U.S. Bureau of the Census, Current Population Survey, unpublished data (Washington, D.C., 2000).

33. D. R. Powell, "Parents' Contributions to the Quality of Child Care Arrangements," *Advances in Early Education and Day Care* 9 (1997), 133–155.

34. P. A. Britner, and D. A. Phillips, "Predictors of Parent and Provider Satisfaction with Child Day Care Dimensions: A Comparison of Center-Based and Family Child Day Care," special issue, *Child Welfare* 74 (1995), 135–1168.

35. V. Peyton, A. Jacobs, M. O'Brien, and C. Roy, "Reasons for Choosing Child Care: Associations with Family Factors, Quality, and Satisfaction," *Early Childhood Research Quarterly* 16 (2001), 191–208.

36. Powell, "Parents' Contributions to the Quality of Child Care Arrangements."

37. D. R. Powell and J. W. Eisenstadt, "Finding Child Care: A Study of Parents' Search Processes," report for the Ford Foundation, June 1980; S. Auerbach-Fink, "Mothers' Expectations of Child Care," *Young Children* 32 (1977), 12–21.

38. C. R. Hill, *The Child Care Market: A Review of the Evidence and Implications for Federal Policy,* report for the Education Resources Information Center, 1977, ED 156 352.

39. S. Low and P. G. Spindler, "Child Care Arrangements of Working Mothers in the United States," (Washington, D.C.: U.S. Children's Bureau and U.S. Women's Bureau, 1968).

40. The Children's Foundation, "The 2003 Family Child Care Licensing Study," Washington, D.C.: The Children's Foundation, 2003.

41. E. E. Kisker, S. L. Hofferth, D. A. Phillips, and E. Farquhar, *A Profile of Child Care Settings: Early Education and Care in 1990,* report prepared for the U.S. Department of Education, Contract No. LC88090001, 1991.

42. E. Galinsky, C. Howes, S. Kontos, and M. Shinn, *The Study of Chil-*

dren in Family Child Care and Relative Care: Highlights of Findings (New York: Families and Work Institute, 1994).

43. See for example, Galinsky et al., *The Study of Children in Family Child Care and Relative Care;* Kisker et al., *A Profile of Child Care Settings;* S. L. Hofferth, K. A. Shauman, R. R. Henke, and J. West, "Characteristics of Children's Early Care and Education Programs: Data from the 1995 National Household Education Survey" (Washington, D.C.: U.S. Department of Education, 1998), 98–128.

44. K. A. Clarke-Stewart, C. P. Gruber, and L. M. Fitzgerald, *Children at Home and in Day Care* (Hillsdale, N.J.: Lawrence Erlbaum, 1994).

45. The Children's Foundation, "The 2003 Child Care Center Licensing Study," Washington, D.C.: The Children's Foundation, 2003.

46. M. C. Whitebook, C. Howes, and D. A. Phillips, *Who Cares? Child Care Teachers and the Quality of Care in America,* final report for the National Child Care Staffing Study (Oakland, Calif., 1990).

47. F. L. Sonenstein, G. J. Gates, S. Schmidt, and N. Bolshun, *Primary Child Care Arrangements of Employed Parents: Findings from the 1999 National Survey of America's Families* (Washington, D.C.: Urban Institute Press, 2002); U.S. Bureau of the Census, "Primary Child Care Arrangements of Preschoolers of Employed Mothers: Spring 1999," Survey of Income and Program Participation Panel, Wave 10, 1996, internet release date: January 24, 2003. The figures reported here are based on the most recent available data on childcare use and reflect an average of the results of two comprehensive national surveys. The results found in these two surveys were very similar, and modest differences in some cases are most likely attributable to the slightly different ways in which different types of childcare were divided in the two surveys.

48. M. R. Burchinal, S. L. Ramey, M. K. Reid, and J. Jaccard, "Early Child Care Experiences and Their Association with Family and Child Characteristics During Middle Childhood," *Early Childhood Research Quarterly* 10 (1995), 33–61; C. J. Erdwins and L. C. Buffardi, "Different Types of Day Care and Their Relationship to Maternal Satisfaction, Perceived Support, and Role Conflict," *Child and Youth Care Forum* 23 (1994), 41–54; R. Fuqua and D. Labensohn, "Parents as Consumers of Child Care," *Family Relations* 35 (1996), 295–303; A. Huston, Y. Chang, and L. Gennetian, "Family and Individual Predictors of Child Care Use by Low-Income Families in Different Policy Contexts," *Early Childhood Research Quarterly* 17 (2002), 441–469; National Center for Education Statistics, *1996 National Household Education Survey* (Washington, D.C.: U.S. Department of Education, 1996).

49. NICHD Early Child Care Research Network, "Type of Child Care and Children's Development at 54 Months," *Early Childhood Research Quarterly* 19 (2004), 203–230.

50. A. S. Johansen, A. Leibowitz, and L. J. Waite, "The Importance of Child-Care Characteristics to Choice of Care," *Journal of Marriage and the Family* 58 (1996), 759–772.

51. NICHD Early Child Care Research Network, "Familial Factors Associated with the Characteristics of Nonmaternal Care for Infants," *Journal of Marriage and the Family* 59 (1997), 389–408.

52. Sonenstein et al., *Primary Child Care Arrangements of Employed Parents.*

53. B. Fuller, S. D. Holloway, and X. Liang, "Family Selection of Child-Care Centers: The Influence of Household Support, Ethnicity, and Parental Practices," *Child Development* 67 (1996), 3320–3337.

54. A. R. Pence and H. Goelman, "Who Cares for the Child in Day Care? An Examination of Caregivers from Three Types of Care," *Early Childhood Research Quarterly* 2 (1987), 312–334.

55. Erdwins and Buffardi, "Different Types of Day Care"; Huston et al., "Family and Individual Predictors of Child Care Use."

56. Data from annual licensing surveys compiled by The Children's Foundation.

57. U.S. General Accounting Office, "Welfare Reform: Implications of Increased Work Participation for Child Care" (Washington, D.C.: May 1997), GAO/HEHS-97-75.

58. K. Schulman, "The High Cost of Child Care Puts Quality Care Out of Reach for Many Families," The Children's Defense Fund (Washington, D.C.: 2000), www.childrensdefense.org.

59. L. Giannarelli and J. Barsimantov, *Child Care Expenses of America's Families* (Washington, D.C.: Urban Institute Press, 2000).

60. K. Smith, "Who's Minding the Kids?"

61. U.S. Department of Health and Human Services, *Access to Child Care for Low-Income Working Families* (1999), www.acf.dhhs.gov.

62. S. Oskamp, Editor's Note, *Journal of Social Issues* 47 (1991).

63. M. D. Keyserling, *Windows on Day Care: A Report on the Findings of Members of the National Council of Jewish Women on Day Care Needs and Services in Their Communities,* report for the Educational Resources Information Center, 1972, ED 063 027).

64. Galinsky et al., "*The Study of Children in Family Child Care and Relative Care.*"

65. Cost, Quality, and Child Outcomes Study Team, *Cost, Quality, and Child Outcomes in Child Care Centers*, 2nd ed., (Denver: University of Colorado, 1995; Whitebook et al., *Who Cares? Child Care Teachers and the Quality of Care in America;* See also J. M. Love, "Quality in Child Care Centers," *Early Childhood Research and Policy Briefs* 1 (1997), for a summary of six studies reporting widespread poor quality in childcare centers.

4. STUDYING CHILDCARE

1. Notable among the few studies that did follow an experimental design are the Abecedarian Project at the Frank Porter Graham Center in North Carolina, directed by C. Ramey, D. Farran, and associates; and the Milwaukee Project in Wisconsin, directed by R. Heber and H. Garber.

2. M. R. Burchinal, D. Cryer, R. M. Clifford, and C. Howes, "Caregiver Training and Classroom Quality in Child Care Centers," *Applied Developmental Science* 6 (2002), 2–11; E. S. Peisner-Feinberg, M. R. Burchinal, R. M. Clifford, M. L. Culkin, C. Howes, S. L. Kagan, and N. Yazejian, "The Relation of Preschool Child-Care Quality to Children's Cognitive and Social Developmental Trajectories Through Second Grade," *Child Development* 72 (2001), 1534–1553; E. S. Peisner-Feinberg, M. R. Burchinal, R. M. Clifford, M. L. Culkin, C. Howes, S. L. Kagan, N. Yazejian, P. Byler, J. Rustici, and J. Zelazo, *The Children of The Cost, Quality, and Outcomes Study Go to School: Technical Report* (Chapel Hill, N.C.: Frank Porter Graham Child Development Center, 2000).

3. T. Harms, D. Cryer, and R. M. Clifford, *Infant/Toddler Environment Rating Scale* (New York: Teachers Press, 1990); T. Harms and R. M. Clifford, *Early Childhood Environment Rating Scale* (New York: Teachers College Press, 1980).

4. J. Arnett, "Caregivers in Day-Care Centers: Does Training Matter?" *Journal of Applied Developmental Psychology* 10 (1989), 541–552; D. Stipek, D. Daniels, D. Galluzzo, and S. Milburn, "Characterizing Early Childhood Education Programs for Poor and Middle-Class Children," *Early Childhood Research Quarterly* 7 (1992), 1–19; C. Howes and P. Stewart, "Child's Play with Adults, Toys, and Peers: An Examination of Family and Childcare Influences," *Developmental Psychology* 23 (1987), 423–430.

5. L. M. Dunn and L. M. Dunn, *Peabody Picture Vocabulary Test,* rev. ed. (Circle Pines, Minn.: American Guidance Service, 1981).

6. R. W. Woodcock and M. B. Johnson, *Woodcock-Johnson Psycho-Educational Battery,* rev. ed. (Allen, Tex.: DLM, 1990).

7. E. S. Schaefer, M. Edgerton, and M. Aaronson, *Classroom Behavior Inventory* (Chapel Hill: University of North Carolina, 1978).

8. R. C. Pianta, ed., *Beyond the Parent: The Role of Other Adults in Children's Lives* (San Francisco: Jossey-Bass, 1992), 25–39.

9. C. Howes, E. Smith, and E. Galinsky, *The Florida Child Care Quality Improvement Study: Interim Report* (New York: Families and Work Institute, 1995); C. Howes, E. Galinsky, M. Shinn, L. Gulcur, M. Clements, A. Sibley, M. Abbott-Shim, and J. McCarthy, *The Florida Child Care Quality Improvement Study: 1996 Report* (New York: Families and Work Institute, 1996).

10. E. Waters and K. Deane, "Defining and Assessing Individual Differences in Attachment Relationships: Q-Methodology and the Organization of Behavior in Infancy and Early Childhood," in I. Bretherton and E. Waters, eds., "Growing Points of Attachment Theory and Research," *Monographs of the Society for Research in Child Development* 50 (1985) 1–2, no. 209, 41–65.

11. L. V. Feagans and D. C. Farran, *The Adaptive Language Inventory* (Chapel Hill, N.C.: The Frank Porter Graham Child Development Center, 1979); C. Howes, "Peer Play Scale as an Index of Complexity of Peer Interaction," *Developmental Psychology* 16 (1983), 371–372; J. L. Rubenstein and C. Howes, "Social-Emotional Development of Toddlers in Day Care: The Role of Peers and of Individual Differences," in S. Kilmer, ed., *Advances in Early Education and Day Care,* vol. 3, (Greenwich, Conn.: JAI Press, 1983), 13–45.

12. L. B. Behar, "The Preschool Behavior Questionnaire," *Journal of Abnormal Child Psychology* 5 (1977), 265–275.

13. Additional details about the history and current status of the study can be found at the study's Web site, www.nichd.nih.gov or secc.rti.org.

14. B. Caldwell and R. H. Bradley, *Home Observation for Measurement of the Environment* (Little Rock, Ark.: Center for Research on Teaching and Learning, 1984). This instrument was adapted for home childcare settings.

15. M. Abbott-Shim and A. Sibley, *Assessment Profile for Early Childhood Programs* (Atlanta, Ga.: Quality Assistance, 1987); M. Abbott-Shim and A. Sibley, *Assessment Profile for Homes with Young Children,* research ed. (Atlanta, Ga.: Quality Assistance, 1993); M. Abbott-Shim, A. Sibley, and J. Neel, *Assessment Profile for Early Childhood Programs,* research ed. (Atlanta, Ga.: Quality Assistance, 1992).

16. NICHD Early Child Care Research Network, "Characteristics of Infant Child Care: Factors Contributing to Positive Caregiving," *Early Childhood Research Quarterly* 11 (1996), 269–306; NICHD Early Child

Care Research Network, "Characteristics and Quality of Child Care for Toddlers and Preschoolers," *Applied Developmental Science* 4 (2000), 116–135.

17. M. C. Hyson, K. Hirsh-Pasek, and L. Rescorla, "The Classroom Practices Inventory: An Observation Instrument Based on NAEYC's Guidelines for Developmentally Appropriate Practices for 4- and 5-Year Old Children," *Early Childhood Research Quarterly* 5 (1990), 475–494.

18. E. S. Schaefer and M. Edgerton, "Parent and Child Correlates of Parental Modernity," in I. E. Sigel, ed., *Parental Belief Systems* (Hillsdale, N.J.: Lawrence Erlbaum, 1985), 287–318; J. K. Posner and D. L. Vandell, "Low-Income Children's After-School Care: Are There Beneficial Effects of After-School Programs?" *Child Development* 65 (1994), 440–456; E. Greenberger and W. A. Goldberg, "Work, Parenting, and the Socialization of Children," *Developmental Psychology* 25 (1989), 22–35; Caldwell and Bradley, *Home Observation for Measurement of the Environment.*

19. M. Ainsworth, M. Blehar, E. Waters, and S. Wall, *Patterns of Attachment: Observations in the Strange Situation and at Home* (Hillsdale, N.J.: Lawrence Erlbaum, 1978); Waters and Deane, "Defining and Assessing Individual Differences in Attachment Relationships: Q-Methodology and the Organization of Behavior in Infancy and Early Childhood"; T. M. Achenbach, C. Edelbrock, and C. T. Howell, "Empirically Based Assessment of Behavioral/Emotional Problems of 2- and 3-Year-Old Children," *Journal of Abnormal Child Psychology* 15 (1987), 629–650; T. M. Achenbach, *Manual for the Child Behavior Checklist/4–18 and 1991 Profile* (Burlington: University of Vermont Department of Psychiatry, 1991); T. M. Achenbach, *Manual for the Teacher's Report Form and 1991 Profile* (Burlington: University of Vermont Department of Psychiatry, 1991).

20. N. Bayley, *Bayley Scales of Infant Development* (New York: Psychological Corporation, 1969); N. Bayley, *Bayley Scales of Infant Development,* 2nd. ed. (San Antonio, Tex.: Psychological Corporation, 1993); B. A. Bracken, *Bracken Basic Concept Scales* (San Antonio, Tex.: Psychological Corporation, 1984); J. Reynell, *Reynell Developmental Language Scales,* U.S. ed. (Los Angeles: Western Psychological Services, 1991); R. W. Woodcock and M. B. Johnson, *Woodcock-Johnson Psycho-Educational Battery—Revised* (Allen, TX: DLM, 1989).

5. EFFECTS OF CARE

1. C. T. Ramey, D. MacPhee, and K. O. Yeates, "Preventing Developmental Retardation: A General Systems Model," in L. Bond and J. Joffe, eds., *Facilitating Infant and Early Child Care Development* (Hanover,

N.H.: University Press of New England, 1982), 343–401; H. B. Robinson and N. M. Robinson, "Longitudinal Development of Very Young Children in a Comprehensive Day Care Program: The First Two Years," *Child Development* 42 (1971), 1673–1683.

2. C. L. Booth and J. F. Kelly, "Child Care Effects on the Development of Toddlers with Special Needs," *Early Childhood Research Quarterly* 17 (2002), 171–196; K. R. Thornburg, P. Pearl, D. Crompton, and J. M. Ispa, "Development of Kindergarten Children Based on Child Care Arrangements," *Early Childhood Research Quarterly* 5, (1990), 27–42.

3. A. M. Hardy and M. G. Fowler, "Child Care Arrangements and Repeated Ear Infections in Young Children," *American Journal of Public Health* 83 (1993), 1321–1325; E. S. Hurwitz, W. J. Gunn, P. F. Pinsky, and L. B. Shonberger, "Risk of Respiratory Illness Associated with Day Care Attendance: A Nationwide Study," *Pediatrics* 87 (1991), 62–69; P. J. Louhiala, N. Jaakkola, R. Ruotsalainen, and J. J. Jaakkola, "Day Care Centers and Diarrhea: A Public Health Perspective," *Journal of Pediatrics* 131 (1997), 476–479; J. L. Paradise, H. E. Rockette, K. Colborn, B. S. Bernard, C. G. Smith, M. Kurs-Lasky, and J. E. Janosky, "Otitis Media in 2,253 Pittsburgh-Area Infants: Prevalence and Risk Factors During the First Two Years of Life," *Pediatrics* 99 (1997), 318–333.

4. S. S. Aronson, "Health and Safety in Child Care," in S. S. Chehrazi, ed., *Psychosocial Issues in Day Care* (Washington, D.C.: American Psychiatric Press, 1990), 177–191; E. K. Oremland, "Childhood Illness and Day Care," in S. S. Chehrazi, ed., *Psychosocial Issues in Day Care,* 193–202.

5. C. Arnold, S. Makintube, and G. R. Istre, "Day Care Attendance and Other Risk Factors For Invasive Haemophilus Influenza Type B Disease," *American Journal of Epidemiology* 138 (1993), 333–340; R. R. Reves, A. L. Morrow, A. V. Bartlett, C. J. Caruso, R. L. Plumb, B. T. Lu, and L. K. Pickering, "Children Care Increases the Risk of Clinic Visits For Acute Diarrhea and Diarrhea Due to Rotavirus," *American Journal of Epidemiology* 137 (1993), 97–107.

6. J. Kotch, *Reduction in Transmission of Infectious Disease in Childcare Settings,* Grant #MCJ-37111, final report submitted to the Maternal and Child Health Research Program, Maternal and Child Health Bureau (1990).

7. NICHD Early Child Care Research Network, "Child Care and Common Communicable Illnesses: Results from the National Institute of Child Health and Human Development Study of Early Child Care, *Archives of Pediatrics and Adolescent Medicine* 155 (2001) 481–488; NICHD Early Child Care Research Network "Child Care and Common

Communicable Illnesses, Ages 37 to 54 Months," *Archives of Pediatrics and Adolescent Medicine* 157 (2003), 196–200.

8. T. Ball, C. Holberg, M. Aldous, F. Martinez, and A. Wright, "Influence of Attendance at Day Care on the Common Cold from Birth Through 13 Years of Age," *Archives of Pediatrics and Adolescent Medicine* 156 (2002), 121–126.

9. T. M. Ball, J. A. Castro-Rodriguez, K. A. Griffith, C. J. Holberg, F. E. Martinez, and A. L. Wright, "Siblings, Day-Care Attendance, and the Risk of Asthma and Wheezing During Childhood," *New England Journal of Medicine* 343 (2000), 538–543.

10. NICHD Early Child Care Research Network, "Asthma Pathogenesis: Child Care, Parenting Stress, and the Productive Activity Hypothesis" (forthcoming). Asthma diagnosed earlier than four and a half years was not related to childcare attendance.

11. C. D. Hayes, P. L. Palmer, and M. J. Zaslow, eds., *Who Cares For America's Children? Childcare Policy for the 1990s* (Washington, D.C.: National Academy Press, 1990).

12. C. L. Creps and L. Vernon-Feagans, "Infant Daycare and Otitis Media: Multiple Influences on Children's Later Development," *Journal of Applied Developmental Psychology* 21 (2000), 357–378.

13. D. L. Vandell, V. K. Henderson, and K. S. Wilson, "A Longitudinal Study of Children with Day-Care Experiences of Varying Quality," *Child Development* 59 (1988), 1286–1292; E. C. Melhuish, E. Lloyd, S., Martin, and A. Mooney, "Type of Child Care at 18 Months-II: Relations with Cognitive and Language Development," *Journal of Child Psychology and Psychiatry* 31 (1990), 861–870.

14. B. Andersson, "Effects of Public Day Care: A Longitudinal Study," *Child Development* 60 (1989), 857–866; M. Burchinal, M. Lee, and C. Ramey, "Type of Day Care and Preschool Intellectual Development in Disadvantaged Children," *Child Development* 60 (1989), 128–137; K. A. Clarke-Stewart, C. P. Gruber, and L. M. Fitzgerald, *Children at Home and in Day Care* (Hillsdale, N.J.: Lawrence Erlbaum, 1994).

15. M. E. Lamb, "Nonparental Child Care: Context, Quality, Correlates," in W. Damon, I. E. Sigel, and K. A. Renninger, eds., *Handbook of Child Psychology,* vol. 4, *Child Psychology in Practice,* 5th ed. (New York: John Wiley and Sons, 1998), 73–134; M. E. Lamb, "Nonparental Child Care," in M. E. Lamb, ed., *Parenting and Child Development in "Nontraditional" Families* (Mahwah, N.J.: Lawrence Erlbaum, 1999), 39–55 for findings regarding advantages and high-quality programs; K. Sylva, E. Melhuish, P. Sammons, I. Siraj-Blatchford, B. Taggart, and K. Elliot,

The Effective Provision of Pre-School Education (EPPE) Project: Findings from the Pre-School Period (London: University of London, 2003); G. W. Ritter and R. C. Turner, "The Impact of Day Care on School Readiness: Using New Data to Examine the Controversy" (paper presented at the biennial meeting of the Society for Research in Child Development, Tampa, Fla., April 2003) for findings regarding advantages of community-based programs.

16. A. G. Broberg, H. Wessels, M. E. Lamb, and C.-P. Hwang, "Effects of Day Care on the Development of Cognitive Abilities in 8-Year-Olds: A Longitudinal Study," *Developmental Psychology* 33 (1997), 62–69 for Swedish study; J. M. Bos and R. C. Granger, "Estimating Effects of Day Care Use on Child Outcomes: Evidence from the New Chance Demonstration" (paper presented at the biennial meeting of the Society for Research in Child Development, Albuquerque, N. Mex., April, 1999) for U.S. study.

17. Lamb, "Nonparental Child Care: Context, Quality, Correlates." However, Differences are not always found; see O. Erel, Y. Oberman, and N. Yirmiya, "Maternal Versus Nonmaternal Care and Seven Domains of Children's Development," *Psychological Bulletin* 126 (2000), 727–747.

18. NICHD Early Child Care Research Network, "The Relation of Child Care to Cognitive and Language Development," *Child Development* 71, (2000), 960–980.

19. NICHD Early Child Care Research Network, "The Relation of Child Care to Cognitive and Language Development"; Andersson, "Effects of Public Day Care"; Bos and Granger, "Estimating Effects of Day Care Use on Child Outcomes"; Clarke-Stewart et al., *Children at Home and in Day Care.*

20. E. C. Melhuish, "Research on Day Care For Young Children in the United Kingdom," in E. C. Melhuish and P. Moss, eds., *Day Care for Young Children: International Perspectives* (London: Routledge, 1991); T. Field, W. Masi, S. Goldstein, S. Perry, and S. Parl, "Infant Day Care Facilitates Preschool Social Behavior," *Early Childhood Research Quarterly* 3 (1988), 341–359; Ramey et al., "Preventing Developmental Retardation."

21. T. Aureli and N. Colecchia, "Day Care Experience and Free Play Behavior in Preschool Children," *Journal of Applied Developmental Psychology* 17 (1996), 1–17.

22. C. O. Eckerman and K. Peterman, "Peers and Infant Social/Communicative Development," in Gavin Bremner and Alan Fogel, eds., *Blackwell Handbook of Infant Development* (Malden, Mass.: Blackwell, 2001), 326–350.

23. T. M. Field, "Quality Infant Day-Care and Grade School Behavior and Performance," *Child Development* 62 (1991), 863–870.

24. J. J. Campbell, M. E. Lamb, and C.-P. Hwang, "Early Child-Care Experiences and Children's Social Competence Between 1.5 and 15 Years of Age," *Applied Developmental Science* 4 (2000), 166–175.

25. Some studies report no differences in peer skills: S. M. Hegland and M. K. Rix, "Aggression and Assertiveness in Kindergarten Children Differing in Day Care Experiences," *Early Childhood Research Quarterly* 5 (1990), 105–116; S. D. Holloway and M. Reichhart-Erickson, "Child Care Quality, Family Structure, and Maternal Expectations: Relationship to Preschool Children's Peer Relations," *Journal of Applied Developmental Psychology* 10 (1989), 281–298; K. H. Rubin, P. Hastings, X. Chen, S. Stewart, and K. MacNichol, "Intrapersonal and Maternal Correlates of Aggression, Conflict, and Externalizing Problems in Toddlers," *Child Development* 69 (1998), 1614–1629; V. M. Schenk and J. E. Grusec, "A Comparison of Prosocial Behavior of Children with and without Day Care Experience," *Merrill-Palmer Quarterly* 33 (1987), 231–240; Thornburg et al., "Development of Kindergarten Children"; see also Erel et al., "Maternal Versus Nonmaternal Care."

26. G. Balleyguier and E. C. Melhuish, "The Relationship Between Infant Day Care and Socio-Emotional Development with French Children Aged 3–4 Years," *European Journal of Psychology of Education* 11 (1996), 193–199.

27. N. Morales and L. J. Bridges, "Associations Between Nonparental Care Experience and Preschoolers' Emotion Regulation in the Presence of the Mother," *Journal of Applied Developmental Psychology* 17 (1996), 577–596.

28. Clarke-Stewart et al., *Children at Home and in Day Care.*

29. NICHD Early Child Care Research Network, "Child Care and Children's Peer Interaction at 24 and 36 Months," *Child Development* 72 (2001), 1478–1500.

30. J. E. Bates, D. Marvinney, T. Kelly, K. A. Dodge, D. S. Bennett, and G. S. Pettit, "Child Care History and Kindergarten Adjustment," *Developmental Psychology* 30 (1994), 690–700; K. J. Sternberg, M. E. Lamb, C.-P Hwang, A. Broberg, R. D. Ketterlinus, and F. L. Bookstein, "Does Out-of-Home Care Affect Compliance in Preschoolers?" *International Journal of Behavioral Development* 14 (1991), 45–65; J. Belsky, "Quantity of Nonmaternal Care and Boys' Problem Behavior/Adjustment at Ages 3 and 5: Exploring the Mediating Role of Parenting," *Psychiatry: Interpersonal and Biological Processes* 62, (1999), 1–20. Thornburg et al., "Development of Kindergarten Children." Not surprisingly, this association is not found in every study: see Hegland and Rix, "Aggression and Assertiveness in

Kindergarten Children Differing in Day Care Experiences"; Balleyguier and Melhuish, "The Relationship Between Infant Day Care and Socio-Emotional Development with French Children Aged 3–4 Years": B. Pier-rehumbert, T. Ramstein, A. Karmaniola, and O. Halfon, "Child Care in the Preschool Years: Attachment, Behaviour Problems and Cognitive Development," *European Journal of Psychology of Education* 11 (1996), 201–214.

31. NICHD Early Child Care Research Network, "Characteristics and Quality of Child Care For Toddlers and Preschoolers," *Applied Developmental Science* 4 (2000), 116–135; NICHD Early Child Care Research Network, "Child Care and Children's Peer Interaction."

32. NICHD Early Child Care Research Network, "Characteristics and Quality of Child Care for Toddlers and Preschoolers." Supporting the suggestion that effects of childcare depend on the child, Bates found that when characteristics of the child were taken into account, the apparent effects of childcare on children's aggression decreased. See Bates et al., "Child Care History and Kindergarten Adjustment."

33. A. B. Smith and S. Barraclough, "Young Children's Conflicts and Teachers' Perspectives on Them," *New Zealand Journal of Educational Studies* 34 (1999), 335–348.

34. K. Tout, M. De Haan, E. Kipp-Campbell, and M. R. Gunnar, "Social Behavior Correlates of Adrenocortical Activity in Daycare: Gender Differences and Time-of-Day Effects," *Child Development* 69 (1998), 1247–1262; A. C. Dettling, M. R. Gunnar, and B. Donzella, "Cortisol Levels of Young Children in Full-Day Childcare Centers: Relations with Age and Temperament," *Psychoneuroendocrinology* 24 (1999), 519–536; S. E. Watamura, A. M. Sebanc, and M. R. Gunnar, "Rising Cortisol at Childcare: Relations with Nap, Rest, and Temperament," *Developmental Psychobiology* 40 (2002), 33–42; M. R. Gunnar, K. Tout, M. De Haan, S. Pierce, and K. Stansbury, "Temperament, Social Competence, and Adrenocortical Activity in Preschoolers," *Developmental Psychobiology* 31 (1997), 65–85.

35. Bates et al., "Child Care History and Kindergarten Adjustment"; Belsky, "Quantity of Nonmaternal Care and Boys' Problem Behavior/Adjustment"; A. Borge and E. Melhuish, "A Longitudinal Study of Childhood Behavior Problems, Maternal Employment, and Day Care in A Rural Norwegian Community," *International Journal of Behavioral Development* 18 (1995), 23–42; J. Belsky and D. Eggebeen, "Cumulative Maternal Employment Hours Across the First Three Years of Life and Children's Adjustment Through Age 12," unpublished data referred to in J. Belsky, "Emanuel Miller Lecture: Developmental Risks (Still) Associ-

ated with Early Child Care," *Journal of Child Psychology and Psychiatry* 42 (2001), 845–859; N. Bayder and J. Brooks-Gunn, "Effects of Maternal Employment and Child-Care Arrangements on Preschoolers' Cognitive and Behavioral Outcomes: Evidence from the Children on the National Longitudinal Survey of Youth," *Developmental Psychology* 27 (1991), 932–945; A. Hausfather, A. Toharia, C. LaRoche, and F. Engelsmann, "Effects of Age of Entry, Day-Care Quality, and Family Characteristics on Preschool Behavior," *Journal of Child Psychology and Psychiatry and Allied Disciplines* 38 (1997), 441–448; Ritter and Turner, "The Impact of Day Care on School Readiness."

36. NICHD Early Child Care Research Network, "Child Care and Children's Peer Interaction" for age two fundings; NICHD Early Child Care Research Network, "Early Child Care and Children's Development Prior to School Entry: Results from the NICHD Study of Early Child Care," *American Educational Research Journal* 39 (2002), 133–164 for age four findings.

37. NICHD Early Child Care Research Network, "Does Amount of Time Spent in Child Care Predict Socioemotional Adjustment During the Transition to Kindergarten?" *Child Development* 74 (2003), 976–1005.

38. R. C Pianta, ed., *Beyond the Parent: The Role of Other Adults in Children's Lives* (San Francisco: Jossey-Bass, 1992), 25–39.

39. When other researchers have identified children who scored in the clinical range on externalizing behavior, they have not found an increased likelihood that they were in childcare; see V. R. Bacharach and A. A. Baumeister, "Child Care and Severe Externalizing Behavior in Kindergarten Children," *Journal of Applied Developmental Psychology* 23 (2003), 527–538; J. M. Love, L. Harrison, A. Sagi-Schwartz, M. H. Van IJzendoorn, C. Ross, J. A. Ungerer, H. Raikes, C. Brady-Smith, K. Boller, J. Brooks-Gunn, J. Constantine, E. E. Kisker, D. Paulsell, and R. Chazan-Cohen, "Child Care Quality Matters: How Conclusions May Vary with Context," *Child Development* 74 (2003), 1021–1033; K. McCartney, S. Scarr, A. Rocheleau, D. Phillips, M. Abbott-Shim, M. Eisenberg, N. Keefe, S. Rosenthal, and J. Ruh, "Teacher-Child Interaction and Child-Care Auspices As Predictors of Social Outcomes in Infants, Toddlers, and Preschoolers," *Merrill-Palmer Quarterly* 43 (1997), 426–450.

40. R. Haskins, "Public School Aggression Among Children with Varying Day-Care Experience," *Child Development* 56 (1985), 689–703; T. M. Field, "Infant Day Care Facilitates Later Social Behavior and School

Performance," in H. Goelman and E. V. Jacobs, eds., *Children's Play in Child Care Settings* (Albany: State University of New York Press, 1994), 69–84; B. Egeland and M. Hiester, "The Long-Term Consequences of Infant Day-Care and Mother-Infant Attachment," *Child Development* 66 (1995), 474–485; E. Harvey, "Short-Term and Long-Term Effects of Early Parental Employment on Children of the National Longitudinal Survey of Youth," *Developmental Psychology* 35 (1999), 445–459.

41. "Does Day Care Breed Bullies?" *ABC News,* April 19, 2001; "Does Day Care Damage Your Child?" *CBS News,* April 19, 2001; "Child Aggression Linked to Hours in Day Care," *CNN News,* April 19, 2001.

42. C. Bok, *Washington Post,* April 23, 2001.

43. Caregiver reports of externalizing behavior at four and a half years = 51 for children in home care + center care for long hours (more than 40 hours/week) vs. 55 for children in center care only for long hours; $F(1, 186) = 4.65, p < .03$ (controlling for family income, mother's education, and childcare quality).

44. Bos and Granger, "Estimating Effects of Day Care Use on Child Outcomes."

45. J. Belsky, "The 'Effects' of Infant Day Care Reconsidered," *Early Childhood Research Quarterly* 3 (1988), 235–272; J. Belsky, "Consequences of Child Care For Children's Development: A Deconstructionist View," in A. Booth, ed., *Child Care in the 1990s: Trends and Consequences* (Hillsdale, N.J.: Lawrence Erlbaum, 1992), 83–94; K. A. Clarke-Stewart, "Infant Day Care: Maligned Or Malignant?" *American Psychologist* 44 (1989), 266–273; K. A. Clarke-Stewart, "Consequences of Child Care For Children's Development," in A. Booth, ed., *Child Care in the 1990s: Trends and Consequences,* 63–82.

46. K. A. Clarke-Stewart and G. G. Fein, "Early Childhood Programs," in P. H. Mussen, M. Haith, and J. Campos, eds., *Handbook of Child Psychology,* vol. 2 (New York: Wiley, 1983), 917–1000.

47. Clarke-Stewart, "Infant Day Care: Maligned Or Malignant?"

48. C. Howes, C. Rodning, D. Galluzzo, and I. Myers, "Attachment and Childcare; Relationships with Mother and Caregiver," *Early Childhood Research Quarterly* 3 (1988), 403–416; F. F. Strayer, E. Moss, and T. Blicharski, "Biosocial Bases of Representational Activity During Early Childhood," in L. T. Winegar, ed., *Social Interaction and the Development of Children's Understanding* (Norwood, N.J.: Ablex, 1989), 21–44.

49. E. M. Verweij-Tijsterman, "Daycare and Attachment" (Ph.D. diss., Free University of Amsterdam, 1996).

50. K. A. Clarke-Stewart, F. A. Goossens, and V. D. Allhusen, "Measuring Infant-Mother Attachment: Is the Strange Situation Enough?" *Social Development* 10 (2001), 143–169.

51. Clarke-Stewart et al., "Measuring Infant-Mother Attachment," Ninety-one percent of these children were classified as "secure."

52. Egeland and Hiester, "The Long-Term Consequences of Infant Day-Care and Mother-Infant Attachment."

53. H. Rauh, U. Ziegenhain, B. Mueller, and L. Wijnroks, "Stability and Change in Infant-Mother Attachment in the Second Year of Life: Relations to Parenting Quality and Varying Degrees of Day-Care Experience," in P. M. Crittenden and A. H. Claussen, eds., *The Organization of Attachment Relationships: Maturation, Culture, and Context* (New York: Cambridge University Press, 2000), 251–276; M. Burchinal, D. Bryant, M. Lee, and C. Ramey, "Early Day Care, Infant-Mother Attachment, and Maternal Responsiveness in the Infant's First Year," *Early Childhood Research Quarterly* 7 (1992), 383–396; M. K. McKim, K. M. Cramer, B. Stuart, and D. L. O'Connor, "Infant Care Decisions and Attachment Security: the Canadian Transition to Child Care Study," *Canadian Journal of Behavioural Science* 31 (1999), 92–106; D. K. Symons, "Post-Partum Employment Patterns, Family-Based Care Arrangements, and the Mother-Infant Relationship at Age Two," *Canadian Journal of Behavioural Science* 30 (1998), 121–131; L. Roggman, J. Lang-lois, L. Hubbs-Tait, and L. Rieser-Danner, "Infant Day Care, Attachment, and the 'File Drawer Problem,'" *Child Development* 65 (1994), 1429–1443; Erel et al., "Maternal Versus Nonmaternal Care"; Field, "Infant Day Care Facilitates Later Social Behavior and School Performance"; Pierrehumbert et al., "Child Care in the Preschool Years."

54. NICHD Early Child Care Research Network, "Child Care and Family Predictors of Preschool Attachment and Stability from Infancy," *Developmental Psychology* 37 (2001), 847–862; NICHD Early Child Care Research Network, "The Effects of Infant Child Care on Infant-Mother Attachment Security: Results of the NICHD Study of Early Child Care," *Child Development* 68 (1997), 860–879.

55. Lamb, "Nonparental Child Care: Context, Quality, Correlates"; Lamb, "Nonparental Child Care."

56. NICHD Early Child Care Research Network, "Child Care in the First Year of Life," *Merrill-Palmer Quarterly* 43, (1997), 340–360.

57. F. B. Glantz and J. Layzer, *The Cost, Quality and Child Outcomes Study: A Critique* (Cambridge Mass.: Abt Associates, 2000).

58. See the NAEYC Web site, www.NAEYC.org.

59. Bayder and Brooks-Gunn, "Effects of Maternal Employment and Child-Care Arrangements" for NLSY boys from high-income families; J. Brooks-Gunn, W.-J. Han, and J. Waldfogel, "Maternal Employment and Child Cognitive Outcomes in the First Three Years of Life: The NICHD Study of Early Child Care," *Child Development* 73 (2002), 1052–1072 for European American children.

60. D. L. Vandell and J. Ramanan, "Effects of Early and Recent Maternal Employment on Children from Low-Income Families," *Child Development* 63 (1992), 938–949; T. L. Parcel and E. G. Menaghan, "Early Parental Work, Family Social Capital, and Early Childhood Outcomes," *American Journal of Sociology* 99 (1994), 972–1009; T. N. Greenstein, "Are the 'Most Advantaged' Children Truly Disadvantaged by Early Maternal Employment?" *Journal of Family Issues* 16 (1995), 149–169; Harvey, "Short-Term and Long-Term Effects of Early Parental Employment on Children of the National Longitudinal Survey of Youth"; W.-J. Han, J. Waldfogel, and J. Brooks-Gunn, "The Effects of Early Maternal Employment on Later Cognitive and Behavioral Outcomes," *Journal of Marriage and the Family,* 63 (2001), 336–354. In the last study researchers found that it was only when mothers started work early in the child's first year and then left the labor force that children did more poorly through age eight.

61. Han et al., "The Effects of Early Maternal Employment on Later Cognitive and Behavioral Outcomes."

62. S. Burgess, P. Gregg, C. Propper, and E. Washbrook, "The Effects of a Mother's Return to Work Decision on Child Development in the UK," (pre-sentation to Bedford Group for Lifecourse and Statistical Studies, Institute of Education, University of London, November 5, 2003) for absence of negative effects on cognitive development; K. Sylva et al., *The Effective Provision of Pre-School Education (EPPE) Project: Findings from the Pre-School Period* for findings regarding advantages of early care.

63. For boys from high-income families, see S. L. Hofferth, "Child Care in the First Three Years of Life and Preschoolers' Language and Behavior" (paper presented at the biennial meeting of the Society for Research in Child Development, Albuquerque, N. Mex., April 1999).

64. Andersson, "Effects of Public Day Care: A Longitudinal Study"; B. Andersson, "Effects of Day Care on Cognitive and Socioemotional Competence of Thirteen-Year-Old Swedish Schoolchildren," *Child Development* 63 (1992), 2036; C. Howes, "A Comparison of Preschool Behaviors with Peers When Children Enroll in Child Care as Infants or Older Children," *Journal of Reproductive and Infant Psychology* 9 (1991), 105–115; K. Sylva et al., *The Effective Provision of Pre-School Education*

(EPPE) Project for findings regarding social skills; Field, "Infant Day Care Facilitates Later Social Behavior and School Performance" for findings regarding number of friends; C. L. Creps and L. Vernon-Feagans, "Preschoolers' Social Behavior in Day Care: Links with Entering Day Care in the First Year," *Journal of Applied Developmental Psychology* 20 (1999), 461–479 for findings regarding positive effects of early care.

65. C. Howes, "Current Research on Early Day Care," in S. S. Chehrazi, ed., *Psychosocial Issues in Day Care* (Washington, D.C.: American Psychiatric Press, 1990), 21–35 for discussion of lack of positive effects.

66. Egeland and Hiester, "The Long-Term Consequences of Infant Day-Care and Mother-Infant Attachment"; A. S. Honig and K. J. Park, "Effects of Day Care on Preschool Sex-Role Development," *American Journal of Orthopsychiatry* 63 (1993), 481–486; J. Belsky and D. Eggebeen, "Early and Extensive Maternal Employment and Young Children's Socioemotional Development: Children of the National Longitudinal Survey of Youth," *Journal of Marriage and the Family* 53 (1991), 1083–1110; Sylva et al., *The Effective Provision of Pre-School Education (EPPE) Project;* Bayder and Brooks-Gunn, "Effects of Maternal Employment and Child-Care Arrangements"; Hofferth, "Child Care in the First Three Years of Life and Preschoolers' Language and Behavior"; L. M. Youngblade, "Peer and Teacher Ratings of Third- and Fourth-Grade Children's Social Behavior as a Function of Early Maternal Employment," *Journal of Child Psychology and Psychiatry* 44, (2003), 477–488; Han et al., "The Effects of Early Maternal Employment on Later Cognitive and Behavioral Outcomes."

67. Balleyguier and Melhuish, "The Relationship Between Infant Day Care and Socio-Emotional Development with French Children Aged 3–4 Years"; Hausfather et al., "Effects of Age of Entry, Day-Care Quality, and Family Characteristics on Preschool Behavior"; E. Tuompo-Johansson, E. Aronen, E. Huikko, A.-C. Kairemo, and F. Almqrist, "Parent-Rated Mental Health of Eight-Year-Old Children and Parent-Rated Quality of Previous Day-Care," *Psychiatria Fennica* 30 (1999), 244–255; A. B. Smith, P. M. Inder, and B. Ratcliff, "Relationships Between Early Childhood Center Experience and Social Behaviour at School," *New Zealand Journal of Educational Studies* 28 (1993), 13–28; Creps and Vernon-Feagans, "Infant Daycare and Otitis Media"; McCartney et al., "Teacher-Child Interaction and Child-Care Auspices as Predictors of Social Outcomes in Infants, Toddlers, and Preschoolers." See also studies of maternal employment: Belsky and Eggebeen, "Early and Extensive Maternal Employ-

ment and Young Children's Socioemotional Development"; T. N. Greenstein, "Are the 'Most Advantaged' Children Truly Disadvantaged By Early Maternal Employment?"; Harvey, "Short-Term and Long-Term Effects of Early Parental Employment on Children of the National Longitudinal Survey of Youth"; Parcel and Menaghan, "Early Parental Work, Family Social Capital, and Early Childhood Outcomes"; Vandell and Ramanan, "Effects of Early and Recent Maternal Employment on Children from Low-Income Families"; Han et al., "The Effects of Early Maternal Employment on Later Cognitive and Behavioral Outcomes"; H. Joshi and G. Verropoulou, *Maternal Employment and Child Outcomes: Analysis of Two Cohort Studies* (London: The Smith Institute, 2000).

68. NICHD Early Child Care Research Network, "Early Child Care and Self-Control, Compliance, and Problem Behavior at 24 and 36 Months," *Child Development* 69 (1998), 1145–1170; NICHD Early Child Care Research Network, "Does Amount of Time Spent in Child Care Predict Socioemotional Adjustment During the Transition to Kindergarten?"

69. L. M. Youngblade, "Peer and Teacher Ratings of Third-and Fourth-Grade Children's Social Behavior as A Function of Early Maternal Employment" for studies controlling for number of arrangements; Bates et al., "Child Care History and Kindergarten Adjustment." In another study, effects of maternal employment during infancy became nonsignificant when concurrent maternal employment was controlled, at least for girls: L. W. Hoffman, L. M. Youngblade, R. L. Coley, A. S. Fuligni, and D. D. Kovacs, *Mothers at Work: Effects on Children's Well Being* (New York: Cambridge University Press, 1999) for studies controlling for the amount of care received.

70. D. Varin, C. R. Crugnola, P. Molina, and C. Ripamonti, "Sensitive Periods in the Development of Attachment and the Age of Entry Into Day Care," *European Journal of Psychology of Education* 11 (1996), 215–229.

71. It is possible, however, that beginning care at the age that attachment is becoming established (in the second half of the first year) is problematic.

72. Burchinal et al., "Early Day Care, Infant-Mother Attachment, and Maternal Responsiveness in the Infant's First Year."

73. NICHD Early Child Care Research Network, "The Effects of Infant Child Care on Infant-Mother Attachment Security"; NICHD Early Child Care Research Network, "Child Care and Family Predictors of Preschool Attachment and Stability from Infancy."

74. Clarke-Stewart et al., *Children at Home and in Day Care.*

75. G. G. Fein, A. Gariboldi, and R. Boni, "The Adjustment of Infants and Toddlers to Group Care: The First 6 Months," *Early Childhood Research Quarterly* 8 (1993), 1–14; Dettling et al., "Cortisol Levels of Young Children in Full-Day Childcare Centers."

76. G. Bohlin and B. Hagekull, "Behavior Problems in Swedish Four-Year-Olds: The Importance of Maternal Sensitivity and Social Context," in P. M. Crittenden and A. H. Claussen, eds., *The Organization of Attachment Relationships,* 75–96.

77. NICHD Early Child Care Research Network, "Early Child Care and Self-Control, Compliance, and Problem Behavior." Children who entered childcare late in their second year or early in their third exhibited more behavior problems.

78. Hofferth, "Child Care in the First Three Years of Life and Preschoolers' Language and Behavior."

79. Howes et al., "Attachment and Child Care: Relationships with Mother and Caregiver"; D. A. Phillips, S. Scarr, and K. McCartney, "Dimensions and Effects of Child Care Quality: The Bermuda Study," in D. A. Phillips, ed., *Quality in Child Care: What Does Research Tell Us?* (Washington, D.C.: National Association For the Education of Young Children, 1987), 43–56.

80. Dettling et al., "Cortisol Levels of Young Children in Full-Day Childcare Centers."

81. F. Osborn and J. E. Milbank, *The Effects of Early Education* (Oxford: Oxford University Press, 1987).

82. E. E. Maccoby and C. N. Jacklin, *The Psychology of Sex Differences* (Stanford, Calif.: Stanford University Press, 1974).

83. D. Botkin and S. Twardosz, "Early Childhood Teachers' Affectionate Behavior: Differential Expression to Female Children, Male Children, and Groups of Children," *Early Childhood Research Quarterly* 3 (1988), 167–177, for findings regarding affection; V. D. Allhusen and M. M. Cochran, "Infants' Attachment Behaviors with Their Day Care Providers" (poster presented at the biennial meetings of the Society for Research in Child Development, Seattle, Wash., April 1991); and NICHD Early Child Care Research Network, "Familial Factors Associated with the Characteristics of Nonmaternal Care For Infants," *Journal of Marriage and the Family* 59 (1997), 389–408, for findings regarding attention; C. J. Carpenter and A. Huston-Stein, "Activity Structure and Sex-Typed Behavior in Preschool Children," *Child Development* 51 (1980), 862–872, for findings regarding proximity; M. A. Clawson, "Day Care Quality: A Model of Relations Between Dimensions and Contributions to Chil-

dren's Social Competence," Ph.D. diss., Auburn University, 1997, abstract in *Dissertation Abstracts International,* Section A: Humanities and Social Sciences 57, N10-A (April 1997), 4254, for findings regarding negative behavior.

84. J. Belsky, L. D. Steinberg and A. Walker, "The Ecology of Day Care," in M. E. Lamb, ed., *Childrearing in "Nontraditional" Families,* 71–116.

85. S. Desai, P. L. Chase-Lansdale, and R. T. Michael, "Mother or Market? Effects of Maternal Employment on the Intellectual Ability of Four-Year-Old Children," *Demography* 26 (1989), 545–561; F. L. Mott, "Developmental Effects of Infant Care: The Mediating Role of Gender and Health," *Journal of Social Issues* 47 (1991), 139–158.

86. Hausfather et al., "Effects of Age of Entry, Day-Care Quality, and Family Characteristics on Preschool Behavior."

87. M. Burchinal, E. Peisner-Feinberg, D. Bryant, and R. Clifford, "Children's Social and Cognitive Development and Child Care Quality: Testing For Differential Associations Related to Poverty, Gender, or Ethnicity," *Applied Developmental Science* 4 (2000), 149–165; Cost, Quality and Child Outcomes Study Team, *Cost, Quality, and Child Outcomes in Child Care Centers,* 2nd. ed. (Denver: University of Colorado, 1995); Han et al., "The Effects of Early Maternal Employment on Later Cognitive and Behavioral Outcomes"; NICHD Early Child Care Research Network, "Early Child Care and Self-Control, Compliance, and Problem Behavior"; NICHD Early Child Care Research Network, "Characteristics and Quality of Child Care For Toddlers and Preschoolers."

88. NICHD Early Child Care Research Network, "The Effects of Infant Child Care on Infant-Mother Attachment Security." NICHD Early Child Care Research Network, "Child Care and Family Predictors of Preschool Attachment and Stability from Infancy"; McKim et al., "Infant Care Decisions and Attachment Security"; K. McCartney and D. A. Phillips, "Motherhood and Child Care," in B. Birns and D. Hay, eds., *The Different Faces of Motherhood* (New York: Plenum, 1988) for results from a combined sample.

89. Fein et al., "The Adjustment of Infants and Toddlers to Group Care: The First 6 Months" for findings regarding emotions and attention; Ramey et al., "Preventing Developmental Retardation: A General Systems Model" for findings regarding cognitive progress.

90. Gunnar et al., "Temperament, Social Competence and Adrenocortical Activity in Preschoolers"; Dettling et al., "Cortisol Levels of Young Children in Full-Day Childcare Centers"; S. E. Watamura, B. Donzella, J. Alwin, and M. R. Gunnar, "Morning to Afternoon Increases in Cortisol

Concentrations for Infants and Toddlers at Child Care: Age Differences and Behavioral Correlates," *Child Development* 74 (2003), 1006–1020; A. C. Dettling, S. W. Parker, S. Lane, A. Sebanc, and M. R. Gunnar, "Quality of Care and Temperament Determine Changes in Cortisol Concentrations Over the Day For Young Children in Childcare," *Psychoneuroendocrinology* 25 (2000), 819–836.

91. Mott, "Developmental Effects of Infant Care: The Mediating Role of Gender and Health."

92. L. Feagans, M. Sanyal, F. Henderson, A. Collier, and M. Appelbaum, "Relationship of Middle Ear Disease in Early Childhood to Later Narrative and Attention Skills," *Journal of Pediatric Psychology* 12 (1987), 581–594; J. E. Roberts, S. Rabinowitch, D. M. Bryant, and M. R. Burchinal, "Language Skills of Children with Different Preschool Experiences," *Journal of Speech Hearing Research* 32 (1989), 773–786.

93. A. W. Miccio, E. Gallagher, C. B. Grossman, K. M. Yont, and Others, "Influence of Chronic Otitis Media on Phonological Acquisition," *Clinical Linguistics & Phonetics* 15 (2001), 47–51, for findings regarding early language development; Creps and Vernon-Feagans, "Infant Daycare and Otitis Media" for findings regarding later verbal ability.

94. L. Vernon-Feagans, M. Hurley, and K. Yont, "The Effect of Otitis Media and Daycare Quality on Mother/Child Bookreading and Language Use at 48 Months of Age," *Journal of Applied Developmental Psychology* 23 (2002), 113–133; L. V. Feagans, E. Kipp, and I. Blood, "The Effects of Otitis Media on the Attention Skills of Daycare-Attending Toddlers," *Developmental Psychology* 30 (1994), 701–708; L. Vernon-Feagans, D. C. Emanuel, and I. Blood, "The Effect of Otitis Media and Quality of Daycare on Children's Language Development," *Journal of Applied Developmental Psychology* 18 (1997), 395–409; Creps and Vernon-Feagans, "Infant Daycare and Otitis Media."

6. VARIATIONS IN CARE

1. S. L. Hofferth, K. A. Shauman, R. R. Henke, and J. West, "Characteristics of Children's Early Care and Education Programs: Data from the 1995 National Household Education Survey," (Washington, D.C.: U.S. Department of Education, 1998), 98–128; S. Scarr, "American Child Care Today," *American Psychologist* 53 (1998), 95–108.

2. M. E. Lamb, "Nonparental Child Care: Context, Quality, Correlates," in W. Damon, I. E. Sigel, and K. A. Renninger, eds., *Handbook of Child Psychology: Child Psychology in Practice*, 5th ed. (New York: John Wiley and Sons, 1998), vol. 4, 73–134. Scarr, "American Child Care Today."

3. D. A. Phillips, K. McCartney and S. Scarr, "Child-Care Quality and Children's Social Development," *Developmental Psychology* 23 (1987), 537–543; this study was conducted in Bermuda. A. G. Broberg, H. Wessels, M. E. Lamb, and C.-P. Hwang, "Effects of Day Care on the Development of Cognitive Abilities in 8-Year-Olds: A Longitudinal Study," *Developmental Psychology* 33 (1997), 62–69; this study was conducted in Sweden. B. Pierrehumbert, T. Ramstein, A. Karmaniola, and O. Halfon, "Child Care in the Preschool Years: Attachment, Behaviour Problems and Cognitive Development," *European Journal of Psychology of Education* 11 (1996), 201–214; this study was conducted in Switzerland. C. Kwan, K. Sylva, and B. Reeves, "Day Care Quality and Child Development in Singapore," *Early Child Development and Care* 144 (1998), 69–77; this study was conducted in Singapore. E. Schliecker, D. R. White, and E. Jacobs, "The Role of Day Care Quality in the Prediction of Children's Vocabulary," *Canadian Journal of Behavioural Science* 23 (1991), 12–24; this study was conducted in Canada. K. Sylva, E. Melhuish, P. Sammons, I. Siraj-Blatchford, B. Taggart, and K. Elliot, *The Effective Provision of Preschool Education (EPPE) Project: Findings from the Pre-school Period* (London: University of London, 2003); this study was conducted in the United Kingdom. M. Burchinal, J. Roberts, L. Nabors, and D. Bryant, "Quality of Center Child Care and Infant Cognitive and Language Development," *Child Development* 67 (1996), 606–620; M. Burchinal, J. Roberts, R. Riggins Jr., S. Zeisel, E. Neebe, and D. Bryant, "Relating Quality of Center-Based Child Care to Early Cognitive and Language Development Longitudinally," *Child Development* 71 (2000), 338–357; C. Howes, "Relations Between Early Child Care and Schooling," *Developmental Psychology* 24 (1988), 53–57; M. C. Whitebook, C. Howes, and D. A. Phillips, *Who Cares? Child Care Teachers and the Quality of Care in America,* final report for the National Child Care Staffing Study (Oakland, Calif., 1990); E. S. Peisner-Feinberg and M. R. Burchinal, "Relations Between Preschool Children's Child-Care Experiences and Concurrent Development: The Cost, Quality, and Outcomes Study," *Merrill-Palmer Quarterly* 43 (1997), 451–477; NICHD Early Child Care Research Network, "Early Child Care and Children's Development Prior to School Entry: Results from the NICHD Study of Early Child Care," *American Educational Research Journal* 39 (2002), 133–164; J. M. Love, L. Harrison, A. Sagi-Schwartz, M. H. van IJzendoorn, C. Ross, J. A. Ungerer, H. Raikes, C. Brady-Smith, K. Boller, J. Brooks-Gunn, J. Constantine, E. E. Kisker, D. Paulsell, and R. Chazan-Cohen, "Child Care Quality Matters: How Conclusions May Vary with Context," *Child Development* 74 (2003),

1021–1033; these studies were all conducted in the United States. S. Kontos, "The Ecology of Family Day Care," *Early Childhood Research Quarterly* 9 (1994), 87–110; S. Kontos, C. Howes, M. Shinn, and E. Galinsky, "Children's Experiences in Family Child Care and Relative Care as a Function of Family Income and Ethnicity," *Merrill-Palmer Quarterly* 43 (1997), 386–403; these studies were conducted in home care settings; Burchinal et al., "Quality of Center Child Care and Infant Cognitive and Language Development"; Burchinal et al., "Relating Quality of Center-Based Child Care to Early Cognitive and Language Development Longitudinally"; Howes, "Relations Between Early Child Care and Schooling"; Whitebook et al., *Who Cares? Child Care Teachers and the Quality of Care in America;* Peisner-Feinberg and Burchinal, "Relations Between Preschool Children's Child-Care Experiences and Concurrent Development"; NICHD Early Child Care Research Network, "Early Child Care and Children's Development Prior to School Entry"; Love et al., "Child Care Quality Matters"; these studies were conducted in child care centers; NICHD Early Child Care Research Network, "The Relation of Child Care to Cognitive and Language Development," *Child Development* 71 (2000), 960–980; this is an example of a study including one-year-olds.

4. W. S. Barnett, "Long-Term Effects of Early Childhood Programs on Cognitive and School Outcomes," *The Future of Children* 5 (1995), 25–50; J. Currie, "Early Childhood Intervention Programs: What Do We Know?" (working paper from the Children's Roundtable, The Brookings Institution, Washington, D.C., 2000); J. P. Shonkoff and S. J. Meisels, *Handbook of Early Childhood Intervention,* 2nd. ed. (New York: Cambridge University Press, 2000); H. Yoshikawa, "Prevention as Cumulative Protection: Effects of Early Family Support and Education on Chronic Delinquency and Its Risks," *Psychological Bulletin* 115 (1994), 28–54; H. Yoshikawa, "Long-Term Effects of Early Childhood Programs on Social Outcomes and Delinquency," *The Future of Children* 5 (1995), 51–75; Lamb, "Nonparental Child Care: Context, Quality, Correlates"; C. T. Ramey and S. L. Ramey, "Early Intervention and Early Experience," *American Psychologist* 58 (1998), 109–120.

5. Lamb, "Nonparental Child Care: Context, Quality, Correlates"; Scarr, "American Child Care Today"; Sylva et al., *The Effective Provision of Pre-School Education (EPPE) Project;* J. J. Campbell, M. E. Lamb, and C.-P. Hwang, "Early Child-Care Experiences and Children's Social Competence Between 1.5 and 15 Years of Age," *Applied Developmental Science* 4 (2000), 166–175; C. Howes, "Current Research on Early Day Care," in S. S. Chehrazi, ed., *Psychosocial Issues in Day Care* (Washington, D.C.:

American Psychiatric Press, 1990), 21–35; S. Kontos, "The Ecology of Family Day Care," *Early Childhood Research Quarterly* 9 (1994), 87–110; NICHD Early Child Care Research Network, "Early Child Care and Self-Control, Compliance, and Problem Behavior at 24 and 36 Months," *Child Development* 69 (1998), 1145–1170; Peisner-Feinberg and Burchinal, "Relations Between Preschool Children's Child-Care Experiences and Concurrent Development"; E. S. Peisner-Feinberg, M. R. Burchinal, R. M. Clifford, M. L. Culkin, C. Howes, S. L. Kagan, N. Yazejian, P. Byler, J. Rustici, and J. Zelazo, *The Children of the Cost, Quality, and Outcomes Study Go to School: Technical Report* (Chapel Hill, N.C.: Frank Porter Graham Child Development Center, 2000); Phillips et al., "Child-Care Quality and Children's Social Development"; D. L. Vandell, V. K. Henderson, and K. S. Wilson, "A Longitudinal Study of Children with Day-Care Experiences of Varying Quality," *Child Development* 59 (1988), 1286–1292; Burchinal et al., "Relating Quality of Center-Based Child Care to Early Cognitive and Language Development Longitudinally"; B. Hagekull and G. Bohlin, "Day Care Quality, Family and Child Characteristics and Socioemotional Development," *Early Childhood Research Quarterly* 10 (1995), 505–526; M. K. Rosenthal, *An Ecological Approach to the Study of Child Care in Israel* (Hillsdale, N.J.: Lawrence Erlbaum, 1994); Love et al., "Child Care Quality Matters."

6. Cost, Quality and Child Outcomes Study Team, *Cost, Quality, and Child Outcomes in Child Care Centers* (Denver: University of Colorado, 1995); A. Hausfather, A. Toharia, C. LaRoche, and F. Engelsmann, "Effects of Age of Entry, Day-Care Quality, and Family Characteristics on Preschool Behavior," *Journal of Child Psychology and Psychiatry and Allied Disciplines* 38 (1997), 441–448; S. Kontos, "Child Care Quality, Family Background, and Children's Development," *Early Childhood Research Quarterly* 6 (1991), 249–262; NICHD Early Child Care Research Network, "Early Child Care and Self-Control, Compliance, and Problem Behavior"; E. Votruba-Drzal, R. L. Coley, P. L. Chase-Lansdale, "Child Care and Low-Income Children's Development: Direct and Moderated Effects," *Child Development* 75 (2004), 296–312.

7. Cost, Quality and Child Outcomes Study Team, *Cost, Quality, and Child Outcomes in Child Care Centers;* E. Galinsky, C. Howes, S. Kontos, and M. Shinn, *The Study of Children in Family Child Care and Relative Care* (New York: Families and Work Institute, 1994); C. Howes, D. A. Phillips, and M. Whitebook, "Thresholds of Quality: Implications for the Social Development of Children in Center-Based Child Care," *Child Development* 63 (1992), 449–460; B. L. Volling and L. V. Feagans, "Infant Day

Care and Children's Social Competence," *Infant Behavior and Development* 18 (1995), 177–188; J. Elicker, C. Fortner-Wood, and I. C. Noppe, "The Context of Infant Attachment in Family Child Care," *Journal of Applied Developmental Psychology* 20, 319–336; S. Kontos, C. Howes, M. Shinn, and E. Galinsky, *Quality in Family Child Care and Relative Care* (New York: Teachers College Press, Columbia University, 1995).

8. A. C. Dettling, S. W. Parker, S. Lane, A. Sebanc, and others, "Quality of Care and Temperament Determine Changes in Cortisol Concentrations Over the Day for Young Children in Childcare," *Psychoneuroendocrinology* 25 (2000), 819–836.

9. Cost, Quality and Child Outcomes Study Team, *Cost, Quality, and Child Outcomes in Child Care Centers;* Peisner-Feinberg and Burchinal, "Relations Between Preschool Children's Child-Care Experiences and Concurrent Development."

10. NICHD Early Child Care Research Network, "The Relation of Child Care to Cognitive and Language Development"; NICHD Early Child Care Research Network, "Child Care and Children's Peer Interaction at 24 and 36 Months," *Child Development* 72 (2001), 1478–1500; NICHD Early Child Care Research Network, "Early Child Care and Self-Control, Compliance, and Problem Behavior."

11. NICHD Early Child Care Research Network, "Early Child Care and Children's Development Prior to School Entry."

12. NICHD Early Child Care Research Network, "Does Amount of Time Spent in Child Care Predict Socioemotional Adjustment During the Transition to Kindergarten?" *Child Development* 74 (2003), 976–1005.

13. NICHD Early Child Care Research Network, "The Effects of Infant Child Care on Infant-Mother Attachment Security: Results of the NICHD Study of Early Child Care," *Child Development* 68 (1997), 860–879; NICHD Early Child Care Research Network, "Child Care and Family Predictors of Preschool Attachment and Stability from Infancy," *Developmental Psychology,* 37 (2001), 847–862; NICHD Early Child Care Research Network, "Child Care and Children's Peer Interaction."

14. NICHD Early Child Care Research Network, "The Relation of Child Care to Cognitive and Language Development."

15. NICHD Early Child Care Research Network, "Child Outcomes When Child Care Center Classes Meet Recommended Standards for Quality," *American Journal of Public Health* 89 (1999), 1072–1077.

16. Burchinal et al., "Relating Quality of Center-Based Child Care to Early Cognitive and Language Development Longitudinally."

17. Peisner-Feinberg and Burchinal, "Relations Between Preschool Children's Child-Care Experiences and Concurrent Development."

18. NICHD Early Child Care Research Network and G. J. Duncan, "Modeling the Impacts of Child Care Quality on Children's Preschool Cognitive Development," *Child Development* 74 (2003), 1454–1475.

19. Love et al., "Child Care Quality Matters."

20. C. L. Creps and L. Vernon-Feagans, "Infant Daycare and Otitis Media: Multiple Influences on Children's Later Development," *Journal of Applied Developmental Psychology* 21 (2000), 357–378; B.-E. Andersson, "Effects of Public Day Care: A Longitudinal Study," *Child Development* 60 (1989), 857–866; Broberg et al., "Effects of Day Care on the Development of Cognitive Abilities in 8-Year-Olds"; Campbell et al., "Early Child-Care Experiences and Children's Social Competence."

21. E. S. Peisner-Feinberg, M. R. Burchinal, R. M. Clifford, M. L. Culkin, C. Howes, S. L. Kagan, and N. Yazejian, "The Relation of Preschool Child-Care Quality to Children's Cognitive and Social Developmental Trajectories Through Second Grade," *Child Development* 72 (2001), 1534–1553; NICHD Early Child Care Research Network, "Early Child Care and Children's Development in the Primary Grades: Results from the NICHD Study of Early Child Care" (forthcoming). Childcare quality was positively related in this NICHD study to achievement and cognitive scores for skills in math (Applied Problems), vocabulary (Picture Vocabulary), and memory (Memory for Sentences) and teacher ratings of social skills and work habits in first and third grades.

22. Barnett, "Long-Term Effects of Early Childhood Programs on Cognitive and School Outcomes"; Currie, "Early Childhood Intervention Programs"; J. P. Shonkoff and S. J. Meisels, *Handbook of Early Childhood Intervention,* 2nd. ed. (New York: Cambridge University Press, 2000); Yoshikawa, "Prevention as Cumulative Protection"; Yoshikawa, "Long-Term Effects of Early Childhood Programs on Social Outcomes and Delinquency"; F. A. Campbell and C. T. Ramey, "Effects of Early Intervention on Intellectual and Academic Achievement: A Follow-Up Study of Children from Low-Income Families," *Child Development* 65 (1994), 684–698; J. Currie and D. Thomas, "Does Head Start Make a Difference?" *The American Economic Review* 85 (1995), 341–364; T. Luster and H. McAdoo, "Family and Child Influences on Educational Attainment: A Secondary Analysis of the High/Scope Perry Preschool Data," *Developmental Psychology* 32 (1996), 26–39; V. C. McLoyd, "The Impact of Poverty and Low Socioeconomic Status on the Socioemotional Functioning of African-American Children and Adolescents: Mediating Ef-

fects," in R. Taylor and M. Wang, eds., *Social and Emotional Adjustment and Family Relations in Ethnic Minorities* (Mahwah, N.J.: Lawrence Erlbaum, 1997), 7–34; Infant Health and Development Program, "Enhancing the Outcomes of Low-Birthweight, Premature Infants: A Multisite, Randomized Trial," *Journal of the American Medical Association* 263 (1990), 3035–3042; L. J. Schweinhart, D. P. Weikart, and M. D. Larner, "Consequences of Three Preschool Curriculum Models Through Age 15," *Early Childhood Research Quarterly* 1 (1986), 15–45.

23. F. A. Campbell, C. T. Ramey, E. Pungello, J. Sparling, and S. Miller-Johnson, "Early Childhood Education: Young Adult Outcomes from the Abecedarian Project," *Applied Developmental Science* 6 (2002), 42–57; Schweinhart et al., "Consequences of Three Preschool Curriculum Models"; H. Yoshikawa, "Long-Term Effects of Early Childhood Programs on Social Outcomes and Delinquency."

24. Campbell and Ramey, "Effects of Early Intervention on Intellectual and Academic Achievement"; F. A. Campbell and C. T. Ramey, "Cognitive and School Outcomes for High Risk African-American Students at Middle Adolescence: Positive Effects of Early Intervention," *American Educational Research Journal* 32 (1995), 734–772.

25. L. J. Schweinhart, H. V. Barnes, and D. P. Weikart, *Significant Benefits: The High/Scope Perry Preschool Study Through Age 27* (Monographs of the High/Scope Educational Research Foundation, 10). Ypsilanti, Mich.: High/Scope Press (1993); L. J. Schweinhart, J. Montie, Z. Xiang, W. S. Barnett, C. R. Belfield, and M. Nores. *Lifetime Effects: The High/Scope Perry Preschool Study Through Age 40.* (Monographs of the High/Scope Educational Research Foundation, 14). Ypsilanti, Mich.: High/Scope Press (2005); W. S. Barnett, J. W. Young, and L. J. Schweinhart, "How Preschool Education Influences Long-Term Cognitive Development and School Success: A Causal Model," in W. S. Barnett and S. S. Boocock, eds., *Early Care and Education for Children in Poverty: Promises, Programs, and Long-Term Results* (Albany: State University of New York Press, 1998), 167–184.

26. Peisner-Feinberg and Burchinal, "Relations Between Preschool Children's Child-Care Experiences and Concurrent Development."

27. NICHD Early Child Care Research Network, "The Relation of Child Care to Cognitive and Language Development."

28. NICHD Early Child Care Research Network, "Does Quality of Child Care Affect Child Outcomes at Age 4½?" *Developmental Psychology,* 39 (2003), 451–469.

29. J. G. Markowsky and A. R. Pence, "Looking Back: Early Adolescents' Recollections of Their Preschool Day Care Experiences," *Early Child Development and Care* 135 (1997), 123–143.

30. L. E. Maxwell, "Multiple Effects of Home and Day Care Crowding," *Environment and Behavior* 28 (1996), 494–511.

31. W. Rohe and A. H. Patterson, "The Effects of Varied Levels of Resources and Density on Behavior in a Day Care Center," in D. H. Carson, ed., *Man-Environment Interactions* (New York: Halsted Press, 1975); K. J. Connolly and P. K. Smith, "Experimental Studies of the Preschool Environment," *International Journal of Early Childhood* 10 (1978), 86–95.

32. S. Fosburg, P. D. Hawkins, J. D. Singer, B. D. Goodson, J. M. Smith, and L. R. Brush, *National Day Care Home Study* (Cambridge, Mass.: Abt Associates, 1980).

33. K. A. Clarke-Stewart, C. P. Gruber, and L. M. Fitzgerald, *Children at Home and in Day Care* (Hillsdale, N.J.: Lawrence Erlbaum, 1994); S. D. Holloway and M. Reichhart-Erickson, "The Relationship of Day Care Quality to Children's Free-Play Behavior and Social Problem-Solving Skills," *Early Childhood Research Quarterly* 3 (1988), 39–53.

34. T. Laike, "The Impact of Daycare Environments on Children's Mood and Behavior," *Scandinavian Journal of Psychology* 38 (1997), 209–218.

35. G. W. Evans, W. Kliewer, and J. Martin, "The Role of Physical Environment in the Health and Well-Being of Children," in H. Schroeder, ed., *New Directions in Health Psychology Assessment* (New York: Hemisphere, 1991), 127–157.

36. L. V. Harper and K. S. Huie, "Free Play Use of Space by Preschoolers from Diverse Backgrounds: Factors Influencing Activity Choices," *Merrill-Palmer Quarterly* 44 (1998), 423–446; Clarke-Stewart et al., *Children at Home and in Day Care.*

37. H. Goelman and A. R. Pence, "Effects of Child Care, Family, and Individual Characteristics on Children's Language Development: The Victoria Day Care Research Project," in D. A. Phillips, ed., *Quality in Child Care: What Does Research Tell Us?* (Washington, D.C.: National Association for the Education of Young Children, 1987), 89–104; Holloway and Reichhart-Erickson, "The Relationship of Day Care Quality to Children's Free-Play Behavior and Social Problem-Solving Skills"; C. Howes and J. L. Rubenstein, "Determinants of Toddlers' Experience in Day Care: Age of Entry and Quality of Setting," *Child Care Quarterly* 14 (1985), 140–151; H. S. Zajdeman and P. M. Minnes, "Predictors of Children's

Adjustment to Day-care," *Early Child Development and Care* 74 (1991), 11–28.

38. NICHD Early Child Care Research Network, "Does Quality of Child Care Affect Child Outcomes at Age 4½?"

39. L. Dunn, S. A. Beach, and S. Kontos, "Supporting Literacy in Early Childhood Programs: A Challenge for the Future," in K. A. Roskos and J. F. Christie, eds., *Play and Literacy in Early Childhood: Research from Multiple Perspectives* (Mahwah, N.J.: Lawrence Erlbaum, 2000), 91–105.

40. E. Brown, "Effects of Resource Availability on Children's Behavior and Conflict Management," *Early Education and Development* 7 (1996), 149–166.

41. K. S. C. Blair, J. Umbreit, and S. Eck, "Analysis of Multiple Variables Related to a Young Child's Aggressive Behavior," *Journal of Positive Behavior Interventions* 2 (2000), 33–39.

42. NICHD Early Child Care Research Network, "Characteristics of Infant Child Care: Factors Contributing to Positive Caregiving," *Early Childhood Research Quarterly* 11 (1996), 269–306; NICHD Early Child Care Research Network, "Characteristics and Quality of Child Care for Toddlers and Preschoolers," *Applied Developmental Science* 4 (2000), 116–135.

43. Sylva et al., *The Effective Provision of Pre-School Education (EPPE) Project;* J. Hadeed and K. Sylva, "Behavioral Observations as Predictors of Children's Social and Cognitive Progress in Day Care," *Early Child Development and Care* 154 (1999), 13–30; Goelman and Pence, "Effects of Child Care, Family, and Individual Characteristics on Children's Language Development: The Victoria Day Care Research Project"; K. McCartney, "Effect of Quality of Day Care Environment on Children's Language Development," *Developmental Psychology* 20 (1984), 244–260; L. B. Miller and J. L. Dyer, *Four Preschool Programs: Their Dimensions and Effects,* Monographs of the Society for Research in Child Development 40, Serial No. 162; K. Sylva, C. Roy, and M. Painter, *Child Watching at Playgroup and Nursery School* (London: Grant McIntyre, 1980); B. G. Warash and C. Markstrom-Adams, "Preschool Experiences of Advantaged Children," *Psychological Reports* 77 (1995), 89–90.

44. McCartney, "Effect of Quality of Day Care Environment on Children's Language Development"; Phillips et al., "Child-Care Quality and Children's Social Development"; Sylva et al., *Child Watching at Playgroup and Nursery School.*

45. NICHD Early Child Care Research Network, "Does Quality of Child Care Affect Child Outcomes at Age 4½?"

46. NICHD Early Child Care Research Network, "The Relation of Child Care to Cognitive and Language Development"; B.-E. Andersson, "Effects of Public Day Care: A Longitudinal Study," *Child Development* 60 (1989), 857–866; J. M. Bos and R. C. Granger, "Estimating Effects of Day Care Use on Child Outcomes: Evidence from the New Chance Demonstration" (paper presented at the biennial meetings of the Society for Research in Child Development, Albuquerque, N. Mex., April, 1999); Clarke-Stewart et al., *Children at Home and in Day Care;* S. Loeb, B. Fuller, S. L. Kagan, and B. Carrol, "Child Care in Poor Communities: Early Learning Effects of Type, Quality, and Stability," *Child Development* 75 (2004), 47–65.

47. Connolly and Smith, "Experimental Studies of the Preschool Environment"; J. E. Johnson, J. Ershler, and C. Bell, "Play Behavior in a Discovery-Based and a Formal-Education Preschool Program," *Child Development* 51 (1980), 271–274; Miller and Dyer, "Four Preschool Programs."

48. N. Wiltz and E. Klein, "What Do You Do In Child Care? Children's Perceptions of High and Low Quality Classrooms," *Early Childhood Research Quarterly* 16 (2001), 209–236.

49. D. Stipek, R. Feiler, D. Daniels, and S. Milburn, "Effects of Different Instructional Approaches on Young Children's Achievement and Motivation," *Child Development* 66 (1995), 209–223. D. Stipek, R. Feiler, P. Beyler, R. Ryan, S. Milburn, and S. Salmon, "Good Beginnings: What Difference Does the Program Make in Preparing Young Children for School?" *Journal of Applied Developmental Psychology* 19 (1998), 41–66.

50. Sylva et al., *Child Watching at Playgroup and Nursery School.*

51. Miller and Dyer, "Four Preschool Programs."

52. Sylva et al., *The Effective Provision of Pre-School Education (EPPE) Project.*

53. T. B. Deal, "The Preschool Mover: A Comparison Between Naturally-Occurring and Program-Directed Physical Activity Patterns," *Early Child Development and Care* 96 (1993), 65–80.

54. S. B. Neuman, "Books Make a Difference: A Study of Access to Literacy," *Reading Research Quarterly* 34 (1999), 286–311.

55. L. Dunn, S. A. Beach, and S. Kontos, "Supporting Literacy in Early Childhood Programs: A Challenge for the Future," in K. A. Roskos and J. F. Christie, eds., *Play and Literacy in Early Childhood: Research from Multiple Perspectives* (Mahwah, N.J.: Lawrence Erlbaum, 2000), 91–105.

56. R. Haskins, "Public School Aggression Among Children with Varying Day-care Experience," *Child Development* 56 (1985), 689–703.

57. N. W. Finkelstein, "Aggression: Is it Stimulated by Day Care?" *Young Children* 37 (1982), 3–12.

58. K. C. Blair, J. Umbreit, and S. Eck, "Analysis of Multiple Variables Related to a Young Child's Aggressive Behavior."

59. Sylva et al., *The Effective Provision of Pre-School Education (EPPE) Project.*

60. C. Stephen, "What Makes All-Day Provision Satisfactory for Three and Four Year Olds? *Early Child Development and Care* 173 (2003), 577–588.

61. Clarke-Stewart et al., *Children at Home and in Day Care.*

62. A. Doyle, J. Connolly, and L.-P. Rivest, "The Effects of Playmate Familiarity on the Social Interactions of Young Children," *Child Development* 51 (1980), 217–223; J. L. Rubenstein and C. Howes, "Caregiving and Infant Behavior in Day Care and in Homes," *Developmental Psychology* 15 (1979), 1–24.

63. J. M. T. Becker, "A Learning Analysis of the Development of Peer-Oriented Behavior in Nine-Month-Old Infants," *Developmental Psychology* 13 (1977), 481–491; A. F. Lieberman, "Preschoolers' Competence with a Peer: Relations with Attachment and Peer Experience," *Child Development* 48 (1977), 1277–1287.

64. L. V. Harper and K. S. Huie, "The Effects of Prior Group Experience, Age, and Familiarity on the Quality and Organization of Preschoolers' Social Relationships," *Child Development* 56 (1985), 704–717; C. Howes, *Peer Interaction of Young Children,* Monographs of the Society for Research in Child Development; J. A. M. Farver and W. Branstetter, "Preschoolers' Prosocial Responses to Their Peers' Distress," *Developmental Psychology* 30 (1994), 334–341.

65. Sylva et al., *Child Watching at Playgroup and Nursery School.*

66. Clarke-Stewart et al., *Children at Home and in Day Care.*

67. N. Morales and L. J. Bridges, "Associations Between Nonparental Care Experience and Preschoolers' Emotion Regulation in the Presence of the Mother," *Journal of Applied Developmental Psychology* 17 (1996), 577–596.

68. Howes and Rubenstein, "Determinants of Toddlers' Experience in Day Care"; S. D. Holloway and M. Reichhart-Erickson, "Child Care Quality, Family Structure, and Maternal Expectations: Relationship to Preschool Children's Peer Relations," *Journal of Applied Developmental Psychology* 10 (1989), 281–298; Sylva et al., *Child Watching at Playgroup and Nursery School;* Whitebook et al., *Who Cares? Child Care Teachers and the Quality of Care in America.*

69. Burchinal et al., "Quality of Center Child Care and Infant Cognitive and Language Development"; Galinsky et al., *The Study of Children in Family Child Care and Relative Care;* Lamb, "Nonparental Child Care: Context, Quality, Correlates"; NICHD Early Child Care Research Network, "Characteristics of Infant Child Care"; L. C. Phillipsen, M. R. Burchinal, C. Howes, and D. Cryer, "The Prediction of Process Quality from Structural Features of Child Care," *Early Childhood Research Quarterly* 12 (1997), 281–303; S. Smith, "The Past Decade's Research on Child Care Quality and Children's Development: What We Are Learning, Directions for the Future" (paper prepared for a meeting on Child Care in the New Policy Context, sponsored by the Office of the Assistant Secretary for Planning and Evaluation, U.S. Dept. of Health and Human Services, Bethesda, Md., April 1998); D. M. Blau, "The Production of Quality in Child-Care Centers: Another Look," *Applied Developmental Science* 4 (2000), 136–148; Cost, Quality, and Child Outcomes Study Team, *Cost, Quality, and Child Outcomes in Child Care Centers;* B. Fink, "Providing Quality Child Day Care in a Comprehensive Program for Disadvantaged Young Mothers and Their Children," *Child Welfare* 74 (1995), 1109–1134; Howes et al., "Thresholds of Quality: Implications for the Social Development of Children in Center-Based Child Care"; Whitebook et al., *Who Cares? Child Care Teachers and the Quality of Care in America;* A. Ghazvini and R. L. Mullis, "Center-Based Care for Young Children: Examining Predictors of Quality," *Journal of Genetic Psychology* 163 (2002), 112–125; Clarke-Stewart et al., *Children at Home and in Day Care;* Elicker et al., "The Context of Infant Attachment in Family Child Care."

70. Howes et al., "Thresholds of Quality: Implications for the Social Development of Children in Center-Based Care"; for findings regarding attachments to caregivers. Love et al., "Child Care Quality Matters;" for findings regarding attachments to mothers. L. Vernon-Feagans, M. Hurley, and K. Yont, "The Effect of Otitis Media and Daycare Quality on Mother/Child Bookreading and Language Use at 48 Months of Age," *Journal of Applied Developmental Psychology* 23 (2002), 113–133; Burchinal et al., "Quality of Center Child Care and Infant Cognitive and Language Development"; Burchinal et al., "Relating Quality of Center-Based Child Care to Early Cognitive and Language Development Longitudinally" for findings regarding language and communication skills.

71. Cost, Quality, and Child Outcomes Study Team, *Cost, Quality, and Child Outcomes in Child Care Centers;* Phillipsen et al., "The Prediction of Process Quality from Structural Features of Child Care"; C. Howes, "Children's Experiences in Center-Based Child Care as a Func-

tion of Teacher Background and Adult:Child Ratio," *Merrill-Palmer Quarterly* 43 (1997), 404–425.

72. C. Howes, E. Galinsky, M. Shinn, L. Gulcur, M. Clements, A. Sibley, M. Abbott-Shim, and J. McCarthy, "The Florida Child Care Quality Improvement Study" (New York: Families and Work Institute, 1996); J. M. Love, P. Ryer, and B. Faddis, "Caring Environments: Program Quality in California's Publicly Funded Child Development Program" (unpublished report on the legislatively mandated 1990–91 Staff/Child Ratio Study, RMC Research Corporation, Portsmouth, N. H., 1992). The change in ratios has to be quite substantial—increasing the ratio from 7:1 to 9:1 was not enough to lead to a measurable decline in the quality of care in the California Staff-Child Ratio Study.

73. NICHD Early Child Care Research Network, "Characteristics of Infant Child Care."

74. NICHD Early Child Care Research Network, "Characteristics and Quality of Child Care for Toddlers and Preschoolers."

75. NICHD Early Child Care Research Network, "Child Outcomes When Child Care Center Classes Meet Recommended Standards for Quality"; NICHD Early Child Care Research Network, "Child-Care Structure—Process—Outcome: Direct and Indirect Effects of Child-Care Quality on Young Children's Development," *Psychological Science* 13 (2002), 199–206.

76. M. Burchinal, C. Howes, and S. Kontos, "Structural Predictors of Child Care Quality in Child Care Homes," *Early Childhood Research Quarterly* 17 (2002), 87–105; Kontos, "The Ecology of Family Day Care"; S. Kontos, et al., *Quality in Family Child Care and Relative Care;* A. R. Pence and H. Goelman, "The Relationship of Regulation, Training, and Motivation to Quality of Care in Family Day Care," *Child and Youth Care Forum* 20 (1991), 83–101.

77. K. A. Clarke-Stewart, D. L. Vandell, M. Burchinal, M. O'Brien, and K. McCartney, "Do Regulable Features of Child-Care Homes Affect Children's Development?" *Early Childhood Research Quarterly* 17 (2002), 52–86; Kontos, "The Ecology of Family Day Care."

78. C. Howes and D. Norris, "Adding Two School Age Children: Does It Change Quality in Family Child Care?" *Early Childhood Research Quarterly* 12 (1997), 327–342.

79. Clarke-Stewart et al., *Children at Home and in Day Care.*

80. R. A. Fabes, N. Eisenberg, S. Jones, M. Smith, I. K. Guthrie, R. Poulin, S. A. Shepard, and J. Friedman, "Regulation, Emotionality, and Pre-

schoolers' Socially Competent Peer Interactions," *Child Development* 70 (1999), 432–442.

81. C. A. Brownell and M. Carriger, "Changes in Cooperation and Self-Other Differentiation During the Second Year," *Child Development* 61 (1990), 1164–1174; D. B. Bailey, R. A. McWilliam, W. B. Ware, and M. A. Burchinal, "Social Interactions of Toddlers and Preschoolers in Same-Age and Mixed-Age Play Groups," *Journal of Applied Developmental Psychology* 14 (1993), 261–276; C. Howes and J. Farver, "Social Pretend Play in 2-Year Olds: Effects of Age of Partners," *Early Childhood Research Quarterly* 2 (1987), 305–314; Fosburg et al., *National Day Care Home Study.*

82. Fosburg et al., *National Day Care Home Study.*

7. THE CAREGIVER'S ROLE

1. W. Fowler, K. Ogston, G. Roberts-Fiati, and A. Swenson, "The Effects of Enriching Language in Infancy on the Early and Later Development of Competence," *Early Child Development and Care* 135 (1997), 41–77.

2. J. Carew, "Experience and the Development of Intelligence in Young Children," *Monographs of the Society for Research in Child Development* 45 (1980); Serial No. 187, K. A. Clarke-Stewart, C. P. Gruber, and L. M. Fitzgerald, *Children at Home and in Day Care* (Hillsdale, N.J.: Lawrence Erlbaum, 1994); NICHD Early Child Care Research Network, "The Relation of Child Care to Cognitive and Language Development," *Child Development* 71 (2000), 960–980; D. A. Phillips, S. Scarr, and K. McCartney, "Dimensions and Effects of Child Care Quality: The Bermuda Study," in D. A. Phillips, ed., *Quality in Child Care: What Does Research Tell Us?* (Washington, D.C.: National Association for the Education of Young Children, 1987), 43–56.

3. A. E. Russon, B. E. Waite, and M. J. Rochester, "Direct Caregiver Intervention in Infant Peer Social Encounters," *American Journal of Orthopsychiatry* 60 (1990), 428–439.

4. E. E. Kisker, S. L. Hofferth, D. A. Phillips, and E. Farquhar, "A Profile of Child Care Settings: Early Education and Care in 1990," report prepared for the U.S. Department of Education, Contract No. LC88090001, 1991.

5. A. R. Pence and H. Goelman, "Who Cares for the Child in Day Care? An Examination of Caregivers from Three Types of Care," *Early Childhood Research Quarterly* 2 (1987), 315–334.

6. D. A. Phillips and M. Whitebook, "The Child Care Provider: Pivotal Player in the Child's World," in S. S. Chehrazi, ed., *Psychosocial Issues in Day Care* (Washington, D.C.: American Psychiatric Press, 1990), 129–146.

7. B. E. Fagot, "Influence of Teacher Behavior in the Preschool," *Developmental Psychology* 9 (1973), 198–206.

8. Clarke-Stewart et al., *Children at Home and in Day Care;* L. B. Miller, M. R. Bugbee, and D. W. Hybertson, "Dimensions of Preschool: The Effects of Individual Experience," in I. E. Sigel, ed., *Advances in Applied Developmental Psychology* (Norwood, N.J.: Ablex, 1985), vol. 1, 25–90.

9. D. H. Arnold, L. McWilliams, and E. H. Arnold, "Teacher Discipline and Child Misbehavior in Daycare: Untangling Causality with Correlational Data," *Developmental Psychology* 34 (1998), 276–287.

10. R. B. Schumacher and R. S. Carlson, "Variables and Risk Factors Associated with Child Abuse in Daycare Settings," *Child Abuse and Neglect* 23 (1999), 891–898.

11. NICHD Early Child Care Research Network, "Characteristics of Infant Child Care: Factors Contributing to Positive Caregiving," *Early Childhood Research Quarterly* 11 (1996), 269–306; NICHD Early Child Care Research Network, "Characteristics and Quality of Child Care for Toddlers and Preschoolers," *Applied Developmental Science* 4 (2000), 116–135; K. A. Clarke-Stewart, D. L. Vandell, M. Burchinal, M. O'Brien, and K. McCartney, "Do Regulable Features of Child-Care Homes Affect Children's Development?" *Early Childhood Research Quarterly* 17 (2002), 52–86.

12. M. K. Rosenthal, *An Ecological Approach to the Study of Child Care: Family Day Care in Israel* (Hillsdale, N.J.: Lawrence Erlbaum, 1994).

13. B. K. Eheart and R. L. Leavitt, "Family Day Care: Discrepancies Between Intended and Observed Caregiving Practices," *Early Childhood Research Quarterly* 4 (1989), 145–162; Kisker et al., "A Profile of Child Care Settings"; M. K. Nelson, *Negotiated Care: The Experience of Family Day Care Providers* (Philadelphia: Temple Press, 1990).

14. J. G. Markowsky and A. R. Pence, "Looking Back: Early Adolescents' Recollections of Their Preschool Day Care Experiences," *Early Child Development and Care* 135 (1997), 123–143.

15. J. Kienbaum, "The Socialization of Compassionate Behavior by Child Care Teachers," *Early Education and Development* 12 (2001), 139–153.

16. F. A. Goossens and M. H. van IJzendoorn, "Quality of Infants' Attachments to Professional Caregivers: Relation to Infant-Parent Attachment and Day-Care Characteristics," *Child Development* 61 (1990), 832–837; C. Howes and C. E. Hamilton, "Children's Relationships with Caregivers: Mothers and Child Care Teachers," *Child Development* 63 (1992), 859–866; M. H. van IJzendoorn, A. Sagi, and M. W. E. Lambermon, "The Multiple Caretaker Paradox: Data from Holland and Israel," in R. C. Pianta, ed., *Beyond the Parent: The Role of Other Adults in Children's Lives* (San Francisco: Jossey-Bass, 1992), 5–24.

17. C. Howes and E. Oldman, "Processes in the Formation of Attachment Relationships with Alternative Caregivers," in A. Goencue and E. L. Klein, eds., *Children in Play, Story, and School* (New York: Guilford Press, 2001), 267–287.

18. C. Howes and C. C. Matheson, "Contextual Constraints on the Concordance of Mother-Child and Teacher-Child Relationship," in R. C. Pianta, ed., *Beyond the Parent: The Role of Other Adults in Children's Lives,* 25–39, for findings regarding length of time with caregiver; B. Pierrehumbert, T. Ramstein, A. Karmaniola, and O. Halfon, "Child Care in the Preschool Years: Attachment, Behaviour Problems and Cognitive Development," *European Journal of Psychology of Education* 11 (1996), 201–214, for relationship with mother.

19. J. Elicker, C. Fortner-Wood, and I. C. Noppe, "The Context of Infant Attachment in Family Child Care," *Journal of Applied Developmental Psychology* 20, 319–336, and K. Seltenheim, L. Ahnert, H. Rickert, and M. E. Lamb, "The Formation of Attachments Between Infants and Care Providers in German Day Care Centers" (paper presented at the meeting of the American Psychological Society, Washington, D.C., May 1997), for findings regarding caregiver involvement; V. D. Allhusen, "Caregiving Quality and Infant Attachment in Day Care Contexts of Varying Quality" (poster presented at the eighth International Conference on Infant Studies, Miami, Fla., 1992); E. Galinsky, C. Howes, S. Kontos, and M. Shinn, *The Study of Children in Family Child Care and Relative Care* (New York: Families and Work Institute, 1994); C. Howes, D. A. Phillips, and M. Whitebook, "Thresholds of Quality: Implications for the Social Development of Children in Center-Based Child Care," *Child Development* 63 (1992), 449–460; S. Ritchie and C. Howes, "Program Practices, Caregiver Stability, and Child-Caregiver Relationships," *Journal of Applied Developmental Psychology* 24 (2003), 497–516; Van IJzendoorn et al., "The Multiple Caretaker Paradox"; findings from these studies all relate to

caregiver sensitivity. Howes and Oldman, "Processes in the Formation of Attachment Relationships with Alternative Caregivers," for findings regarding caregiver comfort.

20. L. L. Hestenes, S. Kontos, and Y. Bryan, "Children's Emotional Expression in Child Care Centers Varying in Quality," *Early Childhood Research Quarterly* 8 (1993), 295–307.

21. R. Cassibba, M. H. Van IJzendoorn, and L. D'Odorico, "Attachment and Play in Child Care Centres: Reliability and Validity of the Attachment Q-Sort for Mothers and Professional Caregivers in Italy," *International Journal of Behavioral Development* 24 (2000), 241–255, for findings regarding cognitive play; C. Howes, "Social-Emotional Classroom Climate in Child Care, Child-Teacher Relationships and Children's Second Grade Peer Relations," *Social Development* 9 (2000), 191–204; C. Howes and C. E. Hamilton, "The Changing Experience of Child Care: Changes in Teachers and in Teacher-Child Relationships and Children's Social Competence with Peers," *Early Childhood Research Quarterly* 8 (1993), 15–32; C. Howes, C. C. Matheson, and C. E. Hamilton, "Maternal, Teacher, and Child Care Correlates of Children's Relationships with Peers," *Child Development* 65 (1994), 264–272; Howes et al., "Thresholds of Quality: Implications for the Social Development of Children in Center-Based Child Care"; Van IJzendoorn et al., "The Multiple Caretaker Paradox"; E. S. Peisner-Feinberg, M. R. Burchinal, R. M. Clifford, M. L. Culkin, C. Howes, S. L. Kagan, N. Yazejian, P. Byler, J. Rustici, and J. Zelazo, *The Children of the Cost, Quality, and Outcomes Study Go to School: Technical Report* (Chapel Hill, N.C.: Frank Porter Graham Child Development Center, 2000); all of these studies report findings regarding interactions with peers. C. Howes, D. Rodning, C. Galluzzo, and L. Myers, "Attachment and Child Care: Relationships with Mother and Caregiver," *Early Childhood Research Quarterly* 3 (1988), 403–416, for findings regarding interactions with adults.

22. E. S. Peisner-Feinberg, M. R. Burchinal, R. M. Clifford, M. L. Culkin, C. Howes, S. L. Kagan, and N. Yazejian, "The Relation of Preschool Child-Care Quality to Children's Cognitive and Social Developmental Trajectories Through Second Grade," *Child Development* 72 (2001), 1534–1553.

23. Howes et al., "Attachment and Child Care: Relationships with Mother and Caregiver."

24. van IJzendoorn et al., "The Multiple Caretaker Paradox."

25. S. Loeb, B. Fuller, S. L. Kagan, and B. Carrol, "Child Care in Poor Communities: Early Learning Effects of Type, Quality, and Stability,"

Child Development 75 (2004), 47–65; K. Sylva, E. Melhuish, P. Sammons, I. Siraj-Blatchford, B. Taggart, and K. Elliot, *The Effective Provision of Pre-school Education (EPPE) Project: Findings from the Pre-school Period* (London: University of London, 2003); Carew, "Experience and the Development of Intelligence in Young Children"; Phillips et al., "Dimensions and Effects of Child Care Quality: The Bermuda Study"; B. Tyler and L. Dittman, "Meeting the Toddler More Than Halfway: The Behavior of Toddlers and Their Caregivers," *Young Child* 35 (1980), 39–46; S. Fosburg, P. D. Hawkins, J. D. Singer, B. D. Goodson, J. M. Smith, and L. R. Brush, *National Day Care Home Study* (Cambridge: Abt Associates, 1980).

26. Clarke-Stewart et al., *Children at Home and in Day Care.*

27. M. Whitebook, C. Howes, and D. A. Phillips, *Who Cares? Child Care Teachers and the Quality of Care in America,* final report of the National Child Care Staffing Study (Oakland, Calif., 1990).

28. NICHD Early Child Care Research Network, "Does Quality of Child Care Affect Child Outcomes at Age 4½?" *Developmental Psychology* 39 (2003), 451–469.

29. J. Arnett, "Caregivers in Day-Care Centers: Does Training Matter?" *Journal of Applied Developmental Psychology* 10 (1989), 541–552; Clarke-Stewart et al., *Children at Home and in Day Care;* C. Howes, "Caregiver Behavior in Centers and Family Day Care," *Journal of Applied Developmental Psychology* 4 (1983), 99–107; Whitebook et al., *Who Cares? Child Care Teachers and the Quality of Care in America;* G. G. Bollin, "An Investigation of Job Stability and Job Satisfaction Among Family Day Care Providers," *Early Childhood Research Quarterly* 8 (1990), 207–220; Clarke-Stewart et al., *Children at Home and in Day Care;* J. Fischer and B. Eheart, "Family Day Care: A Theoretical Basis for Improving Quality," *Early Childhood Research Quarterly* 6 (1991), 549–563; S. Kontos, C. Howes, M. Shinn, and E. Galinsky, *Quality in Family Child Care and Relative Care* (New York: Teachers College Press, 1995); M. Burchinal, C. Howes, and S. Kontos, "Structural Predictors of Child Care Quality in Child Care Homes," *Early Childhood Research Quarterly* 17 (2002), for findings regarding literacy environments, 87–105.

30. Whitebook et al., *Who Cares? Child Care Teachers and the Quality of Care in America.*

31. L. Berk, "Relationship of Educational Attainment, Child Oriented Attitude, Job Satisfaction, and Career Commitment to Caregiver Behavior Toward Children," *Child Care Quarterly* 14 (1985), 103–129.

32. J. M. Love, P. Ryer, and B. Faddis, "Caring Environments: Program Quality in California's Publicly Funded Child Development Program" (report on the legislatively mandated 1990–91 Staff/Child Ratio Study, RMC Research Corporation, Portsmouth, N.H., 1992) for findings regarding appropriate classroom practices; L. Dunn, S. A. Beach, and S. Kontos, "Supporting Literacy in Early Childhood Programs: A Challenge for the Future," in K. A. Roskos and J. F. Christie, eds., *Play and Literacy in Early Childhood: Research from Multiple Perspectives* (Mahwah, N.J.: Lawrence Erlbaum, 2000), 91–105 for findings regarding literacy environments.

33. M. Burchinal, C. Cryer, and C. Howes, "Caregiver Training and Classroom Quality in Child Care Centers," *Applied Developmental Science* 6 (2002), 2–11.

34. Clarke-Stewart et al., "Do Regulable Features of Child-Care Homes Affect Children's Development?"; NICHD Early Child Care Research Network, "Characteristics of Infant Child Care: Factors Contributing to Positive Caregiving."

35. C. Howes, E. Galinsky, M. Shinn, L. Gulcur, M. Clements, A. Sibley, M. Abbott-Shim, and J. McCarthy, *The Florida Child Care Quality Improvement Study* (New York: Families and Work Institute, 1996).

36. A. Ghazvini and R. L. Mullis, "Center-Based Care for Young Children: Examining Predictors of Quality," *Journal of Genetic Psychology* 163 (2002), 112–125. Correlations between caregiver training and caregiving quality exceeded .9.

37. Arnett, "Caregivers in Day-Care Centers: Does Training Matter?"

38. C. Howes, "Children's Experiences in Center-Based Child Care as a Function of Teacher Background and Adult:Child Ratio," *Merrill-Palmer Quarterly* 43 (1997), 404–425.

39. D. G. Klinzing and D. R. Klinzing, "An Examination of the Verbal Behavior, Knowledge, and Attitudes of Day Care Teachers," *Education* 95 (1974), 65–71.

40. Dunn et al., "Supporting Literacy in Early Childhood Programs: A Challenge for the Future."

41. S. Gable, and J. Hansen, "Child Care Provider Perspectives on the Role of Education and Training for Quality Caregiving," *Early Child Development and Care,* 166 (2001), 39–52.

42. S. Kontos, C. Howes, and E. Galinsky, "Does Training Make a Difference to Quality in Family Child Care?" *Early Childhood Research Quarterly* 11 (1996), 427–445; E. Galinsky, C. Howes and S. Kontos, *The*

Family Child Care Training Study (New York: Families and Work Institute, 1995).

43. D. R. Powell and A. J. Stremmel, "The Relation of Early Childhood Training and Experience to the Professional Development of Child Care Workers," *Early Childhood Research Quarterly* 4 (1989), 339–355.

44. Clarke-Stewart et al., *Children at Home and in Day Care.*

45. Whitebook et al., *Who Cares? Child Care Teachers and the Quality of Care in America.*

46. Berk, "Relationship of Educational Attainment, Child Oriented Attitude, Job Satisfaction, and Career Commitment to Caregiver Behavior Toward Children."

47. E. Early, R. Clifford, and C. Howes, "Quality Practices and Barriers in Early Childhood Settings: A National Survey" (paper presented at the annual meeting of the American Educational Research Association, Montreal, April 1999).

48. Dunn et al., "Supporting Literacy in Early Childhood Programs: A Challenge for the Future."

49. L. C. Phillipsen, M. R. Burchinal, C. Howes, and D. Cryer, "The Prediction of Process Quality from Structural Features of Child Care," *Early Childhood Research Quarterly* 12 (1997), 281–303.

50. Clarke-Stewart et al., *Children at Home and in Day Care;* Rosenthal, *An Ecological Approach to the Study of Child Care;* Burchinal et al., "Structural Predictors of Child Care Quality in Child Care Homes"; Galinsky et al., *The Study of Children in Family Child Care and Relative Care;* Kontos et al., *Quality in Family Child Care and Relative Care.*

51. Clarke-Stewart et al., "Do Regulable Features of Child-Care Homes Affect Children's Development?"; NICHD Early Child Care Research Network, "The Relation of Child Care to Cognitive and Language Development"; NICHD Early Child Care Research Network, "Characteristics of Infant Child Care: Factors Contributing to Positive Caregiving."

52. Elicker et al., "The Context of Infant Attachment in Family Child Care"; Howes et al., *The Florida Child Care Quality Improvement Study;* S. Kontos, "The Ecology of Family Day Care," *Early Childhood Research Quarterly* 9 (1994), 87–110; NICHD Early Child Care Research Network, "Characteristics and Quality of Child Care for Toddlers and Preschoolers"; NICHD Early Child Care Research Network, "Characteristics of Infant Child Care: Factors Contributing to Positive Caregiving."

53. D. M. Blau, "The Production of Quality in Child-Care Centers: Another Look," *Applied Developmental Science* 4 (2000), 136–148.

54. S. Rhodes and E. Hennessy, "The Effects of Specialized Training on Caregivers and Children in Early-Years Settings: An Evaluation of the Foundation Course in Playgroup Practice," *Early Childhood Research Quarterly* 15 (2000), 559–576.

55. D. J. Cassidy, M. J. Buell, S. Pugh-Hoese, and S. Russle, "The Effect of Education on Child Care Teachers' Beliefs and Classroom Quality: Year One Evaluation of the TEACH Early Childhood Associate Degree Scholarship Program," *Early Childhood Research Quarterly* 10 (1995), 171–183.

56. Kontos et al., "Does Training Make a Difference to Quality in Family Child Care?"; Galinsky et al., *The Family Child Care Training Study.*

57. Rhodes and Hennessy, "The Effects of Specialized Training on Caregivers and Children in Early-Years Settings."

58. Cassidy et al., "The Effect of Education on Child Care Teachers' Beliefs and Classroom Quality."

59. Kontos et al., "Does Training Make a Difference to Quality in Family Child Care?"; Galinsky et al., *The Family Child Care Training Study.*

60. R. Fiene, "Improving Child Care Quality Through an Infant Caregiver Mentoring Project," *Child and Youth Forum* 31 (2002), 75–83.

61. S. B. Neuman, "Books Make a Difference: A Study of Access to Literacy," *Reading Research Quarterly* 34 (1999), 286–311.

62. D. Passig, P. Klein, and T. Noyman, "Awareness of Toddlers' Initial Cognitive Experiences with Virtual Reality," *Journal of Computer Assisted Learning* 17 (2001), 332–344.

63. J. Johnson, R. Fiene, J. Keat, H. Darling, D. Pratt, and J. Lutcovich, "Effectiveness of Internet Training for Child Caregivers" (unpublished manuscript, Pennsylvania State University, 2000).

64. S. Z. Worotynec, "The Good, the Bad and the Ugly: Listserv as Support," *CyberPsychology and Behavior* 3 (2000), 797–810.

65. E. A. Jaeger, A. B. Shlay, and M. Weinraub, "Child Care Improvement on a Shoestring: Evaluating a Low-Cost Approach to Improving the Availability of Quality Child Care," *Evaluation Review* 24 (2000), 484–515.

66. Arnett, "Caregivers in Day-Care Centers: Does Training Matter?"; Clarke-Stewart et al., *Children at Home and in Day Care;* S. Kontos, H.-C. Hsu, and L. Dunn, "Children's Cognitive and Social Competence in Child Care Centers and Family Day-Care Homes," *Journal of Applied Developmental Psychology* 15 (1994), 387–411; Whitebook et al., *Who Cares? Child Care Teachers and the Quality of Care in America;* Loeb et al., "Child

Care in Poor Communities: Early Learning Effects of Type, Quality, and Stability."

67. Howes, "Children's Experiences in Center-Based Child Care as a Function of Teacher Background and Adult:Child Ratio"; Howes et al., *The Florida Child Care Quality Improvement Study.*

68. M. Burchinal, J. Roberts, R. Riggins Jr., S. Zeisel, E. Neebe, and D. Bryant, "Relating Quality of Center-Based Child Care to Early Cognitive and Language Development Longitudinally," *Child Development* 71 (2000), 338–357; L. Dunn, "Proximal and Distal Features of Day Care Quality and Children's Development," *Early Childhood Research Quarterly* 8 (1993), 167–192; Y.-J. Lee, J.-S. Lee, and J.-W. Lee, "The Role of the Play Environment in Young Children's Language Development," *Early Child Development and Care* 139 (1997), 49–71.

69. M. Burchinal et al., "Relating Quality of Center-Based Child Care to Early Cognitive and Language Development Longitudinally," 338–357.

70. Howes, "Children's Experiences in Center-Based Child Care as a Function of Teacher Background and Adult: Child Ratio"; M. Burchinal, Cryer, Clifford, and C. Howes, "Caregiver Training and Classroom Quality in Child Care Centers," *Applied Developmental Science* 6 (2002), 2–11.

71. NICHD Early Child Care Research Network, "Child-Care Structure→Process→Outcome: Direct and Indirect Effects of Child-Care Quality on Young Children's Development," *Psychological Science* 13 (2002), 199–206.

72. Clarke-Stewart et al., "Do Regulable Features of Child-Care Homes Affect Children's Development?"

73. NICHD Early Child Care Research Network, "Child Outcomes When Child Care Center Classes Meet Recommended Standards for Quality," *American Journal of Public Health* 89 (1999), 1072–1077.

74. Howes, "Children's Experiences in Center-Based Child Care as a Function of Teacher Background and Adult:Child Ratio"; Howes et al., *The Florida Child Care Quality Improvement Study.*

75. Rhodes and Hennessy, "The Effects of Specialized Training on Caregivers and Children in Early-Years Settings" for findings regarding play; Kontos et al., "Does Training Make a Difference to Quality in Family Child Care?"; C. Howes, E. Galinsky, and S. Kontos, "Child Care Caregivers' Sensitivity and Attachment," *Social Development* 7 (1998), 25–36, for findings regarding attachment.

76. S. Kontos and A. Wilcox-Herzog, "Effective Preparation for Early Childhood Education: What Does North America Research Tell Us?" *European Early Childhood Education Research Journal* (forthcoming).

77. NICHD Early Child Care Research Network, "Characteristics and Quality of Child Care for Toddlers and Preschoolers."

78. Burchinal et al., "Structural Predictors of Child Care Quality in Child Care Homes"; S. Kontos and R. Fiene, "Child Care Quality, Compliance with Regulations, and Children's Development: The Pennsylvania Study," in D. A. Phillips, ed., *Quality in Child Care: What Does Research Tell Us?* (Washington, D.C.: NAEYC, 1987), 57–80; Phillips et al., "Dimensions and Effects of Child Care Quality: The Bermuda Study" for negative effects; Kontos, "The Ecology of Family Day Care"; Rosenthal, *An Ecological Approach to the Study of Child Care;* Elicker et al., "The Context of Infant Attachment in Family Child Care"; Clarke-Stewart et al., "Do Regulable Features of Child-Care Homes Affect Children's Development?" for lack of effects.

79. NICHD Early Child Care Research Network, "Characteristics of Infant Child Care: Factors Contributing to Positive Caregiving."

80. Fosburg et al., *National Day Care Home Study.*

81. Phillipsen et al., "The Prediction of Process Quality from Structural Features of Child Care."

82. S. Kontos, C. Howes, and E. Galinsky, "Does Training Make a Difference to Quality in Family Child Care?" *Early Childhood Research Quarterly* 11 (1996), 427–445; Galinsky et al., *The Family Child Care Training Study.*

83. Kontos, "The Ecology of Family Day Care"; A. R. Pence and H. Goelman, "The Relationship of Regulation, Training, and Motivation to Quality of Care in Family Day Care," *Child and Youth Care Forum* 20 (1991), 83–101; Rosenthal, *An Ecological Approach to the Study of Child Care;* Clarke-Stewart et al., "Do Regulable Features of Child-Care Homes Affect Children's Development?" for findings regarding quality; Kontos, "The Ecology of Family Day Care" for findings regarding child outcome.

84. R. C. Ponzio and K. D. Peterson, "Adolescents as Effective Instructors of Child Science: Participant Perceptions," *Journal of Research and Development in Education* 33 (1999), 36–46.

85. R. B. Schumacher and R. S. Carlson, "Variables and Risk Factors Associated with Child Abuse in Daycare Settings," *Child Abuse and Neglect* 23 (1999), 891–898.

86. N. Baydar and J. Brooks-Gunn, "Profiles of Grandmothers Who Help Care for Their Grandchildren in the United States," *Family Relations* 47 (1998), 385–393.

87. E. Larkin and S. Newman, "Benefits of Intergenerational Staffing in Preschools," *Educational Gerontology* 27 (2001), 373–385.

88. D. Gold, M. Reis, and C. Berger, "Male Teachers and the Development of Nursery School Children," *Psychological Reports* 44 (1979), 457–458.

89. Schumacher and Carlson, "Variables and Risk Factors Associated with Child Abuse in Daycare Settings."

90. M. Robb, "Men Working in Childcare," in P. Foley, J. Roche, et al., eds., *Children in Society: Contemporary Theory, Policy and Practice* (Bristol, Pa.: Open University, 2001), 230–238.

91. U.S. Bureau of Labor Statistics, *Occupational Projections and Training Data* (Washington, D.C., 1998).

92. Clarke-Stewart et al., *Children at Home and in Day Care;* B. Bryant, M. Harris, and D. Newton, *Children and Minders* (London: Grant McIntyre, 1980), 114–115.

93. Clarke-Stewart et al., *Children at Home and in Day Care;* Fosburg et al., *National Day Care Home Study.*

94. NICHD Early Child Care Research Network, "Child Care in the First Year of Life," *Merrill-Palmer Quarterly* 43 (1997), 340–360.

95. Whitebook et al. *Who Cares? Child Care Teachers and the Quality of Care in America.*

96. H. Raikes, "Relationship Duration in Infant Care: Time with a High-Ability Teacher and Infant-Teacher Attachment," *Early Childhood Research Quarterly* 8 (1993), 309–325; Whitebook et al., *Who Cares? Child Care Teachers and the Quality of Care in America* for findings regarding caregiver attention and engagement; E. M. Cummings, "Caregiver Stability and Day Care," *Developmental Psychology* 16 (1980), 31–37 for findings regarding caregiver affection.

97. Whitebook et al., *Who Cares? Child Care Teachers and the Quality of Care in America.*

98. NICHD Early Child Care Research Network, "Nonmaternal Care and Family Factors in Early Development: An Overview of the NICHD Study of Early Child Care," *Applied Developmental Psychology* 22 (2001), 457–492.

99. B. E. Vaughn, F. L. Gove, and B. Egeland, "The Relationship Between Out-of-Home Care and the Quality of Infant-Mother Attachment in an Economically Disadvantaged Population," *Child Development* 51 (1980), 1203–1214 for findings regarding attachment; C. Howes and P. Stewart, "Child's Play with Adults, Toys, and Peers: An Examination of

Family and Child-Care Influences," *Developmental Psychology* 23 (1987), 423–430 for findings regarding competent play; V. R. Bacharach and A. A. Baumeister, "Child Care and Severe Externalizing Behavior in Kindergarten Children," *Journal of Applied Developmental Psychology* 23 (2003), 527–538; J. M. Bos and R. C. Granger, "Estimating Effects of Day Care Use on Child Outcomes: Evidence from the New Chance Demonstration" (paper presented at the biennial meetings of the Society for Research in Child Development, Albuquerque, N. Mex., April 1999); J. M. Love, L. Harrison, A. Sagi-Schwartz, M. H. van IJzendoorn, C. Ross, J. A. Ungerer, H. Raikes, C. Brady-Smith, K. Boller, J. Brooks-Gunn, J. Constantine, E. E. Kisker, D. Paulsell, and R. Chazan-Cohen, "Child Care Quality Matters: How Conclusions May Vary with Context," *Child Development* 74 (2003), 1021–1033 for findings regarding behavior problems and cognitive deficits.

100. Cummings, "Caregiver Stability and Day Care"; Elicker et al., "The Context of Infant Attachment in Family Child Care"; Howes and Matheson, "Contextual Constraints on the Concordance of Mother-Child and Teacher-Child Relationship"; Howes, et al., "Attachment and Child Care: Relationships with Mother and Caregiver"; P. K. Smith, "Shared Care of Young Children: Alternative Models to Monotropism," *Merrill-Palmer Quarterly* 26 (1980), 371–389.

101. H. Raikes, "Relationship Duration in Infant Care: Time with a High-Ability Teacher and Infant-Teacher Attachment," *Early Childhood Research Quarterly* 8 (1993), 309–325.

102. M. V. Barnas and E. M. Cummings, "Caregiver Stability and Toddler's Attachment-Related Behavior Towards Caregivers in Day Care," *Infant Behavior and Development* 17 (1994), 141–147.

103. Elicker et al., "The Context of Infant Attachment in Family Child Care."

104. Bollin, "An Investigation of Job Stability and Job Satisfaction Among Family Day Care Providers."

105. Smith, "Shared Care of Young Children: Alternative Models to Monotropism."

106. C. Howes, C. Hamilton, and V. D. Allhusen, "Using the Attachment Q-Set to Describe Non-Familial Attachments" (forthcoming).

107. Galinsky et al., *The Study of Children in Family Child Care and Relative Care.*

108. U.S. Bureau of Labor Statistics, *Occupational Employment Statistics (OES) Program Survey* (Washington, D.C., 1996).

109. M. Whitebook and D. Belle, *Taking on Turnover: An Action Guide for Child Care Center Teachers and Directors* (Washington, D.C.: Center for the Child Care Workforce, 1999); M. Whitebook, L. Sakai, and C. Howes, *NAEYC Accreditation as a Strategy for Improving Child Care Quality: An Assessment by the National Center for the Early Childhood Work Force* (Washington, D.C.: National Center for the Early Childhood Work Force, 1997).

110. Phillipsen et al., "The Prediction of Process Quality from Structural Features of Child Care"; F. B. Glantz and J. Layzer, *The Cost, Quality and Child Outcomes Study: A Critique* (Cambridge Mass.: Abt Associates, 2000).

111. S. Scarr, M. Eisenberg, and K. Deater-Deckard, "Measurement of Quality in Child Care Centers," *Early Childhood Research Quarterly* 9 (1994), 131–151.

112. Whitebook et al., *Who Cares? Child Care Teachers and the Quality of Care in America.*

113. G. I. Zellman and A. S. Johansen, *Examining the Implementation and Outcomes of the Military Child Care Act of 1989* (Santa Monica, Calif.: RAND National Defense Research Institute, 1998); N. D. Campbell, J. C. Applebaum, K. Martinson, and E. Martin, *Be All That We Can Be: Lessons from the Military for Improving Our Nation's Child Care System* (Washington, D.C.: National Women's Law Center, 2000).

114. Kontos et al., *Quality in Family Child Care and Relative Care.*

115. Fosburg et al., *National Day Care Home Study;* Pence and Goelman, "The Relationship of Regulation, Training, and Motivation to Quality of Care in Family Day Care."

116. J. A. Stallings, "An Observation Study of Family Day Care," in J. C. Colberg, ed., *Home Day Care: A Perspective* (Chicago: Roosevelt University, 1980).

117. Clarke-Stewart et al., "Do Regulable Features of Child-Care Homes Affect Children's Development?"

118. Burchinal et al., "Structural Predictors of Child Care Quality in Child Care Homes."

119. H. Goelman and A. R. Pence, "Effects of Child Care, Family, and Individual Characteristics on Children's Language Development: The Victoria Day Care Research Project," in D. A. Phillips, ed., *Quality in Child Care: What Does Research Tell Us?* (Washington, D.C.: National Association for the Education of Young Children, 1987), 89–104.

8. THE FAMILY'S PLACE

1. NICHD Early Child Care Research Network, "Relations Between Family Predictors and Child Outcomes: Are They Weaker for Children in Child Care?" *Developmental Psychology* 34 (1998), 1119–1128.

2. R. D. Hess, G. G. Price, W. P. Dickson, and M. Conroy, "Different Roles for Mothers and Teachers: Contrasting Styles of Child Care," in S. Kilmer, ed., *Advances in Early Education and Day Care,* vol. 2 (Greenwich, Conn.: JAI Press, 1981), 1–28.

3. For example, B. Tizard, H. Carmichael, M. Hughes, and G. Pinkerton, "Four Year Olds Talking to Mothers and Teachers," in L. A. Hersov, A. R. Nichol, and M. Berger, eds., *Language and Language Disorders in Childhood,* (1980), 49–77.

4. Tizard et al., "Four Year Olds Talking to Mothers and Teachers," 69.

5. K. A. Clarke-Stewart, C. P. Gruber, and L. M. Fitzgerald, *Children at Home and in Day Care* (Hillsdale, N.J.: Lawrence Erlbaum, 1994); S. M. Stith and A. J. Davis, "Employed Mothers and Family Day-Care Substitute Caregivers: A Comparative Analysis of Infant Care," *Child Development* 55 (1984), 1340–1348; B. Bryant, M. Harris, and D. Newton, *Children and Minders* (London: Grant McIntyre, 1980), 114–115.

6. M. C. Hyson, L. C. Whitehead, and C. M. Prudhoe, "Influences on Attitudes Toward Physical Affection Between Adults and Children," *Early Childhood Research Quarterly* 3 (1988), 55–75.

7. E. Hock, D. DeMeis, and S. McBride, "Maternal Separation Anxiety: Its Role in the Balance of Employment and Motherhood in Mothers of Infants," in A. E. Gottfried and A. W. Gottfried, eds., *Maternal Employment and Children's Development: Longitudinal Research, Plenum Studies in Work and Industry* (New York: Plenum Press, 1988), 191–229, for findings regarding career orientation; E. C. Melhuish, "Research on Day Care for Young Children in the United Kingdom," in E. C. Melhuish and P. Moss, eds., *Day Care for Young Children: International Perspectives* (London: Routledge, 1991) 142–160.

8. B. Fuller, S. D. Holloway, and X. Liang, "Family Selection of Child-Care Centers: The Influence of Household Support, Ethnicity, and Parental Practices," *Child Development* 67 (1996), 3320–3337, for parents' values; D. A. Phillips, S. Scarr, and K. McCartney, "Dimensions and Effects of Child Care Quality: The Bermuda Study," in D. A. Phillips, ed., *Quality in Child Care: What Does Research Tell Us?* (Washington, D.C.: National Association for the Education of Young Children, 1987), 43–56, for findings regarding parents' education; A. S. Johansen, A. Leibowitz, and L. J. Waite, "The Importance of Child-Care Characteristics to Choice

of Care," *Journal of Marriage and the Family* 58 (1996), 759–772, for findings regarding family size; C. J. Erdwins and L. C. Buffardi, "Different Types of Day Care and Their Relationship to Maternal Satisfaction, Perceived Support, and Role Conflict," *Child and Youth Care Forum* 23 (1994), 41–54, and A. Huston, Y. Chang, and L. Gennetian, "Family and Individual Predictors of Child Care Use by Low-Income Families in Different Policy Contexts," *Early Childhood Research Quarterly* 17 (2002), 441–469, for findings regarding parent beliefs.

9. S. Kontos, C. Howes, M. Shinn, and E. Galinsky, "Children's Experiences in Family Child Care and Relative Care as a Function of Family Income and Ethnicity," *Merrill-Palmer Quarterly* 43 (1997), 386–403, for findings regarding caregiver ethnicity; K. E. Bolger and S. Scarr, "Not So Far From Home: How Family Characteristics Predict Child Care Quality," *Early Development and Parenting* 4 (1995), 103–112, for findings regarding shared values.

10. V. Peyton, A. Jacobs, M. O'Brien, and C. Roy, "Reasons for Choosing Child Care: Associations with Family Factors, Quality, and Satisfaction," *Early Childhood Research Quarterly* 16 (2001), 191–208.

11. Phillips et al., "Dimensions and Effects of Child Care Quality"; E. S. Peisner-Feinberg, M. R. Burchinal, R. M. Clifford, M. L. Culkin, C. Howes, S. L. Kagan, and N. Yazejian, "The Relation of Preschool Child-Care Quality to Children's Cognitive and Social Development Trajectories Through Second Grade," *Child Development* 72 (2001), 1534–1553; Kontos et al., "Children's Experiences in Family Child Care and Relative Care"; M. Burchinal, J. Roberts, L. Nabors, and D. Bryant, "Quality of Center Child Care and Infant Cognitive and Language Development," *Child Development* 67 (1996), 606–620; NICHD Early Child Care Research Network, "Child Care and Mother-Child Interaction in the First Three Years of Life," *Developmental Psychology* 35 (1999), 1399–1413.

12. M. E. Lamb, "Nonparental Child Care: Context, Quality, Correlates," in W. Damon, I. E. Sigel, and K. A. Renninger, eds., *Handbook of Child Psychology: Child Psychology in Practice,* 5th ed., vol. 4 (New York: John Wiley, 1998), 73–134; J. D. Singer, B. Fuller, M. K. Keiley, and A. Wolf, "Early Child-Care Selection: Variation by Geographic Location, Maternal Characteristics, and Family Structure," *Development Psychology* 34 (1998), 1129–1144.

13. M. K. McKim, B. Stuart, and D. L. O'Connor, "Infant Care: Evaluation of Precare Differences Hypotheses," *Early Education and Development* 7 (1996), 107–119.

14. Peisner-Feinberg et al., "The Relation of Preschool Child-Care

Quality to Children's Cognitive and Social Development Trajectories" for findings regarding age of entry into care; S. Kontos, "The Ecology of Family Day Care," *Early Childhood Research Quarterly* 9 (1994), 87–110; A. Hausfather, A. Toharia, C. LaRoche, and F. Engelsmann, "Effects of Age of Entry, Day-Care Quality, and Family Characteristics on Preschool Behavior," *Journal of Child Psychology and Psychiatry and Allied Disciplines* 38 (1997), 441–448; NICHD Early Child Care Research Network, "Familial Factors Associated with the Characteristics of Nonmaternal Care for Infants," *Journal of Marriage and the Family* 59 (1997), 389–408. These studies show no association with quality of care.

15. Cost, Quality, and Child Outcomes Study Team, *Cost, Quality, and Child Outcomes in Child Care Centers,* 2nd. ed. (Denver: University of Colorado, 1995); NICHD Early Child Care Research Network, "Familial Factors Associated with the Characteristics of Nonmaternal Care for Infants"; D. A. Phillips, M. Voran, E. Kisker, C. Howes, and M. Whitebook, "Child Care for Children in Poverty: Opportunity or Inequity?" *Child Development* 65 (1994), 472–492.

16. E. S. Peisner-Feinberg and M. R. Burchinal, "Relations Between Preschool Children's Child-Care Experiences and Concurrent Development: The Cost, Quality, and Outcomes Study," *Merrill-Palmer Quarterly* 43 (1997), 451–477; NICHD Early Child Care Research Network, "Characteristics of Infant Child Care: Factors Contributing to Positive Caregiving," *Early Childhood Research Quarterly* 11 (1996), 269–306. In the CQO and NICHD studies correlations between family characteristics and childcare quality measures ranged between 0.10 and 0.25.

17. M. Burchinal and L. Nelson, "Family Selection and Child Care Experiences: Implications for Studies of Child Outcomes," *Early Childhood Research Quarterly* 15 (2000), 385–411.

18. D. Cryer and M. Burchinal, "Parents as Child Care Consumers," *Early Childhood Research Quarterly* 12 (1997), 35–58.

19. Peisner-Feinberg and Burchinal, "Relations Between Preschool Children's Child-Care Experiences and Concurrent Development"; NICHD Early Child Care Research Network, "Characteristics and Quality of Child Care for Toddlers and Preschoolers," *Applied Developmental Science* 4 (2000), 116–135; NICHD Early Child Care Research Network, "Does Quality of Child Care Affect Child Outcomes at Age 4½?" *Developmental Psychology* 39 (2003), 451–469.

20. In the CQO study, the correlation between childcare quality and language ability with no family selection control was 0.24, whereas with family selection controlled, it was only half that (Burchinal and Nelson,

"Family Selection and Child Care Experiences"). In the NICHD study, the correlation between childcare quality and language ability at age four with no family selection control was 0.23, and with family selection controlled it was less than half that.

21. NICHD Early Child Care Research Network, "Does Amount of Time Spent in Child Care Predict Socioemotional Adjustment During the Transition to Kindergarten?" *Child Development* 74 (2003), 976–1005; J. Belsky, "Quantity of Nonmaternal Care and Boys' Problem Behavior/Adjustment at Ages 3 and 5: Exploring the Mediating Role of Parenting," *Psychiatry: Interpersonal and Biological Processes* 62 (1999), 1–20. Belsky found that when the quality of parenting was controlled, the effect of time in childcare was reduced to nonsignificance.

22. J. E. Bates, D. Marvinney, T. Kelly, K. A. Dodge, D. S. Bennett, and G. S. Pettit, "Child Care History and Kindergarten Adjustment," *Developmental Psychology* 30 (1994), 690–700; A. G. Broberg, C.-P. Hwang, M. E. Lamb, and F. L. Bookstein, "Factors Related to Verbal Abilities in Swedish Preschoolers," *British Journal of Developmental Psychology* 8 (1990), 335–349; H. Goelman and A. R. Pence, "Some Aspects of the Relationship Between Family Structure and Child Language in Three Types of Day Care," in I. E. Sigel, D. L. Peters, and S. Kontos, eds., *Annual Advances in Applied Developmental Psychology,* vol. 2 (Norwood, N.J.: Ablex, 1987), 129–149; Kontos, "The Ecology of Family Day Care"; E. C. Melhuish, E. Lloyd, S. Martin, and A. Mooney, "Type of Child Care at 18 Months-II: Relations with Cognitive and Language Development," *Journal of Child Psychology and Psychiatry* 31 (1990), 861–870; M. E. J. Wadsworth, "Effects of Parenting Style and Preschool Experience on Children's Verbal Attainment: Results of a British Longitudinal Study," *Early Childhood Research Quarterly* 1 (1986), 237–248; Y. J. Lee, J. S. Lee, and J. W. Lee, "The Role of the Play Environment in Young Children's Language Development," *Early Child Development and Care* 139 (1997), 49–71.

23. NICHD Early Child Care Research Network, "The Effects of Infant Child Care on Infant-Mother Attachment Security: Results of the NICHD Study of Early Child Care," *Child Development* 68 (1997), 860–879; NICHD Early Child Care Research Network, "Child Care and Family Predictors of Preschool Attachment and Stability From Infancy," *Developmental Psychology* 37 (2001), 847–862; NICHD Early Child Care Research Network, "Early Child Care and Self-Control, Compliance, and Problem Behavior," *Child Development* 69 (1998), 1145–1170; NICHD Early Child Care Research Network, "Child Care and Children's Peer Interaction at 24 and 36 Months," *Child Development* 72 (2001),

1478–1500; NICHD Early Child Care Research Network, "Child-Care Structure→Process→Outcome: Direct and Indirect Effects of Child-Care Quality on Young Children's Development," *Psychological Science* 13 (2002), 199–206; NICHD Early Child Care Research Network, "The Interaction of Child Care and Family Risk in Relation to Child Development at 24 and 36 Months," *Applied Developmental Science* 6 (2002), 144–156.

24. D. L. Vandell and M. A. Corasaniti, "Variations in Early Child Care: Do They Predict Subsequent Social, Emotional, and Cognitive Differences?" *Early Childhood Research Quarterly* 5 (1990), 555–572; B. Pierrehumbert, T. Ramstein, A. Karmaniola, R. Miljkovitch, and O. Halfon, "Quality of Child Care in the Preschool Years: A Comparison of the Influence of Home Care and Day Care Characteristics on Child Outcome," *International Journal of Behavioral Development* 26 (2002), 385–396.

25. Clarke-Stewart et al., *Children at Home and in Day Care;* Goelman and Pence, "Some Aspects of the Relationship Between Family Structure and Child Language"; Hausfather et al., "Effects of Age of Entry, Day-Care Quality, and Family Characteristics on Preschool Behavior"; S. D. Holloway and M. Reichhart-Erickson, "Child Care Quality, Family Structure, and Maternal Expectations: Relationship to Preschool Children's Peer Relations," *Journal of Applied Developmental Psychology* 10 (1989), 281–298; Kontos, "The Ecology of Family Day Care"; K. J. Sternberg, M. E. Lamb, C.-P Hwang, A. Broberg, R. D. Ketterlinus, and F. L. Bookstein, "Does Out-of-Home Care Affect Compliance in Preschoolers?" *International Journal of Behavioral Development* 14 (1991), 45–65; L. E. Maxwell, "Multiple Effects of Home and Day Care Crowding," *Environment and Behavior* 28 (1996), 494–511; E. Votruba-Drzal, R. L. Coley, P. L. Chase-Lansdale, "Child Care and Low-Income Children's Development: Direct and Moderated Effects," *Child Development* 75 (2004), 296–312.

26. NICHD Early Child Care Research Network, "The Effects of Infant Child Care on Infant-Mother Attachment Security"; NICHD Early Child Care Research Network, "Child Care and Family Predictors of Preschool Attachment and Stability from Infancy."

27. M. K. McKim, K. M. Cramer, B. Stuart, and D. L. O'Connor, "Infant Care Decisions and Attachment Security: The Canadian Transition to Child Care Study," *Canadian Journal of Behavioural Science* 31 (1999), 92–106.

28. R. L. Repetti and J. Wood, "Effects of Daily Stress at Work on Mothers' Interactions with Preschoolers," *Journal of Family Psychology* 11 (1997), 90–108.

29. A. I. H. Borge, M. Rutter, S. Cote, and R. E. Tremblay, "Early Child-care and Physical Aggression: Differentiating Social Selection and Social Causation," *Journal of Child Psychology and Psychiatry* 45 (2004), 367–376.

30. NICHD Early Child Care Research Network, "Before Head Start: Income and Ethnicity, Family Characteristics, Child Care Experiences, and Child Development," *Early Education and Development* 12 (2001), 545–576.

31. NICHD Early Child Care Research Network, "Relations Between Family Predictors and Child Outcomes: Are They Weaker for Children in Child Care?"

32. B. Pierrehumbert, T. Ramstein, A. Karmaniola, and O. Halfon, "Child Care in the Preschool Years: Attachment, Behaviour Problems and Cognitive Development," *European Journal of Psychology of Education* 11 (1996), 201–214.

33. Hausfather et al., "Effects of Age of Entry, Day-Care Quality, and Family Characteristics on Preschool Behavior."

34. NICHD Early Child Care Research Network, "Early Child Care and Self-Control, Compliance, and Problem Behavior"; NICHD Early Child Care Research Network, "The Interaction of Child Care and Family Risk in Relation to Child Development at 24 and 36 Months; Peisner-Feinberg et al., "The Relation of Preschool Child-Care Quality to Children's Cognitive and Social Developmental Trajectories Through Second Grade"; Cost, Quality, and Child Outcomes Study Team, *Cost, Quality, and Child Outcomes in Child Care Centers.*

35. D. M. Bryant, M. R. Burchinal, L. Lau, and J. J. Sparling, "Family and Classroom Correlates of Head Start Children's Developmental Outcomes," *Early Childhood Research Quarterly* 9 (1994), 289–304; M. O. Caughy, J. A. DiPietro, and D. M. Strobino, "Day-Care Participation as a Protective Factor in the Cognitive Development of Low-Income Children," *Child Development* 65 (1994), 457–471; Vandell and Corasaniti, "Variations in Early Child Care: Do They Predict Subsequent Social, Emotional, and Cognitive Differences?"; E. Schlieker, D. R. White, and E. Jacobs, "The Role of Day Care Quality in the Prediction of Children's Vocabulary," *Canadian Journal of Behavioral Science* 23 (1991), 12–24; S. Scarr, J. Lande, and K. McCartney, "Child Care and the Family: Complements and Interactions," in J. Lande, S. Scarr, and N. Gunzenhauser, eds., *Caring for Children: Challenge to America* (Hillsdale, N.J.: Lawrence Erlbaum, 1988), 1–21.

36. M. Burchinal, E. Peisner-Feinberg, D. Bryant, and R. Clifford, "Children's Social and Cognitive Development and Child Care Quality:

Testing for Differential Associations Related to Poverty, Gender, or Ethnicity," *Applied Developmental Science* 4 (2000), 149–165.

37. NICHD Early Child Care Research Network, "Does Quality of Child Care Affect Child Outcomes at Age 4½?"; NICHD Early Child Care Research Network, "The Relation of Child Care to Cognitive and Language Development," *Child Development* 71 (2000), 960–980.

38. Burchinal and Nelson, "Family Selection and Child Care Experiences."

39. L. Vernon-Feagans, M. Hurley, and K. Yont, "The Effect of Otitis Media and Daycare Quality on Mother/Child Bookreading and Language Use at 48 Months of Age," *Journal of Applied Developmental Psychology* 23 (2002), 113–133.

40. P. A. Britner and D. A. Phillips, "Predictors of Parent and Provider Satisfaction with Child Day Care Dimensions: A Comparison of Center-Based and Family Child Day Care," *Child Welfare* 74 (1995), 135–1168; M. Shinn, D. Phillips, C. Howes, E. Galinsky, and M. Whitebook, *Correspondence between Mothers' Perceptions and Observer Ratings of Quality in Child Care Centers* (New York: Family and Work Institute, 1990).

41. E-mail to M. Weinraub, August 25, 2000. This e-mail message was received by a colleague of ours from a young mother in Portland, Oregon, who had consulted her about childcare.

42. S. Farkas, A. Duffett, and J. Johnson, "Necessary Compromises: How Parents, Employers and Children's Advocates View Child Care Today," www.publicagenda.org.

9. MAKING BETTER CHILDCARE CHOICES

1. M. Whitebook, C. Howes, and D. A. Phillips, *Who Cares? Child Care Teachers and the Quality of Care in America* (Oakland, Calif.: Child Care Employee Project, 1990).

2. A. R. Pence and H. Goelman, "Silent Partners: Parents of Children in Three Types of Day Care," *Early Childhood Research Quarterly* 2 (1987), 103–118.

3. K. A. Clarke-Stewart, C. P. Gruber, and L. M. Fitzgerald, *Children at Home and in Day Care* (Hillsdale, N.J.: Lawrence Erlbaum, 1994).

4. Clarke-Stewart et al., *Children at Home and in Day Care;* S. Kontos, H.-C. Hsu, and L. Dunn, "Children's Cognitive and Social Competence in Child Care Centers and Family Day-Care Homes," *Journal of Applied Developmental Psychology* 15 (1994), 387–411.

5. C. Howes and J. L. Rubenstein, "Toddler Peer Behavior in Two

Types of Day Care," *Infant Behavior and Development* 4 (1981), 387–394; E. E. Kisker, S. L. Hofferth, D. A. Phillips, and E. Farquhar, *A Profile of Child Care Settings: Early Education and Care in 1990,* report prepared for the U.S. Department of Education, Contract No. LC88090001, 1991.

6. B. E. Andersson, "Effects of Public Day Care: A Longitudinal Study," *Child Development* 60 (1989), 857–866; J. M. Bos and R. C. Granger, "Estimating Effects of Day Care Use on Child Outcomes: Evidence from the New Chance Demonstration" (paper presented at the biennial meetings of the Society for Research in Child Development, Albuquerque, N. Mex., April 1999); Clarke-Stewart et al., *Children at Home and in Day Care;* NICHD Early Child Care Research Network, "Characteristics and Quality of Child Care for Toddlers and Preschoolers," *Applied Developmental Science* 4 (2000), 116–135.

7. Clarke-Stewart et al., *Children at Home and in Day Care.*

8. B. Fuller, S. L. Kagan, and S. Loeb, "New Lives for Poor Families? Mothers and Young Children Move Through Welfare Reform: The Growing Up in Poverty Project," technical report (University of California, Berkeley; Teachers College, Columbia University; Stanford University; Yale University, April 2002).

9. NICHD Early Child Care Research Network, "Early Child Care and Children's Development Prior to School Entry: Results from the NICHD Study of Early Child Care," *American Educational Research Journal* 39 (2002), 133–164.

10. S. Loeb, B. Fuller, S. L. Kagan, and B. Carrol, "Child Care in Poor Communities: Early Learning Effects of Type, Quality, and Stability," *Child Development* 75 (2004), 47–65.

11. H. Goelman and A. R. Pence, "Effects of Child Care, Family, and Individual Characteristics on Children's Language Development: The Victoria Day Care Research Project," in D. A. Phillips, ed., *Quality in Child Care: What Does Research Tell Us?* (Washington, D.C.: National Association for the Education of Young Children, 1987), 89–104.

12. N. Goodman and J. Andrews, "Cognitive Development of Children in Family and Group Day Care," *American Journal of Orthopsychiatry* 51 (1981), 271–284.

13. B. J. Faddis, P. A. Ryer, and R. M. Gabriel, "Evaluation of Head Start Family Child Care Homes," report submitted to Department of Health and Human Services, Administration for Children, Youth and Families, ACYF, by RMC Research Corporation, Portland, Ore., 1996.

14. S. L. Kagan, "Examining Profit and Nonprofit Child Care: An

Odyssey of Quality and Auspices," *Journal of Social Issues* 47 (1991), 87–104; Whitebook et al., *Who Cares? Child Care Teachers and the Quality of Care in America.*

15. National Association for the Education of Young Children, "Summary of Accredited Programs and Programs Pursuing Accreditation," www.naeyc.org. NAEYC maintains this list, which is organized by state.

16. Cost, Quality, and Child Outcomes Study Team, *Cost, Quality, and Child Outcomes in Child Care Centers,* 2nd. ed. (Denver: University of Colorado, 1995); NICHD Early Child Care Research Network, "Child Outcomes When Child Care Center Classes Meet Recommended Standards for Quality," *American Journal of Public Health* 89 (1999), 1072–1077.

17. S. I. Greenspan, quoted in S. Gilbert, "Turning a Mass of Data on Child Care into Advice for Parents," *New York Times* (accessed online at www.nytimes.com, July 22, 2003).

18. D. R. Powell, "Parents' Contributions to the Quality of Child Care Arrangements," in C. Dunst and M. Wolery, eds., *Advances in Early Education And Day Care* 9 (1997), 133–155.

19. A. S. Ghazvini and C. A. Readdick, "Parent-Caregiver Communication and Quality of Care in Diverse Child Care Settings," *Early Childhood Research Quarterly* 9 (1994), 207–222.

20. M. T. Owen, A. M. Ware, and B. Barfoot, "Caregiver-Mother Partnership Behavior and the Quality of Caregiver-Child and Mother-Child Interactions," *Early Childhood Research Quarterly* 15 (2000), 413–428.

21. M. H. van IJzendoorn, L. W. C. Tavecchio, G. J. J. M. Stams, M. J. E. Verhoeven, and E. J. Reiling, "Quality of Center Day Care and Attunement Between Parents and Caregivers: Center Day Care in Cross-National Perspective," *Journal of Genetic Psychology* 158 (1998), 437–454.

22. K. Kindy and T. Saavedra, "Who's Watching the Children?" *Orange County Register,* March 17, 2002, A1.

23. L. Ahnert, M. R. Gunnar, M. E. Lamb, and M. Barthel, "Transition to Child Care: Associations with Infant-Mother Attachment, Infant Negative Emotion and Cortisol Elevations," *Child Development* 75, (2004), 639–650.

24. R. H. Passman, "Mothers and Blankets as Agents for Promoting Play and Exploration by Young Children in a Novel Environment: The Effects of Social and Nonsocial Attachment Objects," *Developmental Psychology* 11 (1975), 170–177; M. Weinraub and M. Lewis, *The Determinants of Children's Responses to Separation, Monographs of the Society for Research in Child Development* (1977); H. Rauh, U. Ziegenhain, B. Müller,

and L. Wijnroks, "Stability and Change in Infant-Mother Attachment in the Second Year of Life: Relations to Parenting Quality and Varying Degrees of Day-Care Experience," in M. P. Crittenden and H. A. Claussen, eds., *The Organization of Attachment Relationships: Maturation, Culture, and Context* (New York: Cambridge, 2000), 251–276.

25. D. Cryer and M. Burchinal, "Parents as Child Care Consumers," *Early Childhood Research Quarterly* 12 (1997), 35–58.

10. PLANNING BETTER CHILDCARE RESEARCH

1. Several of these ideas were suggested at a meeting held in May 2001, when a multidisciplinary group of sixty-five economists, developmental psychologists, childcare researchers, and policy analysts was invited by the U.S. Department of Health and Human Services to a conference to draw up the next steps for a research agenda in this area; U.S. Dept of Health and Human Services, *The Economic Rationale for Investing in Children: A Focus on Child Care* (Washington, D.C., 2001).

2. D. M. Blau, "The Production of Quality in Child-Care Centers: Another Look," *Applied Developmental Science* 4 (2000), 136–148.

3. S. Scarr, M. Eisenberg, and K. Deater-Deckard, "Measurement of Quality in Child Care Centers," *Early Childhood Research Quarterly* 9 (1994), 131–151; E. K. Beller, M. Stahnke, P. Butz, W. Stahl, and H. Wessels, "Two Measures of the Quality of Group Care for Infants and Toddlers," *European Journal of Psychology of Education* 11 (1996), 151–167.

4. NICHD Early Child Care Research Network, "A New Guide for Evaluating Child Care Quality," *Zero to Three* 21 (2001), 40–47.

5. S. Holloway, S. Kagan, B. Fuller, L. Tsou, and J. Carroll, "Assessing Child Care Quality with a Telephone Interview," *Early Childhood Research Quarterly* 16 (2001), 165–189.

6. Board on Children, Youth, and Families, National Research Council, Institute of Medicine, *Getting to Positive Outcomes for Children in Child Care: A Summary of Two Workshops* (Washington, D.C.: National Academy Press, 2001).

7. NICHD Early Child Care Research Network, "Characteristics of Infant Child Care: Factors Contributing to Positive Caregiving," *Early Childhood Research Quarterly* 11 (1996), 269–306.

8. M. Burchinal and L. Nelson, "Family Selection and Child Care Experiences: Implications for Studies of Child Outcomes," *Early Childhood Research Quarterly* 15 (2000), 385–411.

9. F. B. Glantz and J. Layzer, *The Cost, Quality and Child Outcomes Study: A Critique* (Cambridge Mass: Abt Associates, 2000).

10. J. Brooks-Gunn, L. Berlin, T. Leventhal, and A. Fuligni, "Depending on the Kindness of Strangers: Current National Data Initiatives and Developmental Research," *Child Development* 71 (2000), 257–268.

11. Blau, "The Production of Quality in Child-Care Centers."

12. N. S. Newcombe, "Some Controls Control Too Much," *Child Development* 74 (2003), 1050–1052.

13. W. S. Barnett and C. M. Escobar, "Research on the Cost Effectiveness of Early Educational Intervention: Implications for Research and Policy," in T. A. Revenson, et al., eds., *Ecological Research to Promote Social Change: Methodological Advances from Community Psychology* (New York: Kluwer Academic/Plenum, 2002), 63–92; NICHD Early Child Care Research Network, "Child Outcomes When Child Care Center Classes Meet Recommended Standards for Quality," *American Journal of Public Health* 89 (1999), 1072–1077.

14. C. Howes, E. Galinsky, M. Shinn, L. A. Sibley, M. Abbott-Shim, and J. McCarthy, *The Florida Child Care Quality Improvement Study: 1996 Report.* (New York: Families and Work Institute, 1998).

15. K. McCartney and R. Rosenthal, "Effect Size, Practical Importance, and Social Policy for Children," *Child Development* 71 (2000), 173–180.

16. D. A. Phillips, C. Howes, and M. Whitebook, "The Social Policy Context of Child Care: Effects on Quality," *American Journal of Community Psychology* 20 (1992), 25–51; Scarr et al., "Measurement of Quality in Child Care Centers"; D. Phillips, D. Mekos, D. A. Phillips, D. Mekos, S. Scarr, K. McCartney, and M. Abbott-Shim, "Within and Beyond the Classroom Door: Assessing Quality in Child Care Centers," *Early Childhood Research Quarterly* 15 (2000), 475–496.

17. M. Rosenthal, "Out-of-Home Child Care Research: A Cultural Perspective," *International Journal of Behavioral Development* 23 (1999), 477–518.

18. J. Johnson, E. Jaeger, S. M. Randolph, A. M. Cauce, J. Ward, and the NICHD Early Child Care Research Network, "Studying the Effects of Early Child Care Experiences on the Development of Children of Color in the United States: Toward a More Inclusive Research Agenda," *Child Development* 74 (2003), 1227–1244.

11. IMPLEMENTING BETTER CHILDCARE SOLUTIONS

1. M. M. Cochran, *International Handbook of Child Care Policies and Programs* (Westport. Conn.: Greenwood, 1993); M. E. Lamb, K. J. Sternberg, C.-P. Hwang, and A. G. Broberg, *Child Care in Context* (Hillsdale,

N.J.: Lawrence Erlbaum, 1992); K. Petrogiannis and E. C. Melhuish, *The Preschool Period: Care—Education—Development,* (Athens: Kastaniotis, 2001); P. P. Olmsted and D. P. Weikart, *How Nations Serve Young Children: Profiles of Child Care and Education in 14 Countries* (Ypsilanti, Mich.: High/Scope, 1989); E. C. Melhuish and P. Moss, *Day Care for Young Children: International Perspectives* (London: Routledge, 1991); S. B. Kamerman, "Child Care Policies and Programs: An International Overview," *Journal of Social Issues* 47 (1991), 179–196. All of these works offer excellent reviews of childcare forms and features in other countries.

2. L. Harris and Associates, "Families at Work: Strengths and Strains," *The General Mills American Family Forum* (Minneapolis, Minn.: General Mills, 1981).

3. J. Barling, "Work and Family: In Search of More Effective Workplace Interventions," in C. L. Cooper and D. M. Rousseau, eds., *Trends in Organizational Behavior,* vol. 1 (New York: Wiley, 1994), 63–73. S. Smith, "Family and Work: How the Balancing Act Disadvantages Women in the Workplace," *Sociologists for Women in Society,* http://newmedia.colorado.edu.

4. S. I. Greenspan and J. Salmon, *The Four-Thirds Solution: Solving the Childcare Crisis in America Today* (Cambridge, Mass.: Perseus, 2001).

5. P. Ghedini, "Change in Italian National Policy for Children 0–3 Years Old and Their Families: Advocacy and Responsibility," in L. Gandini and C. P. Edwards, eds., *Bambini: The Italian Approach to Infant/Toddler Care* (New York: Teachers College Press, 2001), 38–48.

6. J. R. Lally, "Infant Care in the United States and How the Italian Experience Can Help," in Gandini and Edwards, eds., *Bambini,* 15–22.

7. M. H. Malin, "Fathers and Parental Leave," *Texas Law Review* 72 (1994), 1047–1089.

8. C.-P. Hwang and A. G. Broberg, "The Historical and Social Context of Child Care in Sweden," in M. E. Lamb et al., *Child Care in Context: Cross-Cultural Perspectives,* 27–53.

9. M. Blair-Loy and A. Wharton, "Employees' Use of Work-Family Policies and the Workplace Social Context," *Social Forces* 80 (2002), 813–845; C. Deitch and M. Huffman, "Family-Responsive Benefits and the Two-Tiered Labor Market," in R. Hertz and N. Marshall, eds., *Working Families: The Transformation of the American Home* (Berkeley: University of California Press, 2001), 103–130; J. Glass and S. Beth, "The Family Responsive Workplace," *Annual Review of Sociology* 23 (1997), 298–313.

10. R. Lynch, *Exceptional Returns: Economic, Fiscal, and Social Benefits of Investment in Early Childhood Development* (Washington, D.C.: Economic Policy Institute, 2004).

11. Education Policy and Issues Center, *An Investment Opportunity That Yields Predictably High Returns,* www.epi-center.org.

12. J. C. Gornick and M. K. Meyers, *Families That Work: Policies for Reconciling Parenthood and Employment* (New York: Sage, 2003).

13. S. B. Kamerman and A. J. Kahn, "Innovations in Toddler Day Care and Family Support Services: An International Overview," *Child Welfare* 74 (1995), 1281–1300; Clearinghouse on International Developments in Child, Youth and Family Policies at Columbia University, www.childpolicyintl.org.

14. Ford Foundation, "Operation Child Care: Does the U.S. Military's Success Hold Promise for Civilians?" (Winter 2001), www.fordfound.org.

15. J. T. Bond, E. Galinsky, and J. E. Swanberg, *The 1997 National Study of the Changing Workforce* (New York: Families and Work Institute, 1998).

16. U.S. Department of the Treasury, "Investing in Child Care: Challenges Facing Working Parents and the Private Sector Response," (Washington, D.C., 1998).

17. U.S. Department of Labor, "Employee Benefits in Medium and Large Private Establishments 1997," bulletin 2517 (Washington, D.C., 1999).

18. U.S. Department of the Treasury, "Investing in Child Care: Challenges Facing Working Parents."

19. E. Galinsky, "Family Life and Corporate Policies," in M. W. Yogman and T. B. Brazelton, eds., *In Support of Families* (Cambridge: Harvard University Press, 1986), 109–145.

20. The Clearinghouse on International Developments in Child, Youth and Family Policies at Columbia University, www.childpolicyintl.org; F. Pistillo, "Preprimary Education and Care in Italy," in Olmsted and Weikart, eds., *How Nations Serve Young Children.*

21. L. C. Johnson, "Patchwork Quilt or Seamless Day? Parent, Teacher and Child Care Staff Views on Early Childhood Education Programs for Kindergarten-Age Children in Canada," *Early Education and Development* 14 (2003), 215–232.

22. C. Howes, E. Smith, and E. Galinsky, *The Florida Child Care Quality Improvement Study* (New York: Families and Work Institute, 1998).

23. H. Blank, A. Behr, and K. Schulman, "State Developments in Child Care, Early Education and School-Age Care, 2000," (Washington, D.C.: Children's Defense Fund, 2001).

24. H. Goelman and A. R. Pence, "Effects of Child Care, Family, and Individual Characteristics on Children's Language Development: The Victoria Day Care Research Project," in D. A. Phillips, ed., *Quality in Child Care: What Does Research Tell Us?* (Washington, D.C.: National Association for the Education of Young Children, 1987), 89–104; S. Fosburg, P. D. Hawkins, J. D. Singer, B. D. Goodson, J. M. Smith, and L. R. Brush, *National Day Care Home Study* (Cambridge: Abt Associates, 1980); E. E. Kisker, S. L. Hofferth, D. A. Phillips, and E. Farquhar, *A Profile of Child Care Settings: Early Education and Care in 1990,* report prepared for the U.S. Department of Education, Contract No. LC88090001, 1991.

25. M. K. Rosenthal, "Daily Experiences of Toddlers in Three Child Care Settings in Israel," *Child and Youth Care Forum* 20 (1991), 37–58.

26. Swedish Institute, *Childcare in Sweden* (2004), http://www.sweden.se/templates/cs/Basic Factsheet_4132.aspx.

Abecedarian Project, 110

Academic development as curricular focus, 120

Accessibility of childcare, 210–213

Achenbach Child Behavior Checklist in NICHD study, 82

Adaptive Language Scale in Florida Child Care Quality Improvement Study, 78

Adolescents as childcare assistants, 142–143

Adult-child ratios. *See* Child-adult ratios; Staff-child ratios

Adult Involvement Scale in Cost, Quality, and Child Outcomes (CQO) Study, 76–77

Adult relative, childcare by, 171–172

Advantaged families, effect of poor-quality childcare on, 161

Aggressive behavior in childcare, 91–92

Ainsworth's Strange Situation assessment, 94–95; test, 99; validity of, 96

American Academy of Pediatrics, 39

American Federation of Teachers, 39

American Psychological Association, 39

Arnett Caregiver Interaction Scale, 75; in Cost, Quality, and Child Outcomes (CQO) Study, 76–77; in Florida Child Care Quality Improvement Study, 78

Arnett, Jeffrey, 133–134

Asthma, risk of, in childcare, 85

At-Risk Child Care Programs, 35

Attachment relationship: with caregivers, 131; childcare quality and, 108

Attachment theory, 12–13

Baby Einstein, 51

Background checks in evaluating quality, 187

Barraclough, Shanee, 91

Bates, John, 99

Bayley Scales of Mental Development, 108, 141; in NICHD study, 82

Behavior: aggressive, in childcare, 91–92; of caregivers, in evaluating childcare quality, 181–184, 194; effect of infancy

Behavior (*continued*)
    programs on, 98–99; effects of
    childcare on, 90–93; praise in
    managing, 128–129
Berk, Laura, 136–137
Biological ties in childcare deci-
    sion, 10–12
Blau, David, 137
Books Aloud program, 120, 139
Bowlby, John, 12–13
Boys, childcare for, 101–102
Bracken School Readiness Scale in
    NICHD study, 82
Brooks-Gunn, Jeanne, 97–98
Burchinal, Margaret, 155, 160, 162
Bush, George H. W., on maternity
    leave, 49150

California, childcare-training re-
    quirements in, 134
California Achievement Test, 110
California Attachment Procedure,
    96
California Licensing Study, child-
    care quality in, 148
Caregivers, 127–149; behavior of,
    in evaluating childcare quality,
    181–184, 194; commitment to
    child and job, 146–149; as
    managers, 128–130; mothers
    versus, 150–153; multifaceted
    role of, 132; as nurturers,
    130–132; stability of, 144–145;
    in structured childcare, 120; as
    teachers, 127–128; in unstruc-
    tured childcare, 120
Caregivers' experience: age in,
    142–143; gender in, 143–144;
    years in the childcare field in,
    141–142
Chicago Study of Child Care and
    Development: caregivers in,

132; childcare choices in, 178;
    group size and child-adult
    ratio in, 123; peers in,
    125–126; social competence
    in, 89
Child abuse: male caregivers and,
    144; risk of, in childcare, 129
Child-adult ratios, 123–125,
    214215; as factor in childcare
    choice, 51; in measuring qual-
    ity, 193. *See also* Staff-child
    ratios
Child and Dependent Care Tax
    Credit, 36–37
Child Care and Development Block
    Grant (CCDBG), 35
Child Care and Development Fund
    (CCDF), 35–36, 37
Child Care Now Action Campaign,
    217
Child development associate
    (CDA) certificate, 134
Child factors in childcare research,
    73–74
Child outcomes: associations be-
    tween childcare quality and,
    202–203; expanded, 195
Child's home, childcare in, 53–54,
    173
Childcare: availability of, 58–59,
    155, 170; behavior problems
    and, 90–93; case descriptions
    on, 5–8, 63–68, 165–170; in
    the child's home, 53–54, 173;
    compensation for family
    disadvantage, 158–160; con-
    trolling for family selection
    of, 155–157; cost of, 59–60;
    educational curriculum in,
    115–121; effects of starting
    early or late, 96–101; as emo-
    tional topic, 9; experimental

studies of, 200–201; financing, 33–37; future of, 191; gender in, 101–104; government involvement in, 32–42; implementing better solutions, 206–218; inconsistent expert opinions on, 15–16; increased accessibility of, 210–213; influence of parents versus caregivers, 157–160; intellectual development and, 86–88; lack of choice on using, 16–17; media coverage of horror stories in, 14–15; military program for, 148–149, 210–211; national ambivalence on, 62; parent choice of, 51–53, 153–155; parents and, 161–164; physical health and development and, 83–86; preparing children for, 188–189; quality of, 60–62; reduced dependence on, 207–209; regulating, 37–42; relationship with mother and, 93–96; role of family in, 150–164; as a service for working-class parents, 27–30; social competence and, 88–89; stability of, 144–146; starting in infancy, 96–99; types of settings in, 171–179; variations in, 105–126; vulnerable children in, 102–104. *See also* Infant childcare

Childcare benefits in employee benefits packages, 212

Childcare centers, 31, 55–56, 175; costs of, 55–56; franchised, 178–179; increased enrollment in, 31; nonprofit, 178; regulation of, 40, 55; structure of, 56; teachers in, 56

Childcare decisions: biological ties in, 10–12; child factors in, 56–58; cultural beliefs and, 13–15; family factors in, 56–58; fathers and, 11; full-time or part-time, 170–171; making better, 169–190; making the best of difficult, 9–16; social pressures and, 13–15

Childcare demand, 43–51; early education and school readiness and, 50–51; economy and, 45–47; family leave programs and, 48–49; lack of extended family and, 49–50; personal fulfillment and attachment to the labor force, 47–48; by single mothers, 44–45

Childcare facilities, history of, 15

Childcare homes, 173–174; child-caregiver ratio in, 125; regulation of, 40–42. *See also* Family childcare homes

Childcare options: care by the father or other adult relative as, 171–172; caregiver behavior as, 181–184; childcare centers as, 55–56, 175; childcare homes as, 53–54, 173–174; consumer endorsements as, 186–187; evaluating and monitoring quality, 179–187; nonrelative care in the child's home as, 173; parent-caregiver relationship as, 185–186; physical setting as, 184–185; preparing children for childcare, 188–189;

Childcare options (*continued*)
structured characteristics in,
180–181182163

Childcare research: broader contexts in, 204–205; control by
design in, 199–201; current,
71–74; early limitations on,
69–71; exemplary studies,
74–82; planning better,
191–205; policy research
in, 201–204; sample size in,
195–198; sampling in,
195–197; valid and comprehensive assessments in,
192–195

Childcare resource and referral services, 211

Childcare supply, 51–62; availability of care and, 58–59; care in
child's home and, 53–54; child
and family factors in childcare
choices, 56–58; childcare
centers and, 55–56; costs of
care and, 59–60; family childcare homes and, 54–55; parent
choice in, 51–53

Childcare workers, wages for, 1

Childhood illnesses, risk of, in
childcare, 84–86

Children: associations between
childcare quality and abilities
of, 108–109; effects of caregiver training on, 140–141;
impact of mother's role satisfaction on, 22–24; optimal
development of, 157–158;
preparing, for childcare,
188–189

Children's Defense Fund, 39

Church-based setting, 179

Circle time, children's dislike for,
117

Classroom Behavior Inventory in
Cost, Quality, and Child Outcomes (CQO) Study, 77

Classroom Practices Inventory in
NICHD study, 81

Clinton, Bill, 49

Cognitive development, quality in,
107

Cognitive outcomes, quality of care
and, 160

Colds in childcare, 84, 85

Commitment of caregiver, 146–149

Communication between parents
and caregivers, 185–186

Community agencies in childcare
choice, 52

Comprehension, tests on, in childcare, 87

Comprehensive Child Development Act, 38

Consumer endorsements in evaluating quality, 186–187

Control variables in childcare
research, 199

Convenience in childcare decision,
155

Corporate involvement in childcare, 212

Cortisol levels: childcare quality
and, 107; childcare research
on, 103; of children in childcare centers, 91

Cost: of childcare, 59–60; of childcare centers, 55–56; as concern in policy studies, 203;
of infant childcare, 60; of
woman's leaving workforce,
46–47

Cost, Quality, and Child Outcomes
(CQO) Study, 74–78; care-
giver training in, 133, 137,
141, 142; child-caregiver

relationship in, 130–131; childcare quality in, 108–109, 111, 147; child-staff ratio in, 124; controlling for family selection in, 156; effects of good childcare in, 163–164; family and quality interactions in, 160; gender in, 102; general education for teachers in, 136–137; limitations of, 192; parents in, 154, 155, 189; quality assessment in, 107–108; samples in, 195–196
Cryer, Debby, 155
Cultural beliefs, childcare decisions and, 13–15

Day nurseries, 28–29; convergence and expansion of, 30–32; early, 28; educational programs in, 29; services offered to mothers in, 29; staffing of, 28; teachers in, 29
Daycare centers, 31
Dependent Care Assistance Plan, 36–37
Divorce rate, growth of single-parent families and, 44, 45
Dual-earner families: financial contribution of wife in, 46; role of fathers in, 20–21; as standard, 46; wages in, 46
Dyer, Jean, 117–119

Ear infections, in childcare, 84, 85
Early childhood education, importance of, for young children, 33
Early Childhood Environment Rating Scale (ECERS), 194; in Cost, Quality, and Child

Outcomes (CQO) Study, 75; in Florida Child Care Quality Improvement Study, 78; in quality assessment, 106, 108, 193
Early Childhood Longitudinal Study, 198
Early education and school readiness, increased focus on, 50–51
Early Head Start Research and Evaluation Project, 197
ECERS-ITERS seven-point scale, 189
Economy, childcare demand and, 45–47
Edelman, Marion Wright, 39
Educational curriculum, 115–121; in measuring quality, 193; structure of, 116–120
Employers, involvement in providing childcare, 212
Expanded child outcomes, 195
Experimental studies of childcare, 200–201
Expert opinions, inconsistent, on childcare, 15–16
Extended family, lack of, and childcare demand, 49–50

Families: controlling for, selection of care, 155–157; as factor in childcare research, 73–74; role of, in childcare, 150–164
Family and Medical Leave Act (FMLA) (1993), 49, 209
Family Child Care and Relative Care study, childcare quality in, 148
Family childcare, preservice training for providers of, 41

Family childcare homes, 54–55; defined, 40; group composition of, 41; number of children in, 54; providers of, 54, 55; state licensure of, 41. *See also* Childcare homes

Family childcare supports, 216–217

Family Child Care Training Study, caregiver training in, 135, 137, 138–139, 142

Family disadvantage, childcare compensation for, 158–160

Family friendly policies, 206

Family functioning, effects of good childcare on, 163

Family leave, as limited, 48–49

Family Support Act (1988), 35

Farel, Anita, 23

Fathers: childcare by, 171–172, 209; childcare decision and, 11; help provided by, 20–22; socialized views of, 21

Federal Interagency Day Care Requirements (FIDCR), 37–38, 194; in measuring quality, 193

Feminist movement, 47

Flextime, 206, 208

Florida Child Care Quality Improvement Study, 78–79; caregiver training in, 133, 141; child-staff ratio in, 124–125; partnering with policy makers in, 202; quality in, 214

Four-thirds solution, 207–208

Franchised childcare centers, 178–179

Friends, development of social competence and, 122–123

Full-time care, part-time care versus, 170–171

Funding, increased, for childcare, 210–211

Gastrointestinal (GI) illnesses, in childcare, 84, 85

Gender gap in wages, 46

Gender of caregiver, 101–104, 143–144

General education, importance of, in childcare training, 136–137

Girls, childcare for, 101–102

Government involvement in childcare, 32–42

Government regulation of childcare, 214–216

Grandmothers in providing childcare, 143

Great Depression, childcare and, 29

Group size, 123–125; as factor in childcare choice, 51

Gunnar, Megan, 91

Hausfather, Albert, 159

Head Start, 33–34, 37, 177; enrichment opportunities offered in, 34; funding for, 34; limitations of, 33–34

Helping hands, 20–22

High/Scope Perry Preschool Program (Ypsilanti, Michigan), in assessing quality childcare, 110

Hock, Ellen, 22

Home-based arrangements, exemptions from licensing requirements, 41

Home Observation for Measurement of the Environment Inventory (HOME), in NICHD study, 81

Howes, Carollee, 134

I Am Your Child Foundation, 217; childcare polls of, 17

Immigrants, need for day nurseries and, 28

Infant childcare, 56–57; behavior problems in, 98–99; boys in, 102; cost of, 60; enriched language experiences in, 127–128; intellectual abilities in, 97–98; social competence in, 98; starting childcare in, 96–99

Infant/Toddler Environment Rating Scale (ITERS): childcare quality and, 108; in Cost, Quality, and Child Outcomes (CQO) Study, 75; in Florida Child Care Quality Improvement Study, 78; in measuring quality, 193; in quality assessment, 106

In-home care, 173; costs of, 53

Innovative work schedules, 207–208

Instrumental variables in childcare research, 199

Intellectual development: childcare and, 178; as curricular focus, 120; effect of infancy programs on, 97–98; effects of childcare on, 86–88

Internet, in childcare training, 139–140

JOBS Child Care Program, 35

JOBS Study, 198

Kaiser, Henry, 1–2

Kaiser Shipyard childcare centers, 1–2; family benefits of, 2

KinderCare Learning Centers, 55

Labor force: participation of women in, 207–209; personal fulfillment and attachment to, 47–48

Lamb, Michael, 96

Language development: childcare quality and, 160; effects of otitis media on, 104

Lanham Act (1942), 29

Large data sets, for secondary analyses, 197–198

Licensing: in childcare choice, 52; link between quality and, 148

Lost-resources hypothesis, 161

Lower-income families, childcare choice by, 57

Low-quality childcare, underrepresentation of, 196

Manager, caregiver as, 128–130

Materials, assessment of, in physical environment, 113–114

Maternal deprivation, 15

Maternal employment and nonmaternal childcare, childcare demand and, 45–47

Maternity leave policies, 48–49

McKim, Margaret, 22

Median wages, level of, 45–46

Memory, tests on, in childcare, 87

Military Child Care Act (1989), 147–148, 210–211

Military childcare program, 147–148, 210–211

Miller, Louise, 117–119

Mommy tax, 26

Montessori materials, 119

Mother-child relationship: childcare decision and, 10–12, 12–13; effects of childcare on, 93–96

Mothers, caregivers versus, 150–153

Motor development, opportunities for, in childcare, 86

Nap time, children's dislike for, 117

National Association for the Education of Young Children (NAEYC), 40; accreditation by, 180, 214; in NICHD study, 81; ratio for infants and, 97; standards sponsored by, 39

National Association of Child Care Resource and Referral Agencies, 217

National Child Care Staffing Study: general education for teachers in, 136; parents in, 154

National Council of Jewish Women, study on childcare quality, 60, 61

National Day Care Home Study: caregiver training in, 142; childcare quality in, 148

National Day Care Staffing Study, caregivers in, 132

National Day Care Study, design of, 201

National Federation of Day Nurseries, 28

National Institute of Child Care and Human Development (NICHD) Study of Early Child Care and Youth Development, 79–82; availability for secondary analysis, 198

National Institute of Child Health and Human Development (NICHD) Study of Early Child Care, 41–42, 57; behavior problems in, 90, 91, 92, 93, 98–99; caregivers in, 132; caregiver training in, 133, 141; childcare choices in, 178; childcare quality in, 108–109, 109, 111; child management in, 130; children from troubled homes in, 159; child-staff ratio in, 125; controlling for family selection in, 156; effects of good childcare in, 163; family and quality interactions in, 160; family variables in, 157; gender in, 102; general education for teachers in, 136–137; infancy care in, 96–97, 97; intellectual development in, 87; limitations of, 192; lost-resources hypothesis in, 161; materials in, 113–114; mother-child relationship in, 99; parents in, 150, 154–155; physical environment in, 115; quality assessment in, 107–108, 194; risks for childcare illnesses in, 84–86; samples in, 195–196; social competence in, 89; stability in, 145; television watching in childcare setting, 115; toddler care in, 100

National Longitudinal Study of Youth (NLSY): gender in, 102; health problems in, 103; infancy care in, 97

National Network for Child Care, 217

National Staffing Study: stability in, 145; staff turnover in, 147

National Study of Child Care for Low-Income Families, 198

National Survey of Families and Households, grandmother caregivers in, 143

Neighborhood resource rooms, in improving quality, 140

Nelson, Lauren, 162

Networks, organizing childcare homes into, 216–217

Never-married mothers, number of, 45

New Chance, 87

New Chance Study, behavior problems in, 93

Nixon, Richard, 38

Nonparental childcare, as complex issue, 9

Nonprofit childcare centers, 178

Nonrelative care in the child's own home, 173

North Carolina Head Start Partnership Study, 160

Nursery schools: convergence and expansion of, 30–32; increased enrollment in, 31; origin of, 30; services offered by, 30; teachers in, 30

Nurturer, caregiver as, 130–132

Object Play Scale in Florida Child Care Quality Improvement Study, 78

Observational Record of the Caregiving Environment (ORCE): in NICHD study, 81; in quality assessment, 106–107

Observation in evaluation of childcare, 181–184

On-site childcare: observations of quality, 192–193; provision of, 212

Organization, assessment of, in physical environment, 112–113

Otitis media(OM) in childcare, 103–104

Panel Study of Income-Dynamics Child Development Supplement, 198

Parental leave, 208–209

Parent-caregiver relationship in evaluating childcare quality, 185–186

Parent co-op, 30

Parent education, 30, 217–218

Parents: in childcare choice, 51–53, 153–155; effect of childcare on, 161–164

Part-time care, full-time care versus, 170–171

Part-time workers, 207

Peabody Picture Vocabulary Test (PPVT), in Cost, Quality, and Child Outcomes (CQO) Study, 76–77

Peer interaction in childcare, 88–89

Peer Play Scale in Florida Child Care Quality Improvement Study, 78

Peers, 125–126

Perry Preschool/High Scope program, 138

Personal fulfillment and attachment, to the labor force, 47–48

Personal Responsibility and Work Opportunity Reconciliation Act (PRWORA) (1996), 35

Phone interview in defining childcare quality, 194

Physical environment, 112–115; materials in, 113–114; organization in, 112–113; space in, 112

Physical growth, opportunities for, in childcare, 86

Physical health and development effects of childcare on, 83–86

Physical punishment, 129

Physical setting in evaluating childcare quality, 184–185

Policy research, 201–204

Poor, childcare as marginal service for the, 29, 30

Praise in managing behavior in childcare, 128–129

Preschool, 31; children of nonemployed mothers in, 51

Preschool Behavior Questionnaire, in Florida Child Care Quality Improvement Study, 79

Preschoolers, childcare for, 57, 100–101

Professional nanny, 53

Professional women, in workplace, 47–48

Profile Assessment for Early Childhood Programs, 193; in NICHD study, 81

Profile of Child Care Settings study, caretaker goals in, 130–131

Profile of Child Care study, 128

Programs and activities, assessment of, 115–121

Project on Human Development in Chicago Neighborhood, 197

Proxy measures, 193–195

Public Agenda, childcare polls of, 17

Public Preschool Evaluation Project, 160

Q-set technique, in Florida Child Care Quality Improvement Study, 78

Quality of care, 105–111; advantaged families and, 161; association between training and, 135–136, 137; associations between child outcomes and, 202–203; associations between children's abilities and, 108–109; background checks in, 187; caregiver behavior in, 181–184; cognitive and social outcomes, 160; consumer endorsements in, 186–187; defining and measuring, 105–106, 193–195; domains of, 39–40; ensuring continued, 188–189; evaluating and monitoring, 179–187; importance of, to children from low-quality home environments, 159–160; length of effects, 109–110; link between licensing and, 148; for military families, 147–148; monitoring, 189; on-site observations of, 192–193; parent-caregiver relationship in, 185–186; physical setting in, 184–185; ranges in, 169–170; regulation of, 214–216; as research focus, 72; structural characteristics in, 180–181; ways of evaluating, 106–107

Quality of life, childcare quality and, 109

Quality time, 18–20

Referral service, in childcare choice, 52

Regulation of care, in policy studies, 203–204

Relationship with mother, effect of infant care, 99

Reynell Developmental Language
    Scales: caregiver training in,
    141; in NICHD study, 82
Role satisfaction, 22–24
Roosevelt, Franklin, 29
Rosenthal, Miriam, 204

Sampling, in childcare research,
    195–197
School readiness, childcare and, 87
Secondary analyses, large data sets
    for, 197–198198
Separation anxiety, 188–189
Single mothers, childcare demand
    by, 44–45
Single-parent families: childcare
    choice by, 16–17, 57; growth
    in number of, 44; use of rela-
    tive care by, 58
Smith, Ann, 91
Social competence: effect of in-
    fancy programs on, 98; effects
    of childcare on, 88–89
Social outcomes, quality of care
    and, 160
Social pressures, childcare deci-
    sions and, 13–15
Social Services Block Grant, 34
Social skills curriculum, imple-
    menting, 121–122
Sociobiological theory, 11
Space, assessment of, in physical
    environment, 112
Spanking, 129
Speech of children in childcare, 87
Stability, of caregivers, 144–145
Staff-child ratios, 41; in NICHD
    Study, 125; regulation of, 40.
    See also Child-adult ratios
Standard intelligence test, in
    measuring children's develop-
    ment, 71

Stay-at-home mothers: investment
    of, 15; pressures on, 15; role
    satisfaction of, 22–24
Stolz, Lois, 1
Strange Situation assessment. See
    Ainsworth's Strange Situation
    Assessment
Stress, on working mothers, 24–26
Structural characteristics, in evalu-
    ating childcare quality,
    180–181
Structured programs: care givers
    in, 116; children in, 116–117;
    curricular content in,
    120–121; teacher and parent
    preference for, 117
Subsidies, for childcare, 34–36

Tax benefits, for childcare, 36–37
Teachers: as caregivers, 127–128; in
    childcare centers, 56; in day
    nurseries, 29; in nursery
    schools, 30
TEACH program, 138; caregiver
    training in, 137
Telecommuting, 208
Television, watching, in child-care
    setting, 115
Temperamental difficulty, childcare
    research on, 103
Temporary Assistance for Needy
    Families (TANF), 35
Time-out, children's dislike for, 117
Title XX, 34
Toddlers: childcare for, 56–57;
    effects of childcare on, 99–100
Total group size, 41; regulation of,
    40
Training: association between
    quality of care and, 135–136;
    in Cost, Quality, and Child
    Outcomes (CQO) Study, 133,

Training (*continued*)
137, 141, 142; effects of, on
children, 140–141; as factor
in childcare choice, 51; in
Florida Child Care Quality
Improvement Study, 133, 141;
general education in, 136–137;
importance of, 133–141; in
improving quality, 140; Internet in, 139–140; links between
quality and, 137; in measuring
quality, 193; need and desire
for, 134–135; regulation of, 40;
standards regarding, 41; in
TEACH program, 137; types
of child, 138–140
Transitional Child Care Program,
35
Traveling teachers, in improving
quality, 140
Tucson Children's Recovery Study,
85
Turnover, in measuring quality, 193
Turnover rates, 144
Two-parent families: childcare
choice by, 57; use of relative
care by, 58

UCLA Early Childhood Observation Form, 75; in Cost,
Quality, and Child Out-
comes (CQO) Study,
76–77
Universal preschool and extended
primary school, 212–213
University-based childcare, 179;
research on, 69–70
Unstructured play, children's preference for, 117
Unstructured programs: caregivers
in, 116; children in, 116–117

Verbal fluency, tests on, in childcare, 87
Vernon-Feagans, Lynne, 162
Verweij-Tijsterman, Els,
94–96
Videotaping care settings,
192–193
Vulnerable children, effects of
childcare on, 102–104

Wages in measuring quality,
193
Welfare Reform in Three Cities,
197–198
Welfare-to-work program, 37;
childcare enrollment, 36
*Who Cares for America's Children:
Child Care Policy for the 1990s,*
85
Women, participation in the labor
force, 207–209
Women's roles, changes in, 6
Woodcock Johnson Achievement
and Cognitive Batteries in
NICHD study, 82
Woodcock-Johnson Test of
Achievement in assessing
quality childcare, 110
Word-of-mouth recommenda-
tions, in selecting childcare,
186–187
Workforce, cost of woman's leaving, 46–47
Working-class parents, childcare as
a service for, 27–30
Working mothers: competing
demands on, 17–18; lack
of choice for, in using childcare, 16–17; need for help,
20–22; personal fulfillment
and attachment to the labor

force, 47–48; pressures placed on, 14–15; quality time and, 18–20; role satisfaction of, 22–24; stress and stain on, 24–26

Work Projects Administration, childcare programs under, 29

Work schedules, innovative, 207–208

Worksite childcare, 179

World War II, need for childcare programs, 29–30

Zero to Three, 217

Zigler, Edward, 37